CLIVE JAMES

May Week was in June

Unreliable Memoirs continued

published by Pan Books

First published 1990 by Jonathan Cape Ltd
This Picador edition first published 1991 by Pan Books Ltd
Cavaye Place, London SW10 9PG
in association with Jonathan Cape Ltd
1 3 5 7 9 8 6 4 2
© Clive James 1990
ISBN 0 330 31522 6

Printed in England by Clays Ltd, St Ives plc

Clive James was educated at Sydney University and Cambridge, where he was President of Footlights. In addition to his bestseller *Unreliable Memoirs* and its equally successful sequel *Falling Towards England*, he has published two novels, *Brilliant Creatures* and *The Remake*; four mock-epic poems; four books of literary criticism; a book of travel pieces, *Flying Visits*; and his poems 1958–85, *Other Passports*. Between 1972 and 1982 he was the television critic for the *Observer* and he appears regularly as a television performer.

in memoriam
Mark Boxer and Tom Weiskel
and to
Gabriella Rosselli del Turco
where she lies sleeping

I realise very well that the reader has no great need to know all this; but I need to tell him.

Rousseau, Les Confessions

I wear a suit of armour made of nothing but my mistakes.

Pierre Reverdy, quoted by Ernst Jünger
in Das zweite Pariser Tagebuch, 21 February 1943

I've never made any secret of the fact that I'm basically on my way to Australia.

Support Your Local Sheriff

Contents

Preface

SOMEBODY ONCE SAID that a trilogy ought ideally to consist of two volumes. Unfortunately he never said anything else, so his name is forgotten. When I set out to write *Falling Towards England*, the second volume of my unreliable memoirs, I honestly meant it to be the end of the enterprise. Gradually it became clear, however, that my entry into the University of Cambridge marked the beginning of a further episode, whose events, while less than awe-inspiring on the scale of cosmology, would suffer distortion if compressed into a few chapters. I could have made more room at the back of the book by cutting the front, but it was already cut. The nuances, after all, were everything. It would not have been enough to say that I was a failure in London. One had to convey the way failure felt: how the clothes slept in to keep one warm looked wrong next day, how a letter of rejection could be distinguished from a letter of acceptance before it was opened, how one drank to quell one's nagging conscience about having borrowed the money with which to drink. In the next generation, young people needed a heroin habit to live like that. I managed it through sheer talent. Cambridge was my way out, if not up.

Once again, though, the raw story would not have been enough. God, said Mies van der Rohe, is in the details. In Cambridge, I began to find my way, but simply to say so would have been to muff the point, because I found my way by getting more lost than ever. It was just that this time, by a bigger than usual dose of my usual extraordinary luck, I was given the chance to become confused in a fruitful, or potentially fruitful, manner. In London, entirely through my own bad management, I had been hunted from pillar to post. In Cambridge I could develop my propensities, such as they were, to the fullest extent possible, and all at once. The result was chaos. Fortunately there is a natural law, whose mathematical basis I don't pretend to understand, which says that chaos isn't always just random. It can have patterns in it. The story in this volume – while being, as before, no more faithful to the facts than the ego finds convenient – is as true as I can make it to the pattern which emerged when my half-formed personality was put back into the scrambler. I won't dignify the process with the name of self-discovery. The self scarcely altered. It might even have become more conscious of itself than ever. But the panic was over. I was still broke, but I had landed in the lap of the only kind of luxury I have ever cared about – a wealth of opportunity. Where once every move had been forced, now there was nothing but choice. For too long the Flash of Lightning had not been free to deploy his cape or put on the mask with the stretched elastic knotted at the back to keep it fitting tightly under the strain of his amazing acceleration. Now once again he was off and running in six different directions.

Cambridge was my personal playground. It would be useless to pretend otherwise. I would be surprised if nostalgia for those easy years did not drip from the following pages like sweat. The place hasn't changed much since. The old Footlights clubroom, together with the whole rat-infested district of which it was the hub, was bulldozed to make room for the Lion Yard development, enraging some but probably saving the city from another outbreak of bubonic plague. The buses have changed colour, there has been a massacre of elms, the old Eagle is ominously surrounded by scaffolding, the Pakistani restaurant on the ground floor of the Friar's House has become a souvenir shop, and fancy goods are now sold in the back room of the Whim where I once sat by the hour writing in my journal. As always, committees of dons do more than the worst developers to inflict horrible buildings on their beautiful city. Yet Cambridge – like Florence, the other main location of this epic – stays what it was. My life didn't. In Cambridge, in the Sixties, my course was altered and fixed, for good or ill. For this reason, though I still spend a good deal of time there, the place is always in the past to me, as epoch-making as my first pair of long pants, and almost as glamorous. The spires, the lawns, the spring alliance of jonquils and daffodils: I hardened my heart against these things, and they all went to my head. Byron kept a low profile in Cambridge, confining himself to booze, broads and leading a live bear around on a string. I was less inclined to hide my light under a bushel. The days of our youth are the days of our glory. He said it, and I believed it.

London, 1990   C.J.

I

Gentlemen, Sport Your Oaks!

ARRIVING IN CAMBRIDGE on my first day as an undergraduate, I could see nothing except a cold white October mist. At the age of twenty-four I was a complete failure, with nothing to show for my life except a few poems nobody wanted to publish in book form. Three years of hand-to-mouth existence in London had led me nowhere but here. For all I knew, Cambridge was receiving me with open arms. They could have had flags out. There could have been a band playing. It was impossible to tell. The white opacity came all the way to my eyeballs. Outside the railway station I stood holding my cardboard suitcase. I couldn't see the station and I could barely see the suitcase. Having been in Cambridge only once before, for a short drunken visit that started well but ended in a haze not unlike, in its texture, the one through which I now groped, I had only the dimmest memories to go on of how to get to town.

Luckily I remembered, when I reached the war memorial, that the statue on top of it was pointing roughly in the right direction. I had to climb the memorial to find out what the direction was. After that I was on the right track to the city centre, where there was enough light to distinguish people from letter boxes. The letter boxes, in my perhaps embittered view, had warmer personalities than the people, but the people, although not notably less taciturn, at least knew how to give directions if they felt like it. I asked a nice little old lady the way to Pembroke, which was to be my college if I ever found it. At first she snarled at me, perhaps because I had located her partly by touch. It took only about a quarter of an hour to calm her fears, however, after which she pointed the way down Pembroke Street and told me to turn left at Trumpington Street. I turned left too early – probably into Tennis Court Road – and ended up at the Fitzwilliam Museum, which I mistook for Pembroke until put right by the man at the desk inside. Before I could get myself and my suitcase back out through the revolving doors he managed to regale me with his entire repertoire of jokes about kangaroos, koalas, dunnies, and walking upside down in the outback, ha ha. As an Australian expatriate I had grown used to the fabled English sense of humour but preferred to steer clear of it when possible, for fear of laughing too hard.

On the far side of the street I found, by stepping into it, a gutter the size of a small canal. This I slowly followed to the left, occasionally crossing the footpath to check the texture of the buildings with my carefully extended right hand. The ashlared front wall of a college crustily identified itself to my fingertips. When stone became wood, I guessed it must be the front gate of Pembroke and turned towards an egg-yolk halo which materialised in the form of the Porter's Lodge. The porter, called Keeps if not Waits, knew an Aussie (which he mispronounced Ossie) when he heard one and was fully informed about kangaroos, koalas and the necessity of walking around upside down when down under, ha ha. Having exhausted the subject and me along with it, he directed me to my set of rooms, D6 in the old court, known as Old Court, above the dining hall, known as Hall. Having asked for 'the smallest possible set of rooms consonant with my playing the clarinet', I found that I had been given an oak-panelled suite which would have been large enough to accommodate Benny Goodman, and his big band along with him. It scarcely needs saying that I couldn't play the clarinet at all, but on the day I made the written application I must have been toying with the idea of taking up that instrument. As I stood beside my suitcase in the middle of the sitting room, a handsome young man in a silk brocade dressing-gown appeared suddenly beside me with a silence made possible by monogrammed leather slippers. 'Abramovitz,' he said, holding out a pampered hand.

I knew that this wasn't my name so I guessed that it must be his. 'I live across the corridor. *Love* that beard. Don't worry, I'm not bent or anything. Just philanthropic. Let me show you the form.'

At least five years younger than I, Abramovitz carried on as if he were fifty years older. He was reading law and naturally assumed that the only reason I was reading English for a second undergraduate degree was in order to give myself time for plenty of extracurricular activities. He advised me to step around to the Societies Fair in the Corn Exchange before I decided finally on trying out for the Footlights. He himself believed the Union to be the only thing that counted if one had one's eye on high government office. I asked him if he was going to be Prime Minister. 'No, Disraeli was the last of our boys they'll ever let in there. Chancellor of the Exchequer: that's the spot.' He explained to me what to do about laundry, of which, as usual, I had more needing to be done than done. He also showed me how to sport my oak. A heavy rolling outer door, the oak was meant to signal that the occupant was at home to nobody, although it was left unclear whether this applied to Abramovitz.

His advice turned out to be good, however. The Societies Fair was indeed a cornucopia of activities, like Orientation Week at Sydney University but on the scale of the Earls Court motor show. Here was my chance to get interested in heraldry, beagling and riding to hounds. Each activity had a booth attended by undergraduates in the appropriate costume. The dramatic societies stood out through having a more abundant, although scarcely lavish, presence of undergraduettes. Careful not to squander my whole grant at once, I did not actually join these dramatic societies there and then, but spent a lot of time standing around being told why I should. Some of the girls from the ADC I thought especially persuasive. But the dramatic society whose booth most impressed me was the Footlights. It consisted of one bare trestle table. Behind it sat a solitary, fine-drawn, bored-looking individual in a tan cashmere jacket. 'How do I join?' I asked. 'You don't,' he said through a barely controlled yawn. 'You audition.' Informing me that his name was Idle, he handed me a roneoed set of instructions saying where, when and how. The auditions were some time off and the chances of selection seemed very slim.

My theatrical urges were further stimulated by the purchase of a gown. Throwing my bearded chin upright and drawing the gown's black drapes around my shoulders, I looked like a Wittelsbach crown prince going mildly ga-ga or a close friend of Count Dracula in search of a meal. When I appeared that evening in Hall there was a hush on the benches and some of the freshmen seemed to feel vulnerable in the area of the neck. Actually I would have done better to dine off them than off the food. This latter proved useful only as a discussion point. The entrée wasn't tender enough to be a paving stone and the gravy couldn't have been primordial soup because morphogenesis was already taking place. 'How *about* this shit?' said a rotund American whose name turned out to be Delmer Dynamo. 'You can bet they're eating something else up *there*.' He angled his pear-shaped head towards High Table, where, surveyed by a plaster bust of William Pitt the Younger, the dons were Dining in Fellowship. They weren't exactly joined together with cobwebs but you couldn't have called them vibrant. It wasn't their age, so much as their well-being, that impressed. Even at a distance you could tell that the dark wine was helping the venison go down to their profound satisfaction. I wondered which of them was the Senior Tutor of Supervisors, whom I was due to meet next day. Or was he called the Senior Supervisor of Tutors?

When I turned up next day to meet him, all the other freshmen in the college turned up too. The Senior Tutor, whose full title turned out to be the Senior Tutor of Junior Supervisors, was obviously shy, but equally obviously he had overcome this disability by a meticulous attention to social punctilio. He made small talk and expected everybody else to do the same. Five minutes after shaking hands with him I found myself left alone with an Iranian biochemist whose name sounded like a fly trapped against a window. This sudden conjunction was blessed with our mentor's assurance that we would have a lot in common. What we had in common was a small glass of sherry and a large measure of awkwardness. I cursed the Tutor for this instead of doing the sensible thing and asking a few questions about biochemistry, a field in which my interlocutor was later to become eminent. If I had asked a few questions about the Senior Tutor I would have found out that he was the world's leading authority on Propertius. Surrounded by distinction, both actual and potential, I was exclusively occupied with not dribbling sherry into my beard. With that, and with the inexplicable presence of Abramovitz. 'What are *you* doing here?' I asked when I had manoeuvred my way to his side through the crowd: 'I thought this was for freshmen.' 'But I *am* a freshman,' said Abramovitz happily. 'I came up the day before you did.' It struck me on the spot that if the English had spent their lives preparing to fit into one of these places, then the only smart thing to do was not to bother about fitting in at all, and I can honestly say that from that moment on I never wasted any time trying. I wasted time doing other things, but not doing that.

Drinks next day with the Master once again featured the full cast, and once again the tipple was warm sherry. The Master was a retired pure mathematician who had no pretensions towards social ease. Wearing a full-length gown, he stood glumly in the centre of the room while we milled around him in our short gowns. Throwing a glass of sherry down my throat and plucking another from a passing silver platter, I assessed him as a nonentity and was duly rewarded for my acumen by finding out, twenty years later, that he had been on the committee which approved the funds for the first Manchester computer just after World War II. Being in possession of that information at the time might have induced enough awe to offset the aggrieved loneliness with which I drank. Apart from the biochemist with the buzzer for a name and the omnipresent Abramovitz, the only face I found familiar was that of Delmer Dynamo. His pear-shaped head, I could now see, was situated on top of a pear-shaped body, which his black gown caused to resemble a piece of fruit going to a funeral. 'How about *this* for a wing-ding?' he shouted conspiratorially. 'You can blow it out your ass. Have you met the Dean yet?' I replied that I was due to meet the Dean the next day. 'You're gonna dig it,' averred Delmer. 'Mind you, he hasn't got this bozo's carefree verve.'

Delmer was only almost right. The Dean, whose name was the Reverend Meredith Dewey, was indeed a picture of inactivity as he sat back in a winged leather armchair and expended just enough energy to keep his pipe alight. But unlike the Master he had overt characteristics. For one thing, his room was full of rocks. The Dean was an amateur geologist who picked up souvenir rocks every time he travelled abroad in order to attend some less-than-crucial ecumenical drone-in. Indeed there were irreverent suggestions that he would accept the occasional invitation – like the one from the Pan-African Convocation of Pastoral Curators in Accra – just so that, between papers and seminars, he could go forth unto the hills and root around for chunks of granite. Doubtless these imputations arose from envy, but only a historian of mining engineering would have been envious: the Dean's rooms were on the first floor and for many years had been arousing concern among the female staff in the linen room below. As they toiled over the ironing of our sheets and pillowcases, they had to live with the mental picture of the creaking ceiling finally bursting open and the Dean's massive collection descending on them like the temple of the Philistines after Samson gave it the push. When you sat facing the Dean you were surrounded by about thirty million years of the Earth's petrified history. While he dutifully enquired after your spiritual welfare you could fill the time by wondering how he got the stuff through customs. There was no problem about how he carried it. Though of only medium height, he had shoulders like Charles Atlas and could obviously lug a tote-bag full of pitchblende for miles. But when those decolonised *douaniers* opened up his luggage and found it crammed with unrefined ore, why didn't they suspect him of stealing their uranium?

The sleepy holiness of his appearance was the only explanation. I told him about my atheism and socialism. His eyelids grew as heavy as sandstone, a large piece of which was poised on a sideboard for purposes of comparison. 'Convinced about that beard, are you?' he enquired tentatively, then lapsed into silence while I explained about radical socialism. I interpreted his apparent torpor as a sherry-fuelled sloth. It was only later on, when I found out how sharp he was, that I realised he was politely but immovably bored rigid at meeting his ten thousandth young saviour of the world. With his direct line to an earlier and better qualified envoy sent on the same task, the Dean was in the position of a senior manager who is required, for form's sake, to go on interviewing candidates after the job has been filled. He released supplicatory puffs of smoke heavenward, tapped his fingertips together, and snuck lazy, longing sideways looks at an inviting lump of lignite.

Overseeing my studies in English was Dr Stewart Frears. Professor Frears, as he later became, was, although the senior English don in the college, only a lecturer at that stage, but he was already an authority on the Metaphysical poets, to which his learned and common-sensical approach had already been more than enough to attract regular vilification from Dr Leavis. In life as in death – between which two states he was currently hovering – Leavis was the most contentious name in Cambridge. Like an old volcano that goes dead in its central crater but unpredictably blows hot holes through its own sides and obliterates villages which thought themselves safe, Leavis was dormant yet still bubbling. Frears caught more than his fair share of the lava and perhaps this accounted at least partly for a pronounced nervous tic. He would periodically click his teeth and twitch his head sideways almost to one shoulder, like a violinist trying to smash his instrument no hands. He won't mind my recalling this trivial affliction because later on it disappeared. (All the many recipients of routine libels from Leavis got a bit flak-happy in one way or another but in almost every case the trouble cleared up after the old warrior passed on to that great Organic Community, which, despite his vehement assurances that it once existed on Earth, has its foundations only in the cloudy soil of the Empyrean.) While it was still happening, however, Dr Frears's flicking tic inevitably attracted some of the attention I was supposed to be directing towards the post-Elizabethans. Actually, to do myself the discredit I had coming, I was having a hard time getting interested again in the Metaphysicals. I had passed through my first Donne period in Sydney and was not to go crazy about him again for another decade or so. In short, I had done Donne. Currently, I was much more under the sway of the Cavaliers, the Romantics and any other historical group except the one I was supposed to be studying. Reading off the course was my temperamental habit. Nowadays I devour whole literatures in sequential order, making notes and writing essays all the way. It's because I don't have to. When I did have to, I couldn't do it.

So it wasn't just my supervisor's neck-snapping twitch that put me off George Herbert. But even had I been as respectful of Herbert as I am now – anyone who tells you that Herbert is negligible beside Donne doesn't understand Donne either – I would have had trouble articulating a clear analysis of *The Temple* if my interlocutor were continually threatening to catch a fly between his cheek and shoulder. I got increasingly nervous about turning up for my weekly supervision. As usual, I lied my way out of trouble, inventing various ailments. Shoving a piece of cotton wool behind my lower lip and pretending to have an abscess was perhaps the silliest trick. Even my better wheezes were schoolboy stuff and the man in charge wasn't fooled. He could have had me rusticated. It sounded like being castrated with a rusty knife and it hurt even worse, because it meant being thrown back into the harsh world where you had to earn a living. Instead, very generously, he passed me further down the line, to those junior dons who were still, as he put it, 'in the first fury of their supervisions'. It sounded too much like work but at least I was still along for the ride.

And the ride meant Footlights. The club held two smoking concerts (called smokers) each term. The first smoker of the first term was the chief audition smoker for new members. The club room was above MacFisheries fish shop in Falcon Yard, off Petty Cury. Required dress was a dinner jacket, which for purposes of the audition I hired. There was no point in buying one outright at that stage, because if I had not got in, there would have been no occasion for wearing it until I graduated. I played Noel Coward in an old Noel-Gertie routine written long ago in Sydney by my three-piece thoroughly Anglicised Australian friend, who had first invited me to Cambridge two years before and was now on the point of graduating. He was a member of Footlights but for some reason had never used the sketch himself. Perhaps he never found a suitable co-star. I was luckier. Though I made Noel Coward sound like Chips Rafferty, I was spurred on by a Gertrude who, although an Australian like me, could act well enough to be believable as anything. Her name was Romaine Rand.

Slightly older than I and already equipped with a degree from Melbourne, Romaine had descended on Sydney University while I was still a second year student. Tall, striking and already famous for her brilliantly foul tongue, she had pursued graduate studies, libertarian polemics, and, for a brief period, me. At the risk of sounding even more conceited than usual, it is important that I record this fact, for a reason which will shortly emerge. At the time I was having published, in the literary pages of the Sydney University student newspaper *honi soit*, a lot of articles, poems and short stories conveying omniscience, poise and worldly wisdom. Publication was not difficult to arrange, because I edited those pages. Correctly intuiting at a glance that I was grass-green in all matters and emerald-green in the matter of sex, Romaine, at her table in the Royal George Hotel, took bets with the Downtown Push that she could seduce me within twenty-four hours. Next day the news reached me before she did. When she appeared, striding like a Homeric goddess, at the door of the cafeteria in Manning House, I cravenly escaped through the side entrance and hid behind the large adjacent gum tree. The rumour that I hid *up* the tree was false but slow to die.

The following year I was a senior and had developed some real confidence, or at any rate had become convinced by my own swagger. This time it was I who pursued Romaine. When the old Union Hall of beloved memory was pulled down and replaced by a new theatre of unparalleled hideousness, I found Romaine sitting behind me at a matinée performance of one of the inaugural plays: some frail, panting comedy by Anouilh which was now receiving the *coup de grâce* from a hunting pack of Australian accents. I held hands with her in the dark: quite a trick when the woman is sitting in the row behind you. It was easy, I told myself, to detect the shy vulnerability which lay beneath this woman's strident show of independence. Consolingly I stroked her palm with my fingertips. They were a bit sweaty, but she didn't object. Later on I walked her home along Parramatta Road. I did my most accomplished heart-winning athletic feat: the one where I grabbed a lamp-post with both hands and stood straight out sideways into the passing traffic. She looked impressed. Running with sweat from these exertions, at her flat I invited myself to take a shower, and did not lose the opportunity to show off the muscular development of my torso, which in those days was arranged with most of the wide bits at the top. Again she looked impressed. Guess what? I didn't get her into bed.

The reason I am telling you all this is that Romaine herself blew the whole story long ago. After she became, deservedly, world famous, she seized the first chance to get back to Australia and tell the most chaotic journalist in the country – whose prose, when he had worked as my assistant on *honi soit*, I had always felt honour-bound to rewrite – the full story of my crummy seduction technique. She evoked my lamp-post lateral extensions and shower-booth biceps-flexing in such hilarious detail that not even the journalist's slovenly verbosity could dull the comic effect. As a champion of truth, a leading light in the struggle against male chauvinism and sexist hypocrisy, Romaine had a right to say all this. I was more appalled by what she didn't say. *She didn't say that she had chased me up that tree.* All right, behind that tree. She didn't say anything about betting the Downtown Push that she could deflower me in twenty-four hours from a standing start. Nothing. Not a word.

But all this was before and later. For the moment, I was standing back to back with Romaine on the tiny Footlights stage, she with her notable bust strapped down under an old A-line satin frock suitably modified – Romaine was always a dab hand at the household tasks against which she later rebelled on behalf of womankind – and I resplendent in watered-down hair and made-up velvet bow tie holding together the collar of one of my old off-white drip-dries. The rented DJ with its stove-pipe pants descended into a brand new pair of black bootees with zips up the inner ankle. Romaine had a cigarette holder the length of a billiard cue and I held my cigarette from underneath, like a Russian spy. With our nostrils given an extra arch of fastidiousness by the smell of halibut rising through the floorboards from the marble display tables of MacFisheries below, we mouthed brittle dialogue. I was awful, she was great, so we both got in. Romaine thus became one of the very first female members of the Footlights, because that was the smoker at which Eric Idle – the slim, dapper and unnervingly deep young President – finally managed to realise his long-laid plan of extending the franchise to the other half of the human race. Up until then, women could appear in Footlights revues only as guests, and most of the dons who congregated around the club's small but thriving bar made it piercingly clear that they had preferred the era of good, straightforward transvestism, with properly shaved legs and no nonsense about it. Keeping her gratitude well under control, Romaine eyed some of the assembled senior members with manifest disdain. 'This place is jumping with freckle-punchers,' she told me confidentially, so that only about thirty of them choked on their drinks. 'You can have it on your own.'

So we immediately split up again. Companionship between Romaine and myself had never been easy, because each of us suspected the other of the desire to conduct a perpetual monologue and neither was inclined to act as the feed-man, or feed-person. In my view she argued exclusively from the emotions and in her view I must have epitomised the kind of arrogant male who would hold such an assumption. Apart from and below all that, however, was a deeper reason: in those days ambitious young Australians left their country in order to discover themselves as individuals. Clinging together when abroad was the last thing they wanted to do. The idea that the Australians in England roll logs for each other has always been exactly wrong. Most of them wouldn't roll a twig. I could barely name two of them who would roll me into an open grave.

Romaine took one look at the English Tripos requirements,

declared them infantile, and by force of argument got herself registered as a PhD student. The University Library, in keeping with the vaguely pre-Columbian threat of its appearance, swallowed her up like a tomb. Perhaps it had absorbed all the other women in Cambridge too. There seemed to be very few of them, and fewer still who were available. From the two women's colleges, Newnham and Girton, only a handful of girls took enough time off from their studies to appear in the vicinity of the dramatic societies. These brave rebels would attend Footlights smokers but otherwise they were to be observed only near Sidgwick Avenue on their way to and from lectures. On ordinary nights in the club there was scarcely a woman to be seen, except the occasional up-and-coming, or more likely down-and-going, actress from a touring company who would take a late-night snort after the evening performance in the Arts Theatre. The relative absence of a civilising female influence made it all the easier to get disgustingly drunk. One was allowed to run up a bar bill. Mine became a bar booklet. The door of the Footlights closed at night long after the front door of my college, so after navigating my way from Petty Cury to the street behind Pembroke I had to climb over the back wall. Climbing in (called Climbing In) was an experience that varied from college to college. Though frowned on, it was an accepted practice. Undergraduates couldn't walk through town after dark without their gowns or else the Beadles would challenge them and, if necessary, give chase. The Beadles wore bowler hats and most of them had RAF moustaches. Wind resistance, however, did nothing to slow them down. But once you had reached the walls of your college there were no patrols to stop you climbing in. The occasional drunken undergraduate who impaled himself on a railing spike received no punishment beyond the scar. When King's had a physically handicapped undergraduate it installed a small hand-rail on one of the walls near the river so that he could climb in without drowning. It was all very English: a rule made to be broken, as long as you didn't kick up a fuss. Within the first two weeks I became adept at scaling the back wall whatever my state of inebriation, crossing the roof of the bike shed and dropping to the ground beside a huge cylindrical metal skip in which rubbish was placed for incineration. In the third week, however, I was so drunk one night that I dropped in the wrong spot, with a noise like a huge gong being softly struck. I woke up inside the skip several hours later, a bleak dawn sky overhead.

2

The Dear Old College

COLLEGE LIFE HAD its attractions. Had I been a few years younger, I might have fallen for them headlong. For undergraduates coming up from public schools, the colleges were no doubt too familiar in their accoutrements to be especially impressive. By public schools, of course, I mean private schools. A boy from Eton might have found even King's or Trinity the same old thing on an only slightly larger scale: the same turrets, crenellations, lodges, fenestrations, cloisters, clerestories, porticos and porters. Those freshmen who came from State schools, however, now met with a concentration of custom and ceremony which had the wherewithal to overwhelm them. It didn't have to hurry. It had all the time in the world. Since I was still a radical socialist, I had no trouble analysing how the system worked. The idea was to tame the intelligent upstart by getting him addicted to privilege. The beautiful architecture had a political function. In Paris, Haussmann's great boulevards were only incidentally grandiloquent: their real purpose was to provide the widest field of fire for the artillery and the quickest access for the cavalry to anywhere the workers might stage a rebellion. In Cambridge, the lovely façades, the sweeping lawns, the intricate crannies opening on distant vistas, were meant not just to lull but to disarm: nobody who had once lived in these emollient surroundings would ever again feel sufficiently alienated from society to be anything more troublesome than a reformist. Gradualism was implicit in every carefully repainted coat of arms and battered refectory table. To remain a revolutionary in such a context you would have had to have treason in the blood, like Kim Philby. Such, at any rate, was the theory, or what I took the theory to be. My college, as I tried my best not to call it, was hardly prodigal with the creature comforts but it knew how to make life convenient. To get my laundry done, all I had to do was put it in a box and leave the box at the head of the staircase. In the course of time, a box of fresh laundry would magically appear in the same place. There are men in British public life to whom this has gone on happening into old age. They are under the impression that their laundry is taken care of by a force of nature. Such coveted hidey-holes for gentlefolk as the Albany in Piccadilly aren't selling the luxury of the Savoy: they are selling the invisible services of the dear old college. The oak-panelled walls are there to remind the inhabitants of school and university. The laundry box is there to reassure them that there is still a linen room somewhere which they will die without ever having to visit.

All this I could anatomise with the piercing insight of Marx and Engels. But I put my laundry into the box just the same. It was too handy to pass up. Similarly the bedder was an institution which could not be defended but was impossible to forego. The bedder was a woman who made your bed. Many of us were ashamed that a woman who might otherwise have been employed doing useful work for society, not to mention fulfilling herself spiritually, was earning a pittance by squaring up our crapulous sheets and blankets. Not many of us ever met her, however. I met mine just once, and just long enough to learn that she valued the work without necessarily valuing me, whose standards of hygiene she found questionable. 'I have to speak frankly, Mr James,' she quacked unprompted. 'Frankly, the best thing to be said for you is that Mr Abramovitz is even worse, frankly.' Her name was Mrs Blades and she looked tough enough to need no defending. So I decided to put off the moment of going to the barricades on her behalf. Very soon I left my bed unmade without giving it a thought, and came back in the afternoon to find it made without giving that a thought either. After all, the same thing had happened at home for the first eighteen years of my life.

Similarly, my initial impressions of the food served in Hall were soon modified. At first I had thought the food was terrible and that I would never be able to eat it. After a few weeks I had come round to the opinion that the food was terrible but that I could eat it. Here again, the arrangements were just too convenient to pass up. Breakfast was there for the taking. I rarely took it. Usually I got up just in time for lunch. It didn't taste of anything, but that could have been the fault of my mouth, fur-lined after a heavy evening. For dinner, you had your choice of first or second sitting, as on board ship. The advantage of the first sitting was that the High Table was empty. At the second sitting, if you looked up from your plate of burnt offerings and denatured vegetable matter, you were faced with the spectacle of the dons Dining in Fellowship off a haunch of venison while they circulated the claret with the speed of happy children playing pass-the-parcel. On the other hand the second sitting enabled you to linger over an extra half pint of acceptable bitter before gravitating to the graduates' parlour for a noggin of port or three. Either way, I could get from my rooms to dinner simply by dragging on a gown and falling downstairs. Falling off a log would have been harder, and I wouldn't have got fed.

This cosy, effortless taking-on of sustenance had an irresistible appeal, especially considering that I was under no compulsion to fraternise with my fellow undergraduates beyond rubbing gowned elbows with them at the long low table. I entered the Junior Common Room only, if ever, to read the newspapers. My in-college hangout was the graduates' parlour, where one could sign for one's drinks and comport oneself almost as a don. Another Australian affiliate, Brian C. Adams, overdid this to the point of not even hanging up his gown. He stood around pontifically in full drag, his accent, during the course of one term, losing all trace of antipodean colouring, and acquiring, during the course of a second term, an affinity with that of Princess Margaret. 'Eigh-ow,' he would neigh, 'rarely?' He meant 'Oh really?' but the expression emerged like a chicken which had been strangled in a letter box and then pushed out through the slit. Not that Adams was stupid. He was merely quicker than most to go native. He was arrogant, but at least he was honest. Reading

English like me, he was after first class honours, and said so. His unprompted disquisitions on critical theory made me wonder if I would be able to get a third even if I worked. He had already read everything, and was now reading it again. He talked learnedly about the Spirit of the College, I suppose with some justification, because he never left its front gate except to attend lectures in Sidgwick Avenue, visit the University Library, or sit at the feet of F. R. Leavis in Downing. In Pembroke, the Gray Society was a literary organisation which met monthly to hear a paper. Brian C. Adams became secretary of the Gray Society before I had even heard that it existed. In Australia, while still an undergraduate, he had published a slim but substantial critical work, *Johnson's Boswell: the Man-made Self.* Two copies of this booklet promptly appeared in Pembroke College Library, with the signature of Brian C. Adams on the donor's bookplate. Brian C. Adams was a College Man.

If, however, you had gagged him, stripped the gown off him, and viewed him from a suitable distance, Brian C. Adams might just conceivably have been mistaken for an ordinary human being. The true embodiment of the College Spirit was Delmer Dynamo. Though his satirical verbal assaults on the college food and facilities never ceased, it was clear that Delmer had found his promised land. His tailoring becoming more gentlemanly by the week, he would manoeuvre his low-slung posterior into position against the open fire of the graduates' parlour, part the rear wings of his Savile Row tweed jacket, and toast himself like a marshmallow while lovingly discussing the Dean's proclivities, real and imagined. 'The question isn't how he gets his rocks *in*,' Delmer would announce loudly. 'The question is how he gets his rocks *off*.' Delmer called the graduates' parlour the grad pad, a designation which eventually all its habitués, even the English, took up. There could be no doubt that the grad pad's cosiest amenity was Delmer himself. He was in there like the furniture. Similarly he was as prominent in Hall as Spenser's portrait or Pitt's bust. Every graduate was invited once a year to dine at High Table. Delmer wangled it three times in his first term. Dining on offal down in the pit, we would look up at him while he sat there being waited on. He would be attacking the venison while the stringy beef was attacking us. At assimilating himself to the English establishment, Delmer Dynamo left Disraeli looking like Guy Fawkes. It was because he was so interested. He knew all the college gossip. Few dons could resist the way he talked about their colleagues. The college was a microcosm which he took at its own estimation, as a macrocosm. Not even the Dean could do without Delmer, who had mugged up the whole history of Pembroke's most precious architectural possession, the Wren chapel. 'Sometimes I can't believe that boy's Jewish,' the Dean was heard to say. 'He really does know an *awful* lot about stained glass.' The Dean would invite Delmer to sherry and show him geological treasures kept in thin glass-topped drawers in locked cabinets: slivers of silver, chips of chalcedony, amulets of anthracite, lollipops of lapis lazuli. Delmer feigned interest far into the night, plugging his yawns with a fat Havana cigar. The Dean liked Delmer's cigars, of which Delmer's father, once a term, sent him a dove-tailed box the size of a small suitcase.

The Master and his wife asked Delmer to dinner in the Lodge, where Delmer, maddened by the Madeira, announced his intention of willing his personal library to the college. He was lucky that the Master laughed the offer off. Delmer's book-buying already represented a large, if indiscriminate, investment. In receipt of all the rare book catalogues, he chose from them almost at random, and within a seemingly unlimited budget. If he purchased a set of, say, Maria Edgeworth better than the one he already had, he gave the old one to the college library, where the bookplate marked 'From the collection of Delmer Dynamo' was soon familiar. Delmer's declared aim was to rival the learning, taste and munificence of the legendary Aubrey Attwater, who, at the turn of the century, had been the college humanist *par excellence*, a byword for fine wine, fine bindings and fine manners. Delmer founded the Aubrey Attwater society, electing himself both president and secretary. When it turned out that he was also the entire membership, he prorogued the next meeting *sine die*, but without giving up on his ambition to emulate Attwater's luxurious indolence. For Delmer, college was more than a context. It was a niche, a cradle. It was an egg-cup.

I saw the point but wanted something else. Perhaps my brain just wasn't subtle enough for me to sit around until all hours amidst the softly lit oak panelling while discussing why Selwyn was an obscure college, Sidney Sussex was more obscure, and Fitzwilliam was even more obscure than either. In my view, the differences between colleges were impossible to detect. I had, and still have today, enough trouble telling the difference between Cambridge and Oxford, too many of whose products flatter themselves that they have been stamped by the one with some indelible hallmark which informs the discerning that they did not go to the other. No doubt Pembroke had enjoyed more than its fair share of poetic talent – as well as the aforesaid Spenser and Gray, Christopher Smart and Ted Hughes had both been there – but the fund of creativity wouldn't be added to by feeling smug about it while warming one's behind at the fireplace of the grad pad. Without feeling disloyal to my college, I felt under no compulsion to make it my sole stamping ground. A wider stage beckoned: fairly begged, in fact, to be occupied.

Like Oxford, Cambridge was, as it still is, an aggregate of colleges. The university as a whole existed only in two ways: one, as a means to examine the undergraduates, and two, as a display case for their extracurricular activities. Into these latter I purposefully entered. Actually, I did not have much of a plan, but since I was four or five years older than most of my fellow undergraduates – a big gap at that age – I was, although unusually immature, a bit less unsure of myself than they were, and in my principal activity, writing, I had the immense advantage of having been at it a while longer. Cambridge was full of aspiring writers. To publish their works, there was a whole range of periodicals: the weekly newspaper *Varsity* and the irregularly appearing but dauntingly historic *Granta* were only the two most prominent. There were poetry magazines with names like *Pawn*, *Solstice*, *Inverse*, and – a token of seriousness, this – *Poetry Magazine*. There was a stapled, cyclostyled weekly called *Broadsheet* which reviewed everything: the penniless prototype of the listings magazines which ten years later were to strike it rich. The *Cambridge Review*, for which William Empson had once written and in whose letter columns the Leavisites would still occasionally immolate a colleague, was put out by graduates, but otherwise the whole immense publishing effort was produced by a few young men, and fewer young women, all *in statu pupillari*. They were in constant search of publishable material. They were about to meet the right man. They had the demand and I had the supply. In prose even more than in verse, I was still trying to bring my style under control, but in comparison to all the other hungry young geniuses I had the odd scrap of solid information to offer along with the strained metaphors and the overloaded syntax. When I reviewed a film, for example, I could quite often refer to other films by the same director. All those tickets to the National Film Theatre, paid for by my dear lost love Lilith Talbot, were now to have their effect. The great age of the undergraduate film buff had not yet arrived. Nowadays every university in the country boasts a dozen young aspiring film critics who know everything about their subject, even if, because they have seen so many films so fast, they know nothing about anything else. In my day, such a range of reference was less common. I was a harbinger. For *Varsity*, reviewing *Muriel*, I launched into a survey of Resnais's entire *oeuvre*, including the rarely seen *Nuit et Brouillard*. For *Broadsheet*, reviewing *Cuba Si!*, I questioned whether Chris Marker in a state of certainty could ever be as interesting as he was in *Letter from Siberia*, when he was in a state of doubt. Other undergraduate would-be cultural journalists might have been cleverer than I was – as I was later to discover, several of them were – but they hadn't been alive long enough to have that kind of scope. Beyond that, I had the virtue of my chief drawback. My childish imagination was still vivid with the gaudy bric-a-brac which had helped to form it. I wrote about Tarzan and Jane as if they were still real to me. They were, so I sounded convinced, and to sound convinced is the first and longest step towards sounding convincing. My prose pieces gave the effect, strained for though it might be, of a sort of panoptic pop. For the undergraduate editors, always too short of publishable contributions, I was a gift horse who ran off at the mouth.

Soon I was appearing in every publication. The poetry magazines I supplied from the dog-eared back catalogue of finished masterpieces that lined my cardboard suitcase. Here again, there were other undergraduate aspirants more talented. But they were in the first phase of their development and I was in the second of mine. I had got to the point where I would keep working on a poem until it sounded, to my ears at least, like a finished product, not just a promise. It hardly needs saying that my judgment was often faulty: no amount of finishing touches will compensate for a bad design. Much of what I then published seemed to me so immature in retrospect – and retrospect began only a few years later – that at one recent stage I seriously planned to buy up all surviving copies of the relevant magazines and burn them. But at the time it must have seemed, and not just to me, that my work had an authority lacking in the average undergraduate's contribution. It would have been surprising if this had not been so. The poets and editors – all the editors were poets and most of the poets were editors – were admirably poised in their reserved demeanour but they were terribly young. They wore tweeds and corduroys. One of them smoked a pipe and ate seed cake with his sweet tea. Another hid his acne with his hand. The occasional poet-editor was a classless *arriviste*, called something like Steve Bumption, who wore a white leather jacket and talked about Graphics, but at that point trendiness had barely impinged. 'Graphics,' he would say, 'is where it's *all happening*.' But he was saying it into a void. It was all happening in Carnaby Street, not in Cambridge. Mostly the young people who ran the university literary scene looked and sounded as if they belonged in a wartime BBC radio studio along with C. Day Lewis and Louis MacNeice. They crouched beside the gas fire in their rooms pasting up the layout of the next issue on the threadbare carpet while they drank Nescafé from chipped mugs. Doubtless they had ambitions of their own but this failed to occur to me when I burst in and brow-beat them into running a two-page layout of what I cheerfully assured them was my best stuff.

Since I never took 'no' for an answer, their only way to reject my work was to accept it and then try to forget it. I wouldn't let them forget it. Even in that first year, about two-thirds of everything I submitted got published, which, since I submitted a lot, was a lot. My self-assurance must have been a bit tough on the nerves of some of the young poets who had been around for two years already and might have hoped to shine unrivalled during their third year. None of them sought to make me aware of this, or even, in my hearing at any rate, objected to a colonial taking over. There might, of course, have been the odd snide comment I missed. There probably wasn't much I didn't miss, come to think of it. I had never been much of a one for the hidden message. Nor did it occur to me that a lack of editorial resistance might not necessarily be a good thing. What I really needed was discouragement.

Fate decreed that in the theatrical field, if in no other, I would soon get what was coming to me. At the second Footlights smoker in the first term I was on stage in half a dozen different sketches. The Footlights club room, while it had a curtained stage, had no deep wings or any other means of concealment while you waited your turn to go on. Under the windows on the Falcon Yard side of the clubroom there was a wooden bench where you had to wait. It was *de rigueur* to look up at the stage and pretend to enjoy the act preceding yours. As I write, I can feel the curve of that wooden bench under my buttocks: it grew so familiar. Like the oiled stench coming up through the floor from MacFisheries below, and the thump of the dancing feet coming down from the Yacht Club through the ceiling above, the pinch of the bench evoked a cocktail of fear and triumph. You couldn't have the triumph without feeling the fear first. Thus the basic structure of any theatrical experience was laid out cold. Without having in any way begun to refine my sketches – it still hadn't crossed my mind that they would have to be constructed at least as carefully as poems – I went out to the little stage often enough to make an impact. Also I had an angle. My stuff was literary. With the aid of an unsuspecting Canadian who played Alice B. Toklas, I performed a sketch I had written about Gertrude

Stein. Nobody really understood it – I'm sure of that because I didn't either – but at least the number had a tone of its own. At that time, the Footlights was going through one of its recurring periods of looking for a new style. A few years before, *Cambridge Circus*, essentially a Footlights May Week revue with a bigger budget, had conquered London and eventually the world. The Footlights, which had recovered from the success of supplying half the cast of *Beyond the Fringe*, was once again plunged into the necessity of not repeating itself. In London, the satire boom was already commercialised to the point where joining it would have looked slavish. The challenge, as always, was to find your own voice, and the problem, as always, was to find out where that had been mislaid. The club was full of precociously accomplished young performers but as yet they had little to say. I had a lot to say, even if I was not accomplished. This put me in the dangerous position of playing uncle: my worst role. Like most people who organise their lives badly, I just love giving advice.

The Footlights committee were advised by their new recruit to climb on a train and go up to London to see the opening night of *The Charge of the Light Fandango*. The revue I had written with my erstwhile Svengali and long-term collaborator Spencer had found a backer: Spencer's father-in-law. My share of the writing had largely been completed before I came up to Cambridge. Employing the odd weekend *exeat*, I had attended a few rehearsals and helped Spencer to rewrite those of our songs and sketches which threatened to be insufficiently obscure. The cast were all Australian expatriates with high hopes. Some of them had been abroad long enough to be wondering if the big break would ever come. Spencer himself had high hopes, strangely enough. His dedication to obliquity was unimpaired but somehow he expected that his efforts to alienate the audience would meet with rapturous applause. Less forgivably, I expected the same result. I not only should have known better, I *did* know better: but I had been caught up. Any theatrical event has a momentum of its own: any theatrical event except *The Charge of the Light Fandango*. The Lyric Theatre, Hammersmith, had been hired at colossal expense. The Footlights committee were sitting with me in a box. To say that the disaster unfolded would be to exaggerate its pace. The disaster developed at the speed of stale cheese growing blue hair. It was all low points, but perhaps the lowest was a song about a jewel robbery which Spencer and I, greatly pleased with our own ingenuity, had written to the tune of Ravel's *Bolero*. Six of the cast were meant to sing it while tip-toeing in intricate patterns around the stage. If they had merely forgotten the words it would have been a mercy. Pummelled by the waves of indifference from the auditorium, however, they remembered the words, but in the wrong order. Since the choreography was cued by the lyrics, the actors were soon out of sequence. Eventually two of them were out of sight, having taken craven advantage of their proximity to the wings. It was hard to blame them. The song was a *tour de force* and nothing else.

The whole show was like that. It was all technique. Even at that time I half-realised it: a pretty drastic self-appraisal after more than a year's work. The Lord Chamberlain, who at that time still exercised his baleful influence on the British theatre, had insisted that my best sketch be left out. It was an all-purpose Queen's speech, in which the sovereign assured some foreign country that her best wishes, warm blankets or aircraft carriers were on their way towards it. The idea was that she could cross out what did not apply. When the Lord Chamberlain crossed out the whole thing, I tried to convince myself that censorship had wrecked our chances. The dutiful chuckles of the Footlights committee should have told me the truth. They stayed to the end, in sharp contrast to the majority of the audience, which drained away steadily throughout the first half, leaving the second half to be watched only by friends and relatives. The party afterwards was a wake in all respects except the failure of Spencer's father-in-law to realise that he was the corpse. Either he enjoyed losing money or else he was simply relieved about not having been on stage. It would have been disloyal to renounce my expatriate colleagues, who had all tried hard. Also I honestly felt (self-deception always feels particularly honest) that we had done something new and challenging. Privately, however, far back, in a dark part of my mind which admitted light but was slow to reflect it, I was getting ready to begin again. In Sydney, though I had found Spencer's influence overwhelming, I had always harboured secret desires to establish a contact with the audience. In Cambridge, the undergraduate thespians, however green, shared the same impulse. The polite young men I was with wanted to be entertainers and so did I. On the train back up to Cambridge we talked about something else. They were so kind and tactful that they frightened me. Where had they *got* it, this sensitivity to the pain of others? School must have been Hell, like the trenches in World War One, which could have been the subject of the reviews that *The Charge of the Light Fandango* got next day. I read them in the Junior Common Room and resisted the temptation to rip them out of the newspapers so that nobody else would see them. This forbearance might have been, had it been conscious, a correct guess about the tactical advisability of not reacting to criticism. In reality, however, I was so drained of energy that the effort of tearing a sheet of newspaper would have left me breathless.

Luckily a chance to work off my embarrassment offered itself straight away. Footlights was not the only institution to stage smokers. Some of the colleges had an annual smoker of their own. These college smokers were staffed almost exclusively by Footlights members who were not necessarily members of the college concerned. In other words, the Footlights were pulling a fast one. The relevant university bye-law, fiercely enforced by the proctors, allowed the Footlights only two smokers per term plus the annual May Week revue. In order to work up the best material from the twice-a-term Footlights smokers into a form which might possibly make it into the May Week revue, the Footlights infiltrated the college smokers. Any Footlights member who wasn't enrolled at the college concerned was invited in as a guest. A sufficiently fanatical Footlights performer could thus tread the boards in the club room, in his own college and as a guest in every other college, so that he was in a constant rhythm of rehearsing and performing for as long as the academic year lasted. In a college smoker, especially, he would get plenty of practice at playing to a wider audience, because a college smoker could be attended by anybody from that college or any other college, since the tickets were on the open market.

Of all the college smokers, the most reliably successful was the Pembroke smoker. When Peter Cook had been up, agents from London would attend the Pembroke smoker and try to purchase the material. On one occasion Cook sold the whole show to the West End. The effect of his professionalism, though not necessarily of his originality, had lingered on. It was a hard act to follow, and when the Footlights committee suggested that I might like to direct the next Pembroke smoker I was not hasty in saying yes. Without question I was the natural choice. The only other Footlights member from my college was some kind of scientist who had been elected to the club by accident after giving what the audience had taken to be a brilliant impersonation of a man who had forgotten a terrible script. When the fact finally percolated that the script had really been terrible and that he had, indeed, forgotten it, he settled down for three years of enjoying the bar facilities and left the field clear for me. But although I had no doubts about the desirability of going back to basics and learning to please an audience, I had several doubts about whether this was the right time to do it. First of all, there was the question of my studies, which so far were non-existent. Also my confidence was not at its highest. The quality of the silence with which the audience had greeted *The Charge of the Light Fandango* was still ringing in my ears like a blow to the side of the head with the flat of the hand. I could still hear every cough, every wild, bitter laugh of disbelief, every bang of the safety exit double-doors as the steel bar across them was hit loudly by the uncaring fist of another customer baling out like a test pilot from a prototype spinning to its doom. Finally, the doors had been held open by the usherettes. They had nodded knowingly. I didn't want to see that knowing nod again.

I was talked out of my gloom and into the job. Actually, the show couldn't lose. Eric Idle was in it and he knew all the ropes. Above all, he knew that what really mattered was the wine. Into Pembroke's old library, called Old Library, were carried many boxes of a cheap but acceptably smooth Beaujolais from Peter Dominic, who also supplied the glasses. Many of these were broken on the first night by the Hearties. The show ran for four nights and everybody came. The Hearties were merely the noisiest element. Large, boat-rowing types with low foreheads, thick necks and annoyingly pretty female companions imported from London, they laughed at everything, including the love songs. Everyone else enjoyed the show too, although most of them would have been hard put to give a clear account of it afterwards. All the men were in black tie and all the women in evening gowns. Some of the male dons would have liked to have been in evening gowns also, but they confined themselves to lipstick and rouge. The stage, constructed from beer-crates for the occasion, was only about six feet square and stood uncurtained in one corner of the room, so that you could make an entrance through the door leading to the book-stack. The rest of the room was packed with small low tables tightly surrounded by increasingly happy people. The oxygen was quickly used up. So was the wine, except that our waiters kept replacing it. The heat was terrific. Breathing neat nitrogen, with only an unlimited supply of plonk to stave off dehydration, the entire audience was already drunk before the lights went down on the first act. Even the dons were shouting. But the level of physical behaviour remained decorous if you didn't count the periodic attempts by the Hearties to smash their table by dancing on it.

The show, I am bound to say, merited an enthusiastic response. A cast of all the best Footlights guest artists did their stuff, topped off by Romaine Rand's fabled strip-tease nun routine, making its first appearance since the Sydney University revue several years before. For its reincarnation in the Pembroke smoker, she had hand-sewn a whole new Carmelite nun's habit. She wore a particularly daring bikini underneath. Luckily, the Dean didn't see the show until the last night, when he bit through the stem of his pipe. Though Romaine pulled the walls in, really there was nothing in the show which did not go down a storm, mainly because the audience was clinically intoxicated, but partly because, in my role as producer, I had arranged the running order with some care, making sure that the up-beat songs came at the end of the half and stuff like that. I even got away with my own monologue. A whimsical little number about two railway locomotives in love, it went on for so long that the Hearties, from a sitting start, managed to reduce their table to matchwood before I was half-way through. But the show had built up too much impetus to be easily stopped. Since the whole of the university's theatrical establishment turned up over the course of the four nights, this small success could be counted as my first tangible impact on the broader Cambridge scene. For anyone with the right set of personal inadequacies, an applauding audience is a wine far more heady than anything that you can buy in a bottle. I was especially pleased to see the women putting their hands together admiringly. The wine having flowed freely for the cast as well as the audience, it was with a fond eye made foolish that I peeped low around the corner of the book-stack door while some other act was on stage and checked out those pretty faces looking up, lit as if they were spectators at a ballet by Degas. I felt love. I felt grief. I felt sick. Where had they been?

Wherever they had been, they were gone again when the fifth day dawned and there was no more Pembroke smoker to draw them out of their hiding-places. A life without women made it hard to be temperate. Theoretically, I was undeviatingly loyal to my near-fiancée, Françoise. Having left Australia the year after I did, she was now studying in Florence. Italy was a long way away. My close Catholic acquaintance, Robin, was still in London, but even London needed an *exeat* and Robin was going through one of her recurring phases of being reconciled with the Church. Questions of fidelity aside, to know a girl in Cambridge would have been the answer, but where were they? The few that I clapped eyes on seemed capable of transferring themselves from the Sidgwick Avenue site to the safety of their Newnham sitting rooms within a matter of seconds, or else cycling back up Castle Hill to Girton as if competing successfully in the Tour de France. Perhaps I should have paid more attention to my personal appearance. Many a young man has worn himself to a frazzle practising verbal approaches when what he should have done was wash his hair. But even supposing I had squeaked with cleanliness, who would have seen the shine? Sitting through lectures at Sidgwick Avenue was too high a price to pay, and if the undergraduettes weren't working there, they were working in the University Library, the faculty libraries or their rooms. Study was all they ever did. Abramovitz had the answer but it took his kind of unembarrassable self-confidence. He toured the schools in Station Road where the foreign girls came to learn English, picked himself a strapping German with paradigmatically chiselled Aryan features, brought her back to his rooms and gave her English lessons. The fee was not in cash but in kind. Through Abramovitz's frequently sported oak, the squeals of his guest penetrated with ease. What was he doing to her in there? When I met him in the gyp room while brewing tea he would explain, trembling with repletion, that he was doing his bit for historic justice. 'I've *enslaved* her, dear boy. It's the guilt. She's putty in my hands.' I think he taunted her during the throes of need. Anyway, there was a big scandal when his ancient bedder – the same Mrs Blades who was my bedder too – tottered into his bedroom one morning and found half a dozen loosely knotted, awesomely heavy condoms festooned all over the decor. The one draped over the lampshade had started to fry. Presumably Mrs Blades had seen one or two of those things before, back around the time of the Battle of Jutland, because when she eyeballed six of them at once the shock of recognition drove her backwards all the way down the stairs and across the court into the Dean's office, where she had hysterics among the haematite. Convulsions amid the chrysoprase. She passed out into the porphyry. The Dean proclaimed the matter out of his spiritual jurisdiction and got in touch with the Chief Rabbi, who happened to be Abramovitz's uncle. Abramovitz should have had another year of living in college but he was told that next year he would have to take digs in town. He was lucky not to get sent down. He had luck running out of his ears so maybe the reprieve was just normal. Abramovitz was among the blessed. Some of the English he taught Helga apparently got her into a lot of trouble back in Stuttgart. 'Wasn't it remarkable,' he asked me years later, 'how *much* she looked like Heydrich?'

3

Sleeping Tiger

PREPARING FOR PART TWO of the English Tripos was supposed to take me two academic years, and the first was already gone in a drunken haze. As usual, I had done quite a lot of reading. Again as usual, little of it was on the course. I had started teaching myself French by construing Proust a sentence at a time – the complete job was to take only slightly less than fifteen years – but to satisfy the examination requirements I would have done better to teach myself a bit more English from the English Moralists, some of whom I could not recognise even by name, let alone by their opinions. The unspoken policy in Cambridge was to give affiliated students like myself a long rein in their first year, although a certain proportion – mainly Americans, strangely enough – persisted in regarding the long rein as enough rope, and hanging themselves with it. Suicide from loneliness was unnervingly common. One of the many hazardous prospects of a bedder's job was to enter a young gentleman's oak-panelled sitting room in the morning and find him suspended from the central light-fitting. This possibility was rendered less likely in my case by the news that I too, like Abramovitz, might have to spend the following academic year lodged in the town, where oak panelling was less lavishly supplied. I was also officially advised that during the long vacation it might be profitable to attain at least nodding acquaintance with the curriculum, and thus stave off the already likely possibility that I would receive a degree classified so low it would be tantamount to a certificate of mental disability. But all these admonitions were easy to take lightly now that it was May Week in Cambridge.

May Week, one need hardly point out, took place in June. Only if it had been called April Week would it have taken place in May. Your first academic year in Cambridge is so arranged that you must learn to appreciate your surroundings in winter, when the trees are waterlogged traceries and the buildings are doomy silhouettes between sky and fen. Captain Cousteau diving without lights saw more colour under a continental shelf than you will see in Cambridge between November and March. Also he kept relatively dry. So you either hang yourself from despair inside one of the venerable edifices or else learn to love them for their shape alone. The perfect little lidless cube of Clare College unpacks its form most reluctantly, but eventually most completely, when the grass of its courtyard is covered with a tablecloth of snow. In Garret Hostel Lane, the dark chimneys of Trinity's south wing are already cut out clearly against the sodden clouds. The trick is to see the brilliance of the set design before the spotlights are switched on. After that, not even the blind could miss it. When spring pumps the water out of the panorama, the lawns of King's light up and throw their radiance into walls that suddenly look as edible as wafers. The blue sun-dials in the courts of Caius reveal what they have been mimicking: a clear sky. The Wren library in Trinity fills up with sunlight underneath, a baroque hovercraft on fire. The backs of the colleges are like Dresden reborn in a garden, like an Ideal Chateau Exhibition on a toytown Loire. The whole undergraduate population takes to the punts. Released from their examinations, the girls whose very existence you had begun to doubt reveal their delicious corporeality in thin cotton frocks vaporised by sunlight. Horrible young men in blazers and straw boaters momentarily attain the fluent beauty of a river party by Renoir, before their neighing voices – 'I say Simon! Simon! Don't let those oiks nab that punt!' – shatter the illusion. The illusion forms again. Everyone is outdoors. Everyone except those concerned with the Footlights May Week Revue. They are inside the Arts Theatre, facing the horrendous prospect of not being loved.

46

That first year I calamitously failed the audition to join the cast, but got the job of assistant stage manager. Being a bit older than anyone else involved, I was in a potentially humiliating position, but felt, with the flop of *The Charge of the Light Fandango* still reverberating in my dreams, that a stretch of being humble couldn't hurt. It could be argued that Cambridge was already eroding my spirit of protest. A more likely explanation, however, was that I had temporarily suspended my self-assertiveness in order to submit myself to a new discipline. I was falling back in order to jump better. The French, I had just learned from Proust, had a phrase for it: *reculer pour mieux sauter*. I couldn't pronounce it very well, but it sounded like the right idea.

As a Footlights May Week revue assistant stage manager, I was diligence personified. The previous year's revue had apparently been only one step up from a fiasco. It had tried to ape its successful predecessor *Cambridge Circus* without the wherewithal in either personnel or material. This year's had improved the position to the point of being merely something of a dud. Romaine had been coaxed out of the library to join Eric Idle at the head of an accomplished cast, but good material was at a premium, and most numbers were little better than workmanlike. But being little better than that, they were never worse than that either. The music, in particular, seemed astonishingly inventive and accomplished to anyone who, like myself, had spent several years arduously fitting lyrics on to ready-made melodies because he didn't know anyone who could write new ones. In the Footlights there were young men who could read and write music. In the depths of my conceit I didn't really believe that any of these youngsters could write words better than I could, but when it came to putting black dots between staves – or between keys or whatever it was that they did – there was no question that they had me whipped. Nearly everybody could sing. Even those who could only speak could speak in tongues. They could do accents, for example, which I couldn't, and indeed still can't. So there was an air of professionalism about the whole business, to which I contributed with some ruthlessly efficient assistant stage management. When the show was touring the provincial towns, the set had to be secured to the stage with sixty-four separate screws. I had them all colour-coded. With one of those pump-action screwdrivers I could do the whole job in the dark. When Idle sprinted on stage as the Olympic torch-bearer, his flaming torch had been primed by me with exactly the right amount of inflammable fluid. When Idle came sprinting off again, barely had the lights snapped out before I had propelled Romaine, dressed as a Russian peasant woman and sitting in an old armchair on top of a wheeled platform, smoothly into position for her appearance as Tolstoy's widow. The whole lexicon of backstage terminology – tabs, flats, spots, dimmers – was easy on my lips. On the entire tour I made no mistakes at all. It turned out that I was saving them all up for the opening night in London.

Perhaps the venue spooked me. Once again, by the cruellest coincidence, it was the Lyric, Hammersmith. The memory still haunted me of how the audience, during the early stages of *The Charge of the Light Fandango*, had fought among themselves at the crowded exits. That night at the wake, I had poured Spencer's bereaved father-in-law a full glass of whisky because he had been still too stunned to say 'when'. This night I must have been reliving that night, because when the time came to prime Idle's Olympic torch with inflammable fluid I overdid it by a pint. As he ran on, his torch was already sending flames almost to the proscenium arch, and before he was half-way through his monologue there were fireballs falling all around him. Trouper that he was, he kept going to the end, but the audience found it harder to laugh as it became more likely that his incipient demise would entail theirs. Shortly before the end of the number the torch, as if disappointed at having failed to burn down the theatre, sputtered out, just in time to ruin Idle's punch-line, which depended on its still being alight. When he came running off into the wings he cursed me with admirable restraint, but by now I was rattled, and I pushed Romaine's trolley into the blackout with too much force, so that it rolled several feet past the marked position. When the fixed spotlight which should have illuminated her was switched on, it illuminated a circular area of empty stage instead. She delivered the first part of her monologue in total darkness, during which time, it transpired, she had got out of her chair and begun the job of pushing the trolley back towards the right position. When the lighting operator at last figured out what had gone wrong, he killed the fixed light and picked her up with a follow-spot, thereby revealing her toiling away like Mother Courage at the exact moment when she was describing what it was like to be paralysed on her death bed. The audience was either sophisticated enough to be wondering politely how Brecht had got into the act, or else had correctly judged that something was amiss.

The show would probably have been no great smash hit anyway, but I had helped scotch what chance it had. The notices were death threats. David Frost, acting as a guest critic in *Punch*, was generously kind, but a turkey, once cremated, declines to be a phoenix. Though the revue ran for the scheduled two weeks, it was full only from Thursday to Saturday, with hellish matinées during which the cast ran some of the sketches backwards to see whether the old age pensioners would notice. I got some valuable training in how to keep slogging away at a show after it had been pronounced dead. Also, I was getting paid: the first real money I had ever made in show business. Though the stipend wasn't very large, it was larger than the one I earned next. When the show folded, there was still a lot of the Long Vacation stretching ahead, and before I could get to Italy I would need to earn the fare. One of the regular staff at the Lyric told me that the circus at Olympia had an opening for a roustabout. I applied for the job and got it before I found out that the opening was at the back of a tiger.

My job was to clean out the tiger's cage. In later years, when telling this story, I didn't always remember to mention that the tiger was removed from the cage before I got in there with my bucket and short shovel. Actually there wouldn't have been much danger if the tiger had stayed put. He had probably thrown the occasional scare into Clive of India, but to Clive James he posed no threat. So old that only his stripes were holding him together, he had teeth that couldn't dent the tennis ball with which he had been provided. Already safer than if he had been stuffed, he was rendered definitively innocuous by drugs. Some form of tranquilliser was fed to him in his morning hunk of raw meat, zonking him to the point where he couldn't suck his tennis ball without dribbling. The trainer plus three assistants removed the savage beast from its cage by rolling two long poles under the dozing corpse and lifting it out like a litter full of rag and bone. Then in I would go, a man in control of his fear, showing the ice-cool nerve of those who work close to the big cats. In I would go and scoop up those sadly depleted droppings. The poor shagged-out old moggie could scarcely shit a pretzel. The stuff was a sort of dark green, if you're wondering. Or perhaps, in that mysterious part of the brain which Baudelaire conquered like a new country, one of my memories has taken colour from another.

Flashback

When I was about twelve years old in Sydney I was allowed for the first time to attend the Royal Easter Show on my own, carrying two whole pounds with which to buy sample bags. I bought the Minties sample bag so that I could assemble the Minties cardboard gun, which was meant to fire cardboard discs but could fire lead slugs if you doubled the rubber band. Having assembled the gun, I ate all the Minties. I bought the Jaffas sample bag and ate all the Jaffas. So my stomach already had a lot to deal with before I bought not just one Giant Licorice sample bag, but two. My plan was to take one of the Giant Licorice sample bags home to my friend, Graham Gilbert, who was bedridden with German measles. Before I had finished eating the contents of my own Giant Licorice sample bag, this plan was already starting to fade, and during the long wait for the Doll's Point bus that was to take me home I ate the contents of the second bag as well. There was an incredible amount of licorice in a Giant Licorice sample bag, and all of it was black. There were logs of black licorice, straps of black licorice, coils of black licorice, cables of black licorice. By the time the bus came I had eaten everything and could make my way only with caution up the stairs to the top deck. Just past Brighton-le-Sands the road along the beach met President Avenue. From the junction it was an easy walk to Kogarah, so that was where I usually got off. It was where I got off this time, too, but not as usual. I pressed the upstairs bell to halt the bus at the next stop, but I couldn't move without feeling strange. The conductor appeared on the downstairs rear platform and looked up the staircase to see who had pressed the bell in an irresponsible manner, a misdemeanour to which a statutory penalty was attached. As I swayed at the top of the stairs I could see him in the stair-well mirror, so he must have seen what I did next. I vomited. I did the big spit. In the resulting avalanche, large fragments of Minties and Jaffas appeared merely as reinforcement, like gravel in liquid concrete. The basic thrust of the whole thing, the burden as it were, was an unspeakable tide of half-digested licorice. Yet what struck me with most force, even as the first wave of the descending onslaught struck the conductor, was how strange it was that what had gone in black had come out green. It was a dark green, admittedly: a green deeper than bottle green, thicker than heavy jade. But still it was green. From where I crouched heaving at the head of the stairs, it all went bouncing down like a baroque cascade of duckweed nougat. When, void and light-headed, I started walking home, the bus was still there: all the passengers had been ordered off because the conductor had refused to continue.

*   *   *

But that was to digress. I like to think that in adulthood I have acquired a certain polish, and that if I were now offered two sample bags full of Giant Licorice I would have the will-power to turn one of them down. There is no use pretending, however, that my sensibilities were either refined or usefully mortified by squeegeeing the effluent of a senile feline whose only contribution to the big cat act was a slow hop on to a stool and another slow hop down again, the two manoeuvres being separated by a growl in response to a crack of the trainer's whip. The growl sounded like a long yawn from the audience, a comparison which could readily be verified. It wasn't much of a circus, yet I rarely failed to watch the performance. The show didn't run to a trapeze act but there was a good-looking and sumptuously shapely girl in a silver-spangled scarlet leotard who climbed up a rope into the roof, hung on by her teeth to a short silver bar, and then spun rapidly round. It's an old act – Degas and Lautrec both did a picture of it – but it never fails if the girl has the right equipment, and Pearl had. She was billed as Pearl the Girl in a Whirl and in addition to her athletic attainments she demonstrated an excellent understanding of my poems for someone whose usual reading matter was the novels of Barbara Cartland. Pearl was all strength. When she flashed her teeth you tended to cross your legs involuntarily. But underneath the finely tuned muscles there was something tender. Unfortunately the ringmaster thought so too. Pearl was his mistress. When the circus broke up they left for Benidorm together. I left for Florence, this time able to pay for my own ticket, with only a small subsidy from Robin so that I could buy two cartons of duty-free Rothmans filters – which in Italy were as good as gold, because the Nazionale cigarettes produced by the state tobacco monopoly tasted like burning polystyrene.

Another wise precaution was to remove my beard. This transformed my reception in Florence almost as much as it transformed my face, which emerged pale, small and pointed at the bottom, like a talking turnip. Some of the things it said were in the local language, which with Françoise's encouragement I had mastered to the point of being able to speak platitudinously on the subject currently under discussion, instead of the subject that had been changed five minutes before. In those last few beautiful summers before the floods, the young university people of Florence had an open air party every evening as the sun went down behind the cypresses lining the informal garden of some villa on the other side of the Arno, usually on the slope leading up between the Gardens of Boboli and the Piazzale Michelangelo. Sunset left the horizon rimmed with a light like crème de menthe. Young men wore cravats, allegedly of English origin, thus adding extra casualness to their tan lightweight suits, the jackets of which were hooked on one shoulder in the warm air. Young women wore silk and sandals. To indicate nonconformity they smoked like old trains. Feminism had not yet arrived but the girls were already feeling, if not their power, certainly the need for it. They could all talk a streak. One of them, called Adriana, was so witty she literally took away your breath: you were scared to respire in case you missed a wisecrack. Incorrectly judging her eyes to be too small, she drew circles of mascara around them, which made her look like a pangolin. At dinner in Gabriella's apartment across from the façade of the Pitti Palace, Adriana would palpitate on the spot with the fecund splendour of her own verbal invention, her cigarette waving around her head like a magic wand, ashing gaily into the ice-cream pudding. 'The sweet is my ashtray,' she would cry in her own language: 'it sounds like my autobiography.' Gabriella ate the affected area, as a gesture of apology for her money and titles. Larger gestures would be demanded later, but this was before the young Italian intellectuals had taken their rebellion much beyond a daring thesis reinterpreting Gramsci, or an interest in the poetry of Pier Paolo Pasolini. When crocked on chianti they sang the old songs of the partisans. With the hangover came the eternal question of who would be appointed whose research assistant when and where. '*Bella ciao*,' they sang rebelliously, '*bella ciao bella ciao bella ciao ciao ciao*.' But the system was hard to buck. If music could have changed the antiquated Italian university system it would have had to be the kind of music that changed Jericho. Even Gabriella must have been concerned about how and where she would fit in. If she was worried, though, it was hard to tell. In addition to the apartment opposite the Pitti Palace, Gabriella owned a villa in the country. She was an aristocrat. Her hospitality was extended not only to her friends, but to the friends of her friends, such as myself. She had nobility. There is nobility in every class but if an aristocrat has it she finds it easier to exercise it. My beliefs, at the time, being dead set against privilege in all its forms, I found it disturbing to like her style. Though not beautiful, she had the grace that brought beauty towards her. Everyone was at his best near Gabriella. Françoise's fine intelligence burst into flower, and Adriana became a semantic fountain. Keeping, or trying to keep, up with what Adriana said was the best possible training, a linguistic advanced motorist's course. A supplement to the course was La Lucciola Estiva, the Summer Firefly, an open air cinema in the dry pebbled bed of the Arno which showed the comedies of Ugo Tognazzi and Nino Manfredi on a continuous basis. *L'Immorale*, a comedy directed by Pietro Germi and starring Tognazzi, was the first Italian film whose dialogue I was able to follow. Tognazzi played a soft-hearted *amoroso* who kept two wives and a mistress ecstatically happy by lying to all of them while he ran from one to the other on a split-second timetable. He never missed a trick. Remembering every birthday and anniversary, he always bought the correct flowers, turned up on time for the intimate little dinner by candlelight, knocked himself out being wonderful with the children. Finally, in a post office, while mailing three separate sets of letters and postcards, he expired quietly from a heart attack. The audience laughed helplessly at his demise, so perfectly was the film paced. I saw it three times and enrolled it among the all-time film masterpieces. Perhaps it wasn't, but the thrill was authentic: the state of grace when we break through into understanding a new language is, after all, only the recurrence, this time fully conscious, of the long euphoria in which we first attained comprehension of the tongue to which we were born. For those of us who work with words, a periodic return to that initial urgency is essential. Don't listen to the pedant who says that because you have not mastered the whole speech of another language there is no point learning to read it. Smatterings are well worth having. They help strip the world bare again of its cloaking vocabulary. Dante's few lines about how paper burns took me back to the first principles of evocation in a way all of Shakespeare's plays could not, because with Shakespeare I had forgotten that the word and the thing are different things. Florence was my unofficial university. In my few weeks there I read more than in the whole of the previous year. My whitewashed room in the Antica Cervia, an obscure *locanda* behind the Palazzo Vecchio, was like a warehouse of sand-coloured BUR paperbacks. Two streets further down towards Piazza Santa Croce was the Trattoria Anita, a cheap restaurant favoured by whores, pimps and cigarette-smugglers. There I read and ate, spattering the pages of Cesare Pavese with spots of meat sauce. In the Biblioteca Nazionale I was part of the furniture, taking short lunches so that I could wolf down Sapegno's history of pre-Renaissance literature, the note-books of Leopardi and the major works of Benedetto Croce. Very little of this would come in handy when I sat the Italian paper in Part Two of the Cambridge English Tripos, but my guardian angel was still working overtime to protect me from utilitarian values. His representative on Earth was Françoise, who seemed dutybound to push the right books in front of me so that I could devour them. What satisfaction she got out of my single-mindedness I didn't bother to ask. The question never occurred to me, any more than it occurred to me to wonder why she didn't choose between her several other suitors, all of them serious and one with a very large Mercedes. Perhaps that was my secret. Having left ordinary self-absorption behind, I was a self trying to absorb all creation, and must have been as hard to ignore as a vacuum cleaner.

Michaelmas term was already a week old when I caught a crowded train north to Milan. Reading Eugenio Montale's first book of essays, I scarcely noticed that I spent the whole journey on my feet. The plane was delayed by a day. The airline paid for a night in a cheap hotel but such necessary extras as cigarettes ate up my remaining cash and when asked for the airport tax I was once again embarrassingly not able to produce it. The last time that had happened to me, a nice man from Calcutta had taken pity and offered assistance, no strings attached. This time there was no Indian Samaritan on hand to overhear my entreaties and fork out the money. All the Indians were back in India. The airport tax official, noting the book I was carrying, must have independently decided that a foreigner's incipient love of the world's most lovely language should be encouraged by subsidy. Dumb luck. Don't think it doesn't bother me now, how my falling bread always landed with the buttered side up. It even bothered me then. But there was a mass of compensatory trouble waiting for me in the chill air of the fens. In my Junior Common Room pigeon-hole was a series of progressively more curt notes from the Dean requiring my presence at once. Either he was digging a mine-shaft down into the linen room and needed help, or I was in deep shit.

4

Unquiet Flow the Dons

I NEARLY GOT thrown out. Squatting gnome-like in his rocky grotto, the Dean examined the bowl of his pipe as if he had not yet given up hope of discovering small but valuable mineral deposits within its charred circumference. Mature students of a certain theatrical *réclame*, he informed me, could get away with a lot, but to come up late for term, without a previous written application, was to invite rustication at the very least. Also it was just plain bad manners. To one *in statu pupillari* such as myself, he explained, the college was *in loco parentis*. Gazing at the Dean as he sat framed among feldspar, I found it hard not to reflect that he was about as loco as any parent could well get, but this unworthy thought was chased away by my uncomfortable realisation that he had a point. Offering my apology on the spot, I pleaded, with some truth, that the educational stimulus of Tuscany had distracted me from my normal loyalties. The Dean accepted these protestations with a Christian heart, though it was clear that Italy for him meant either the presence of the Scarlet Woman or an absence of suitable rocks. Perhaps the customs officers had once opened his bags in the Brenner Pass and found them full of Carrara marble. This year, he told me, I would not be offered a set in college. He understood that there was a room going at the Eagle, in the centre of town. The Eagle being a pub, it scarcely counted as approved lodgings, but it would do until I found something better. He made it sound as if I had better find something better pretty quickly, or else die of privation. He did not, on the other hand, offer the alternative of staying on in college until something classier than a room at the Eagle should become available. 'Trot along,' he insisted, 'and rent it straight away.' My packed suitcase, he added, was in the care of the housekeeper. Naturally I could eat in Hall as usual, but perhaps it would be an advantage both to myself and the college if I no longer had to scale the walls after dark. There was such a thing as dignity, and too many nights spent in the incinerator skip could entail its loss. 'One can only advise,' he puffed.

He left me to find out for myself that the incinerator skip knocked spots off the Eagle as a place of abode. The Eagle was the most romantic pub in Cambridge, if not the whole of England. During the war, bomber crews from all over East Anglia had come to the Eagle to spend, in hilarious conviviality, what was statistically likely to be one of their last evenings alive. Riding on each other's shoulders, into the deep red linoleum ceiling of the saloon they burned the numbers and nicknames of their squadrons with naked candle flames: a portent, doubly hideous for its innocence, of their own fate, and a grim token of the fiery nemesis they were bringing every night to the cities of Germany. To this day I can't enter that room without hearing their laughter, which becomes steadily more unmanning as I grow older. All my sons. Twenty years ago I was not all that much older than they had been when they were snuffed out. It was a hall of fame, a temple of the sacred flame, a trophy room for heroes. Unfortunately my room was somewhere above it, and not quite so grand. The door to my room opened off the first floor gallery which ran around the courtyard where the coaches had once stopped. When I opened the door and stepped into the darkened room, I fell across the bed and smacked my forehead smartly on the opposite wall. Luckily the wall, under many geological layers of plaster and paint, was sufficiently resilient to absorb most of the impact. It was also quite moist. When I found the light switch, a twenty-watt bulb dispelled just enough of the gloom to reveal that the moisture was not my blood. It was rising damp. It was also descending damp, with a good deal of transverse damp mixed in. The smell of mould was tropical. The temperature of the air, on the other hand, was arctic. There was a two-bar electric fire, one of whose bars worked reasonably well for half its length. I had lived like this in London. I had no wish, and no capacity, to live like this again. Squeezing my cardboard suitcase into the space not occupied by the bed, I lay down in the half-light and tried to decide whether I was near tears or had simply begun, like my new surroundings, to deliquesce. There was a pillowcase on the pillow but there was something on the pillowcase. It was wet dust.

I had not really been punished. Nobody ever was. The ancient universities looked after their own. When a currently famous poet lived on my stair at Pembroke, he not only invited women friends to stay the night and the next night as well, he advertised the fact by encouraging them to dry their stockings out of his window, which overlooked the old court, called Old Court. After about a year of indecision, the Senior Tutor for Junior Supervisors finally grasped the nettle. He knocked timidly on the poet's seemingly permanently sported oak. Nothing happened. The Tutor went away. The next day he went back and knocked again. Still nothing. The day after that, he knocked again. At last the oak rumbled open to reveal the poet, stark naked with his arms thrown apart, shouting 'Crucify me!' Within seconds the Senior Tutor was having tea with the Dean. Together they decided that nothing had occurred, even though blasphemy, as the celebrated case of Mark Boxer had recently demonstrated, was the only reason why anyone ever *was* sent down. The Tutor went on to become the Master, the poet went on to become Poet Laureate – I name no names – and the Dean went on. Continuity was the keynote. Any amount of eccentricity was tolerable as long as not publicised. If my friend Boxer, rather than publishing a mildly secular poem in *Granta*, had practised voodoo in his rooms, he would have gone on to get his Gentleman's Third, instead of being carried symbolically out of Cambridge in an open coffin. But merely to state his case is to show the truth. To be thrown out was to be kept in. Oxbridge had you even when it let you go. Oxford threw Shelley out but kept his name. You can get sprung only on probation. It drives some alumni bananas, so that they write whole cycles of plays and novels about how they don't really care about not having become dons. One of the several candidates for the dubious title of Cleverest Man in England always tells his interviewers that the one real failure of his life was his not being elected a Fellow of All Souls. Can you imagine, say, Leonardo da Vinci, who had a reasonable claim to the title of Cleverest Man in Italy, confessing his disappointment at being refused membership of any institution at all, no matter how exalted? Though I had reason to be grateful to Cambridge, I was already thanking God that it hadn't caught me young, before the world had given me some measure by which to get its insidious cosiness into proportion. As things stood, I had the memory of how Masaccio's frescoes looked on the wall of the Church of the Carmine in Florence to remind me of what intellectual distinction was really like. The dons could impress me with what they knew, but it took more than their port and walnuts to impress me with what they were.

And some of them were as crazy as loons. To give a star student free board and lodging for life might well protect his future productivity from quotidian distraction but it is rarely good for the personality and can lead to behaviour patterns indistinguishable from those that get people in other walks of life locked up. Either Trinity or Trinity Hall, I forget which, elected a History Fellow in the 1930s who seemed set fair to be the next Edward Gibbon. From that day forward he never did anything except walk the streets with a bundle of old newspapers under his arm. If they had always been the same newspapers he might have retained some historical interest. You could have stopped him and found out what the *Daily Express* had said about Ribbentrop. But he changed the newspapers at random, just as he never took the same route twice on his endless walks to nowhere.

A don didn't need to be carrying a bundle of newspapers in order to manifest an unhinged walk. It was a Fellow's privilege, when crossing a courtyard, to walk diagonally across the grass instead of, like everyone else, keeping to the flagstones around the edge. Dons whose behaviour was near normal in all other respects would exercise this grass-treading privilege even when it would have been more convenient to everybody, including themselves, if they had not. In summer they would amble across the grass and then wonder loudly why they had been followed by a large party of tourists from Osaka. The answer was obvious: the tourists from Osaka had not been able to judge from the Fellow's gowned appearance that he was any more uniquely privileged than a bad imitation of Batman. But the Fellow's training had equipped him to deal only with the abstruse. Though he could deliver a learned paper about Ulrich von Wilamowitz-Moellendorff's refutation of A. B. Drachmann's theories about *Antigone*, or preferably compose a scathing review of somebody else's learned paper on that subject, he couldn't deal with the proposition that the really smart way to preserve the grass would be to deny access not just to most people, but to everybody. One don, in a college I had better not name, walked diagonally across the grass even in winter. This would have made sense if he had worn wellingtons. He invariably wore the patent leather dancing pumps which had been bequeathed to him by Ivor Novello. The snow could be three feet deep and you would see his tracks going through it like the wake of a caribou. The short cut would have made some sense if he had been saving mileage at the beginning of a route march to Land's End. He was only going as far as the Porter's Lodge to see if there was any news of the Jamaican steel band he invited over every year to play calypsos to him in his rooms. Blessed with a large inheritance, he had a healthy bank balance which the gift of a suite of rooms, all found, did nothing to diminish, but his emotional propensities were more questionable, although rumour had it that not all the members of the steel band were asked to remove their clothes, only some. The rest just took off their overcoats and galoshes.

In Cambridge there was a good deal of High Table homosexuality, some of it still struggling in the closet but a lot of it out in the open and dancing around on tiptoe. Recently the full story has been told of how the homosexual mathematician, Alan Turing, most gifted of all the many Queens of King's, saved Britain's life in World War II. With a then unusual combination of mathematical and engineering genius – two departments which the English educational system had always worked hard to keep separate – Turing devised the mechanism by which radio signals encoded through the German Enigma machine could be read in time to produce the stream of useful, often vital, secret intelligence known as Ultra. It was the society outside Cambridge which hounded Turing to an early grave. Cambridge itself, even if it did not precisely cherish him, at least offered him its tolerance and protection. Even more than Keynes's or Wittgenstein's, Turing's case, it seems to me, is decisive. Though it could be said that Cambridge was equally tolerant and protective of a whole succession of Foreign Office and MI5 prodigies who subsequently turned out to have been drawing an extra salary from the Soviet Union, nothing can alter the fact that Hitler, who threatened the whole of civilisation, owed his defeat in a large part to a high-voiced but not very predatory invert who threatened nobody, and that the dons of King's, who knew all about Turing's proclivities, did nothing to sabotage this desirable outcome. Where victimless crimes are concerned, tolerance is an absolute good. Cambridge will probably never get round to formally approving homosexuality, but the type of homosexual involved perhaps prefers a blind eye to public acknowledgment, and meanwhile a tacit understanding seems to provide liberty enough. In my time as an undergraduate, however, I sometimes had to concentrate very hard on how horrible most of the boat-rowing heterosexuals were if I was to offset my distaste for some of the more epicene dons, of which Footlights had a full quota among its senior membership. Dating from the long era when every May Week revue had been a big-budget exercise in make-up and drag, they would turn up at term-time smokers and form a swooping group at the back of the room, muttering archly at the pretty pass to which things had come. One of them was among the nicest men I had ever met, but I didn't go for his pals. They obviously thought I was too butch to be plausible, and I was constantly afraid of being knocked flat by their flailing wrists. I bottled it up, though. Human nature is various, and I have never been pleased enough about my own nature to be fully contemptuous about anybody else's, provided he isn't homicidal. These weren't that: they were just a bit high-pitched. The kind of undergraduates who swarmed around them certainly weren't being misled, unless sugar misleads ants.

In order to be weird, however, a don didn't have to carry bundles of old newspapers, cross snow-filled courtyards diagonally with only his head showing, or make up his eyelids with the very lightest touch of blue shadow. Some of them could maintain an unbroken rectitude of deportment while still going comprehensively haywire, especially if they were involved in the humanities. Cambridge science having done such earth-shattering things, it was sometimes suggested that non-scientists were suffering from an inferiority complex. If so they kept it well hidden. A more likely explanation concerns the relative difficulty of keeping work separate from life. A physicist can't live his physics. A humanist can live his humanism and after too much Madeira might find it impossible not to. One of the young Cambridge philosophy dons specialised in aesthetics and made sure you knew it. He dressed the part, wearing a black leather jacket, tight trousers and high boots. He had not, at that stage, produced any of the substantial writings in which he has since expounded his viewpoint, but such was the level of personal invective he maintained in conversation that you always knew where he stood. He stood on his opponent's throat. He was a Leavisite, junior model. He had taken his master's principles of literary criticism and applied them to the other arts as well. Thus it came to light that in each field of artistic endeavour there were only three or four master practitioners, all the others being enemies of civilisation. In music the three or four were reduced to one: Wagner. I once heard this terrifying young man say that one of the many great things about Wagner was that when you realised his true greatness it obviated the necessity of listening to pipsqueaks like Puccini. I searched his face for a sign of humour but could see nothing except certainty. It was Leavis that had made him certain. On the rare occasions when the black-leather Wagnerian could be tempted into print, it was usually an encomium in the *Cambridge Review* for some collection of addle-pated late essays by Leavis, or else it was a passionate attack on a book, any book, by someone who, at some point in the past, no matter how distant, had disagreed with Leavis or merely failed to endorse his every opinion. Even Wagner came second to Leavis.

Leavis himself, though nearing the end of his career, was, as I have mentioned, still active around Cambridge and more irascible than ever, particularly against his disciples. To do him credit, he could never be depended upon to go on lapping up the hosannahs of his sycophants indefinitely. At some unpredictable moment he would turn on his arselickers and deliver a series of stunning kicks to their pursed lips. Later on, almost with his dying breath, he publicly repudiated the Wagnerian for having 'misrepresented my views'. Far from having misrepresented Leavis's views, the Wagnerian had endorsed them even at their most fatuous. When Leavis wrote his last-gasp, break-through essay in which Tolstoy was discovered to be a great novelist, the Wagnerian, either having forgotten about the existence of Matthew Arnold or else never having heard of him, announced that nobody had dared to proclaim Tolstoy's eminence so courageously before. With his tongue thus applied to the heel of his master's boot, the acolyte was ill-prepared to receive its toe in his teeth. The Wagnerian never fully recovered. He took to wearing a Harris tweed jacket and ordinary shoes, and not long ago, at a dinner party in a private home, I caught him red-handed listening to other people instead of just laying down the law as of old.

Really he shouldn't have taken it so hard. Leavis's views were almost impossible not to misrepresent, because they were designed so that only he could hold them. This was partly true even in the early, fruitful part of his career, and became completely true later on, when dogma took over from doctrine. Those who opposed him he merely insulted, but to support him invited vilification, and anyone who arrived at one of his conclusions before he did suffered treatment that differed from character assassination only in being prolonged like torture. When he gave his famous Dickens lectures the hall was jammed. I was there along with the worshippers, the admirers and the merely gullible. Brian C. Adams was sitting in the front row, with two fountain pens ready in case one of them ran out. He was doing his best to appear critically detached but there was no mistaking his look of exaltation when Leavis came trotting briskly in. Leavis was Seriousness personified. He even had a serious way of being bald. Though I had, and for some years to come retained, respect for the intensity of his commitment, I suppose I was the only person present who actively disapproved of him. There were plenty who detested him, but they had stayed at home. I wanted to see at least the vestiges of the mental force he must once have had in order to cause those decades of fuss and bother. I hadn't tried to enroll in his seminars because I had passed the age of being caught up in his rhetoric. This will sound like light-mindedness to all those Cambridge graduates – many of them now prominently placed in the theatre, radio, television and journalism as well as the academic world – who think that Leavis made them serious about literature. But literature would have made them serious about literature. They met him at an impressionable age, and they have matured since only to the extent that his influence has been ameliorated by the thing he preached of but saw with such distorting strictness – life. It depends not just on who your mentor is, but on when you meet him, and I no longer needed Leavis to tell me that Shakespeare was a greater poet than Shelley. If Leavis had had something to say about the kind of poet Shelley would have been had he lived to middle-age, I might have listened. But the good Doctor dealt in absolutes. Nevertheless I was prepared, as that bald-eagle head bent over its pile of notes and cleared the gaunt throat in its open collar, to admit that he had something, if he had.

What he had, alas, was a long series of attacks on all those critics who had made the unpardonable mistake of calling Dickens a genius before he did. Humphry House came in for an avalanche of abuse, clearly because Humphry House had given half his life to Dickens while Leavis had still been proclaiming that only *Hard Times* merited serious attention. The names Graham Hough and John Holloway also kept cropping up, although their connection with Dickens was not clear. 'We know what to think of Dr Hough,' sneered Leavis, as though no further explanation were necessary. 'We know what to expect from Dr Holloway.' Perhaps Hough and Holloway had not only been prematurely pro-Dickens, they had also been anti-Leavis, or, even worse, pro-Leavis without permission. Then a strange thing began to happen. The names Hough and Holloway went on cropping up, but they cropped up mixed up. 'This is the kind of misrepresentation, I need hardly point out, which we have learned to associate with the name of Dr Houghoway.' Not long afterwards there was a reference to Professor Hollohough. Some of Dr Leavis's pages seemed to be in the wrong order. He shuffled them, apparently at random, and read on. This should have been a touching, if not exactly comic, grace-note to the performance, but the outpouring of venom forbade sympathy. As the hour neared its end, there was a peroration against Edmund Wilson, who had pioneered the movement which, long before Leavis got around to joining it, had brought the critical appraisal of Dickens into line with public appreciation. 'We doubt Edmund Wilson's qualifications to discuss Dickens,' said Leavis, and although I am quoting from memory the memory is so indecently vivid I would swear by its accuracy. 'We doubt Edmund Wilson's qualifications,' he wound up triumphantly, 'to discuss *any* literature.' Beside me, an Indian girl student in a sari noted it down: 'doubt E. Wilson quals. discuss *any* lit.' In a blessed life, that moment was as close as I have so far come to witnessing clerical treason in its pure form, dogma distilled into a pathogen. One day I might write a book about how I think cultural memory is transmitted, and perhaps I had better put off discussing this sad business until then, but for now I should say, in order to stave off charges of frivolity, that I thought any amount of frivolity preferable to the Leavisite parade of seriousness. Better Lord David Cecil at his most fruitily fluting than Leavis's Vyshinskyite tirade, his inquisitorial denunciations. The hall was full of students who would have profited immensely from reading Edmund Wilson's literary criticism, which was, and is, full of discovery and judgment. Wilson's appreciation of Dickens was just what they should have been encouraged to read. Instead they had been given an excuse to do something for which students need no encouragement: not to read.

Not much of a reader on the course myself, I was in no fit state to climb on a high horse. Helping me to contain my rage was the suspicion that this event was more parody than reality. The Leavisite brand of *odium theologicum* had all the characteristics of totalitarian argument, right down to the special hatred reserved for heretics. But the patterns of thought which had filled the concentration camps of Europe proper had arrived in England in the mercifully diluted form of university politics. The ruckus surrounding Leavis, though too nasty to be a farce, was not toxic enough to be a tragedy. You could always have gone somewhere else. Leavis himself could have gone somewhere else, but fought to stay on in Cambridge. It couldn't be said while he was alive, and is still considered bad taste when said now, but the reason he was shut out of university preferment had little to do with his supposedly challenging originality. It was personal. People will submit to having their opinions contradicted, but not to having their characters attacked at the same time. They can't watch their fronts *and* their backs. They would rather shut the door. So Leavis, as he put it, became part of the real Cambridge: the Cambridge in spite of Cambridge. He was part of the landscape. You became accustomed to seeing him walk briskly along Trinity Street, gown blown out horizontal in his slipstream. He looked as if walking briskly had been something he had practised in a wind tunnel. Not long before he died I was in Deighton Bell's second-hand bookshop looking over the rain-ruined books of the literary booze-artist John Davenport, who must have left the library doors open on the stormy night of his suicide. Suddenly Leavis's wife, Queenie, appeared at my shoulder. 'Nasty piece of work, Davenport,' she muttered, having no reason to know me from Adam. 'While he was up here he was the leader of a *particularly odious set.*' Seeing me buy Davenport's cracked and stained Pléiade edition of Rimbaud, she nodded approval. Almost any teacher, no matter how intransigent his or her views, can be moved to tears by the sight of a student voluntarily purchasing a book, but the light in Queenie's eye was one of reminiscence. 'With Frank it was Laforgue. He nearly broke us, buying up those Frenchmen. On to it quite independently of Eliot. In France you couldn't get him past a bookshop. We were there a lot when we were young.' She sniffed for a while at a row of damaged books which Davenport had failed to return to the London Library. Then she left. In later years I have remembered that chance encounter as part evidence that in matters of the spirit the truly dangerous poisons are refined from flowers. In her husband's youth she must have found him as easy to love as in his last days I found him easy to loathe. I tried not to hate him, though. Of all the moral lessons he had to teach, the one that stuck was the one he taught inadvertently. In his later books he libelled his literary opponents so scandalously that when he tried to condemn Stalin he had no harsh words left over. If he had been asked to give his opinion of Hitler and Himmler, he would not have been able to summon up any terms of disapprobation that he had not already lavished on Houghaway and Hollohough. He had given up his sense of reality, and all in pursuit of the very study which, he went on insisting, was the only thing that could give you a sense of reality. He was a self-saboteur.

5

Yanks on the Cam

YOU CAN MAKE a good case for even the weirdest don if he stimulates the young to anything, if only anger. At my age I didn't need the goad. Though I was still too idle a student to put much time into the business of seeking out a sound teacher and listening to what he had to say, at least I recognised such a one when I heard him. Theodore Redpath, for example, was an old man by then and his lectures on tragedy didn't sparkle. You had to strain to listen. But when he talked about Sophocles he was responding to the Greek text. His little book on Tolstoy took in all the Russian scholarship. He was unspectacular, but I had come just far enough to know that he was worth listening to, and precisely because he had no big ideas. He talked nothing except sense. Younger undergraduates couldn't be blamed for wanting stronger stuff. In Pembroke, the star students in English were nearly all Americans. Some of them went to hear George Steiner, recently installed at Churchill College, talk eloquently about how the crisis of Western civilisation had reached a point where it would be better if everybody stopped talking. Others went to hear Leavis talk about how the crisis of western civilisation had been made worse by Steiner. Some of them went to hear both, took verbatim notes from each, intercalated the results and served up the synthesis in their weekly essays. Sharing practical criticism seminars or group supervisions with the Americans, I would marvel at the seriousness with which they took it all. But there would be ample time for them to become less gullible later, and for the time being their all-fired keenness was probably more fruitful, and certainly more attractive, than my indolence. They had a hard enough time fathoming the English, so my own transitional persona must have seemed as out of focus as a chameleon crossing a kilt.

They, to me, looked perfect. Whether Ivy League WASPS, New York Jews or third generation Polacks and Bohunks with names full of 'c's and 'z's, they were fully in character and inexhaustibly supplied with authentic all-American dialogue. They were all very bright, of course, which helped. Fulbright scholars and Phi Beta Kappa almost to a man, they were reading the second part of the English Tripos, like me. Unlike me they had degrees which had been won by hard work against deadly competition at Yale, Princeton, Harvard, Columbia and Amherst. Of the Ivy League types, the outstanding example was Stradlington Westwood Blantyre III, called Strad for short, like an expensive violin. And indeed he was a finely tuned instrument, though built like an upper East Side brownstone. Six feet four in his triple-welted brogues, he had grown a moustache out of shyness and looked apologetic that it had hidden no more than his upper lip. The expression 'modest to a fault' had been invented for him. President of Triangle when at Princeton, he had a fine line of songs and monologues, but could be forced on to the Footlights stage only at gunpoint. The only male graduate who could cycle past Newnham and make its inhabitants appear at the windows spontaneously – the rest of us could not have obtained the same results had we thrown tear gas – he never noticed the sensation he caused. Every day he was invited to tea at Girton, more than once by the dons themselves. He was actually *invited* to that heavily defended castle full of unattainable females. The rest of us would have been picked up by the searchlights and fixed machine guns before we had even cut our way through the barbed wire and reached the moat full of alligators. But what did he do when he got there? He discussed Thackeray. As the inmates passed him cucumber sandwiches with trembling hands, he quietly made clear that there was a fiancée waiting for him at home. Pending his graduation and marriage – the two events were apparently scheduled to take place simultaneously – energies left over from study were expended on rowing. He rowed for the college and would probably have done the same for the university if he had not been so intelligent. In the grad pad after Hall, when the affiliated students would stand around drinking port or coffee in a vain attempt to quell memories of what they had eaten for dinner, I would accuse Strad of wanting to do all the right things. 'No,' he said, after thinking it over, 'I just want to do things right.'

He thought himself conventional but made an art of the conventions. I admired his good manners and perhaps he relished my lack of them. At any rate he took me some way into his secret life. One afternoon, in his rooms, he poured me another inch of Bourbon and put an LP on his record-player. 'It is important to be *cool*,' he said, with characteristic terseness. 'These three women are called the Supremes. Notice how *cool* they are.' While the sublime riffs and harmonies of 'You Can't Hurry Love' came lilting into my life for the first time, Strad was rolling a peculiar-looking cigarette. 'Now let's hear that again while we take a drag on this object, which we call a *joint*.' I would like to say that the experience was transformative, but like most first-time pot-smokers I missed the point through not taking a sufficient quota of air. The Supremes were enough to get me high all by themselves, however. Strad was like that: he played it dead square, but there was always another side to him. His façade had facets.

Of Delmer Dynamo I have already given a preliminary description, but he, too, was many-sided, if someone so bulb-shaped could be that. In his second year he had put out shoots and tendrils. He had not relinquished his sardonic commentary on the college and its facilities. (Famously he had said 'blow it out your ass' within earshot of the Dean, but had got away with it because the Dean, misled by the American pronunciation of the word, had thought that Delmer was making some arcane reference to a biblical animal.) Delmer had, however, embraced English cultural values with the determination of a Greek ship-owner angling for election to White's. He was a college man yet more than a college man. He was practically a college building. His large supply of money from home was poured into first editions of

George Eliot and the novels of Dickens in the original monthly parts. In his rooms there was a matched pair of Purdey shot-guns, one of which had not been fired, and the other of which, by Delmer's own account, had been aimed at a partridge and accounted for a beater. There was fly-fishing equipment. Where once there had been a rack of Savile Row suits and tweed hacking jackets, there were now two racks, while on the appropriate pegs and shelves, specially installed, there were Burberry overcoats with detachable linings, oiled Barbours, opera capes, deerstalker hats and green wellingtons. Late night discussions in front of Delmer's fireplace were fortified with a hamper from Fortnum and Mason's. Most impressive of all, kept in a small car-park off Trumpington Street, was Delmer's car. It was a Bentley with a very rare H. J. Mulliner double-shell body of aluminium. A measure of Delmer's Englishness was that he did not call aluminium 'aloominum'. Delmer's newly anglicised diction, seemingly acquired from manuscripts which P. G. Wodehouse had rejected as too characteristic, shed any last overtones of self-mockery where his car was concerned. 'Care for a spin, old bean?'

Strad, who adored Delmer, warned me to play along. 'He's serious. Don't call him on it or he'll crash the goddam thing.' The big drawback was that Delmer couldn't drive. He had an international licence but he must have bought it off a crooked cop in Atlantic City. In the car-park, Strad and I had to wait a long time while Delmer tried to turn the key. Not in the ignition: in the door. When we got into the car there was another long wait while he got it to start. 'Tally ho!' he cried, when the flooded carburettor at last coughed life into the engine. 'Wizard prang! Now let's toodle off into the landscape.' Then he couldn't get out of the car-park. With too much pride to let anyone else try instead, he crabbed toward the exit, backed up, twisted the wheel, lurched forward again, but couldn't line the front wheels up with the way out. Part of the trouble was the driving position. With his feet on the pedals he had to tilt his head back in order to see over the walnut dashboard. Eventually it was time for Strad to go rowing, so he got out. That left me. After a while

I got out too and tried to guide Delmer between the posts. It didn't work. Though the engine of the Bentley wasn't very loud even when revved in desperation, there was a terrific silence after Delmer switched it off. He climbed out, shut the door, and looked for a long time at his most expensive acquisition. His hands were in his pockets. I got the impression that if they hadn't been he would have punched a dent in the front door. The lustrous toes of his ox-blood shoes, which had been handmade in St James's, were twitching. But the revenge he took on his recalcitrant purchase was not physical. Recrimination had gone beyond that. With his hands still in his pockets he threw back his head and cried out to Heaven. 'BLOW IT OUT YOUR ASS!'

Strad and Delmer both slaved over their books like gladiators in training, but always with a sense of their limitations. Strad would one day go to work in the family publishing firm, Delmer in the faculty of English at Columbia. They would serve literature, not create it. JFK, their best hope and only President, was dead; the Vietnam war, though still rated officially only as a police action, already beckoned with an evil welcome for contemporaries who had been less lucky; they were troubled for their country and grateful for small mercies. But Bob Marenko was Captain America. An Amherst Phi Bete who as a high school tight end had already been scouted by every team in the newly-formed National Football League, he had turned his massive shoulders on sport in order to put his head down and charge at literature, fourth down and goal to go. In his rooms he had two copies of Yeats's collected poems, one to be kept sacred and the other to be marked up. In the marked copy every line was underlined and annotated in the margin. 'Elision of "the" and "indifferent" conveys casualness of swan after consummation, while abruptness of terminal word "drop" mimics action. Develop.' Unsurprisingly for one so young and keen, Marenko's own poems aped those of his idol, yet you couldn't fail to be impressed by the sheer number of them. He never sent them out for publication in the university newspapers and magazines. Instead he passed them around the college, listening attentively to criticism before going back to his rooms and writing far into the night. It was clear that if he did not become a great poet he would become a great critic. The latest books and articles by Harold Bloom, Northrop Frye, Yvor Winters and Stephen Marcus were all collected and cross-referenced by Marenko as if they were jazz records. He felt the same way about jazz records, but they had to be modern. Thelonious Monk was about as far back as Marenko's tastes went, and he really started to feel comfortable only with John Coltrane, whose interminable solos could be listened to and argued about until dawn broke. Marenko wanted to discuss things. Above all, he wanted to discuss Vietnam. He was serious about it: much more serious than the anti-war agitation which was by now building up throughout the Western lands. If Marenko thought it was a just war, he would put his head down and run at the Viet Cong. If he thought it was unjust, he would put his head down and run at his own government. Hence the necessity to talk things over. The debates lasted half the night every night, except when there was live jazz to be heard. Every Wednesday night there was a guest soloist at the Red Lion in Lion Yard, usually a good, solid British sax player such as Ronnie Ross, Art Themen, Don Rendell or Kathy Stobart. Colin Edwards, a townsman, was the resident drummer, and Mike Payne, a retired Vampire pilot, played the bass. For a few shillings it was a feast of danceable mainstream music. On top of that, once in a great while an American legend came to town. Duke Ellington came to Great St Mary's and gave his Sacred Music concert, which proved to be a bit too sacred for my taste, while Marenko merely found it antediluvian. I tried to explain that Ellington's great period had been in the early 1940s, when every three-minute recording was like a miniature symphony. Marenko's eyes were suffused with pity. But when Thelonious Monk played at the Union, even Marenko got excited. We went with Delmer. Monk-mad myself, I did my best to understand as the mighty man – backed by a susurrating post-bop rhythm section in which the drummer seemed to hit nothing except the cymbals and the bass player did everything he could to avoid the beat – punched clusters of notes apparently at random and climaxed a half-hour rendition of 'Monk's

Dream' by jabbing all his fingers into the lid of the key-board. 'Jesus H. Christ on a crutch,' said Delmer at interval, 'this guy is stoned.' Marenko tried to set Delmer straight. 'I can relate to how you might feel that, Delmer,' said the star student compassionately, 'but the aleatory component was always implicit in Monk's music. He's merely taking that element to its logical conclusion.'

'Blow it out your ass,' Delmer replied. '*I'm* going *home*.' Marenko and I stayed for the second half, during which Monk twice missed the piano altogether. But over cocoa late that night Marenko was persuasive about our having witnessed an important step in modern music. Marenko's passionate erudition was hard to resist. He knew so much, and cared so much more. Long before dawn, he had me convinced that every move of Monk's hands had been a miracle of controlled self-expression. Late next morning we were waiting outside the Blue Boar Hotel in Trinity Street to pay homage when Monk checked out. When he appeared, he wasn't precisely being carried by the drummer and the bass player, merely supported by them, but his feet were only vaguely in contact with the ground and his eyes looked like blood-capsules. 'Where we *at*, man?' I heard him enquire softly. 'Still in England,' muttered the bass player. 'Stay cool till we're in the car.' Monk's toes were touching the pavement but they were dragging behind his heels. His puce eyeballs rolled upwards to look at the narrow brim of his black felt hat while his lips, between his toothbrush moustache and his vestigial goatee, imitated a little doughnut. 'Where we *at*?' he moaned.

Marenko took this setback philosophically, the way he took everything. Dutifully he would enlarge his world view to fit the world. In college I spent more time with the Americans than with the British because the Americans were more interested in everything, including Britain. They certainly made better Europeans. They worked hard at their languages and got across to the continent in every vacation. They looked on self-improvement as a sacerdotal obligation. Democratic without being philistine, studious without feeling superior, the Americans were my solace inside the college. Outside the college, I necessarily spent much of my time with the natives.

By that stage, I was publishing poems and articles in every issue of *Varsity*, *Granta* and the *Cambridge Review*, with the overspill going into the aforesaid gaggle of evanescent literary magazines unread by anybody except the committed *literati*. These latter life-forms were now becoming easier for me to classify into their various weights and types. There were flashbacks called Algernon who dressed and sounded as if they were auditioning for a tea party thrown by Harold Acton or Maurice Bowra. There were ultra-grey ex-grammar school types who wrote something called Concrete Poetry and were called Ken. Both groups, had I but known it, were on their way up in the world. The Algernons were all from minor public schools. In the new mood of classlessness they could plausibly carry on as if they came from major ones. (As the cachet enjoyed by the editorial staff of *Private Eye* had already demonstrated, the principal effect of the Sixties social revolution was to make young men who had been to Shrewsbury feel less miserable about not having been to Eton.) The Kens were amassing points for their future careers: a BBC general traineeship would fall most easily to the *curriculum vitae* which showed evidence of artistic endeavour, if not actual achievement. Over the secret desires and lurking ambitions of both Algernon and Ken I rode rough-shod. Algernon wrote crepuscular sonnets and Ken assembled, probably with tweezers, microscopic unpunctuated stanzas from which the ghosts of ideas gestured feebly, like lice in raindrops. There was a lot of white space left over, which I filled. My verse was still a long way from the clarity which I was eventually to realise should be my aim – I would rather my work were thought prosaic than poetic, and there are some who would say that I have been granted my wish – but compared with the eye-dropper out-squeezings of my undergraduate rivals it was a torrent of candour. Also, after a year's practice, I had become almost impossible to turn down. Having grown another beard even more farouche than its predecessor, when I fronted up at an undergraduate editor's door I must have looked less like an aspiring contributor than someone who had been hired to collect a debt. I was only about five years older than the average final-year literatus but in your twenties a *lustrum* is like a canyon. Most of these young scribblers, I guessed, would one day give up, whereas I had already diagnosed myself, correctly, as having the disease in its chronic form. I was a lifer. Being that, perhaps I should have sent my work out to the professional magazines, but if these amateurs resented my crabbing their act they didn't show it. Not that I would have noticed if they had, because I spent as little time socialising with them as possible. If, to them, I was just too insensitive, to me they were just too callow. Except for the Algernons, who were living in Echo Park, all that concerned them was Experimental Writing, and I had come far enough to know that there is no such thing as experimental writing. There is only writing. The arts do not advance through technique, they accumulate through quality. One evening I went to a literary tea in Newnham. The editor of a magazine called something like *Samphire* had invited me as guest of honour. If the editor had been male, I need hardly state, I would have found the invitation much easier to refuse. All the Cambridge poets were there, the Algernons in their velvet jackets and the Kens in their anoraks. During the muffled course of a desultory conversation in which tea-cake crumbs were carefully retained in the cupped hand, Anselm Hollo was proposed as a touchstone contemporary poet. My contention that they would all be better off learning MacNeice's *Autumn Journal* by heart was greeted with tolerant smiles by the Kens. The Algernons were more ready to entertain the notion but they were outnumbered. The balance was shifting. Revolution was in the air. An aerosol can of crazy foam was passed around. We were supposed to close our eyes and shape the foam between our hands while improvising on the theme of primal creation. One of the Kens squirted the crazy foam into his long hair. I left, not because I didn't like them but because what they had on their hands, under the crazy foam, was time, and time was what I was already running out of.

At such moments I wondered whether I had any legitimate business being in a university, which is, after all, a place where young people discover themselves. Those who have already done so should clear out. These misgivings were reinforced by what went on in the Union debating chamber. Abramovitz was elected Secretary of the Union in the first term of his second year: the fastest climb to power on record. I attended his inaugural debate with some vague intention of speaking from the floor. I was ready to lie down on it and go to sleep before the paper speeches were half over. Though Abramovitz himself conducted the proceedings suavely enough, the frolicsome puns and points of order from the resident wits would have tried the patience of a saint. A moustached madman called Peregrine Sourbutts-Protheroe kept jumping to his feet and proposing that the motion be put, or that the point of order be promulgated, or whatever. Since the motion was some balls-aching foolery along the lines of 'That this House would rather rock than roll', I was all in favour of its being got out of the way as soon as possible, but apparently Sourbutts-Protheroe was out of order. He certainly looked it. Instead of the black tie favoured by the committee he wore full white-tie evening dress, except that he also wore plimsolls. Abramovitz informed me that Sourbutts-Protheroe was tolerated for the amusement he provided. The humourless, keen to be thought otherwise, love to laugh but need to be told when, so they are always glad if a clown dresses the part. With my eyes closed I listened in despair as the evening wore on. It was just possible that something serious could be said in such a context of bad jokes and braying laughter. But something funny never could. I vowed never to speak in a university union debate. In later years I was to rescind that vow several times each in Cambridge and Oxford, but always with subsequent regret for a largely wasted evening. If only they would cut the malarkey and get on with the oratory. Nothing speeds up your heart like speaking on your feet.

There was plenty of opportunity for that in the Footlights, where I continued to meet young British people who were to influence my life deeply. Some of them have become well-known since. I will try not to single them out merely on that basis. Stylistic gymnastics ensue when one tries to drop a name softly, while simultaneously indicating that one was present at the birth of, and perhaps even helped breathe life into, the future star. ('The name Marlon Brando didn't mean much then, but when he watched you act you knew that someone very special was analysing your every move, your every vocal inflection,' etc.) Besides, some of those who impressed me most have never become stars, but have lived normal lives instead: a destiny to be preferred, in my opinion, unless the strength of inner compulsion leaves no choice.

Eric Idle had gone down to begin a professional career as a performer on stage and screen. Since the road to Monty Python was longer and harder than most of the journalists who write about the subject are capable of taking in, he won't thank me for saying that he had future stardom written all over him. He was a consummate performer. He was, however, still somewhat short of material at that time, having not yet found his true comic vision, which was within him, but needed a context to bring it out. His successor as President of Footlights was Andy Mayer, whose originality was already fully established, and probably had been when he was still in the cradle. Mayer must have lacked the neurotic requirement for the limelight, because nowadays he is happy to work behind the camera. At the time his precocity floored me. He went on stage with his own stuff, and it was unique. So was his style of delivering it. A smallish young man with a huge Beatles-style helmet of dead straight dark hair whose fringe was cut square across the eyes so that he had to tilt his head back to look at the audience, he had a weird sort of negative timing which made pauses go on longer than they should, except when, as he often did, he got a big laugh, which he would try to talk straight through, as if he couldn't hear it. Staccato and legato at the same time, his monologues were short and apparently incoherent collages of verbal fragments. A routine in which he pretended to be an American evangelist had me simultaneously roaring with laughter and breathless with admiration, wondering how he packed so much in. 'Jesus Christ! Remember the name. Said. (Long pause) Or is *said* to have said. (Longer pause) God! (Inconceivably long pause) I put it to you that he *noo*! *I* dunno. (Looks at watch, nods into wings.) So! (Extends forefinger, finds it fascinating, becomes transfixed, shakes head.) Write away! Write away *right* away to the following *ad*dress ... ' There were only about a hundred words in the piece but it took him five minutes to get through it, so panic-stricken was the audience. They would hold on to each other and howl.

Pronounced by so young a man, these comic ramblings, when I stopped laughing to reflect, stung like a reproach. My own monologues were still running at about ten minutes minimum and Mayer was taking half the time to say twice as much, with four times the effect. When it was announced that President Johnson's daughter, Lucy Baines Johnson, was engaged to be married, I presaged the nuptials with a monologue which was my first really big hit in the Footlights. But the emphasis was on 'big'. Cast in the form of a running commentary, as if the wedding ceremony were a football match, the piece went on and on like a novel by Thomas Wolfe before Maxwell Perkins had persuaded him to cut it down to merely mammoth proportions. The foreign policy of the United States was starting to worry me almost as much as it was starting to worry my American friends. I had a lot to say on the subject. Partly because my American friends were present in the audience, my 'Lucy Gets Married' monologue went down a storm in the Falcon Yard clubroom, but it was a long storm, with several lulls included. Chastened by Andy Mayer's gift for brevity, I trimmed my masterpiece by several minutes before going public with it in the Pembroke smoker. At the cost of sacrificing some of the more obviously political content, the laugh lines were brought closer together. What I was then engaged in, I realised much later, was the first stage in a laborious process of learning to remove the connecting tissue so that the argument could be unified by tone rather than logic. In the long run this painfully acquired discipline would enable me to write a thousand-word article which sounded as if I was just saying it (detractors who called my television column in the *Observer* a cabaret turn were exactly right) but at the time it was painful to go on and die, and even when I had a hit, like 'Lucy Gets Married', the hit could be alarmingly hit and miss. A laugh that I got on Thursday night wouldn't be there on Friday night. What had I done wrong? I had produced the show successfully enough – the wine had once again done its work on the audience – but I was less adept at producing myself. This was to remain a pattern. When it came to criticising and arranging the work of others, the shaping spirit operated in good order. When it came to my own work, the enthusiasm of invention made me deaf to my own better judgment. Always I had to go into hiding and lick my wounds before I found the wherewithal to improve. When I did improve, it was often in the wrong direction, towards a more polished performance, when what I needed to do was to perform less: the deader my pan, the better my words worked. An anti-talent, I needed a non-style.

Romaine Rand: now *there* was a performer. After her striptease nun routine the previous year, I was well aware that her absence from the Pembroke smoker would not be tolerated. The Hearties would dismantle the place if she did not show up. By now I was in digs on the Newnham side of the river, having got out of my room in the Eagle only just in time to avoid being consumed by the killer mould. My new room was rented from a nice young couple of graduate scientists who needed the money. Apart from my habit of smoking in bed while drunk, from their viewpoint I must have been the ideal tenant, because I was busy in Footlights almost all the time. They seldom saw me, and my memory of them is hazy. I changed my sheets about once a term, but never slept in them long enough on any given night to turn them any very deep shade of grey. A pot of jam that I left with its lid off for two or three months was mysteriously removed. Apart from that there was no interference with my freedom. Rather better organised as usual, Romaine lived in a Newnham hostel not far away. Her sitting room had a diamond-leaded casement, through which, from outside the building, I debonairly inserted my upper body before launching on an eloquent appeal for her participation in the Pembroke smoker. Walled in by stacks of books about Elizabethan rhetoric, she tried to stave me off by pleading pressure of work. I had the answer to that. Since, as I have related, she had managed to persuade the university authorities that she should be allowed to forget the Tripos and register for a PhD, it was *my* year for sitting examinations, not hers. Then she tried to stall me by saying that she didn't have a number ready. I countered by telling her that it would be enough for her just to show up and go on. It didn't matter what she did, but if she wasn't there then I was a gone goose. This appeal to her compassion was unavailing, because although Romaine's emotions were powerful, they came and went, and this was a Tuesday, whereas her day for compassion was Wednesday. Tuesday was her day for patriotism. When I pointed out that if the Pembroke smoker flopped it would be bad news for Australia, she began to melt, and when I wound up by suggesting, in broad terms, that no essay in the art of cabaret and intimate revue could be fully alive without the galvanising influence of her genius for improvisation, it became clear that I had finally touched her heart. Her day for self-obsession was every day. Since the same went for me, it had taken time for me to switch the centre of attention from me to her, but having once got around to it I could congratulate myself on my cunning. 'Don't get your hopes up,' she said dismissively, already engrossed again in the exquisite scholastic filigree of *Love's Labours Lost*. 'I'm fucked if I'll work my tits off for a pack of dick-heads who row boats.' She promised, however, to put in an appearance of some kind. Romaine had her drawbacks but her word was her bond. She had said she would be there, so I was saved. It was with an inexpressible sense of relief, then, that I backed down the gardener's ladder up which I had climbed to her window. Although elated, I was careful not to hurry. Her sitting room was only on the second floor, but the gravel driveway looked as hard as a proctor's heart.

Though Romaine did indeed turn up on the first night of the Pembroke smoker, she terrified me by announcing that she intended to do nothing except sing 'Land of Hope and Glory'. She had brought the sheet music for this, so that our piano player could accompany her. She was also carrying a dark blue straw hat with a stuffed bird on it. She put in a request to go on last, so that she would have time to practise her piece out in the corridor. My own view was that it was her look-out. The standard of numbers was quite high that year. We had a jazz quartet powered by the compulsive mainstream drumming of Colin Edwards, who was moonlighting from his regular gig at the Red Lion. Under the low ceiling of the Old Library, with the audience far gone into the rapture of the deep, that band sounded like a destroyer passing close overhead. All the Footlights who had aspirations towards being included in the May Week revue were parading their audition pieces in highly polished form. I'm bound to say that I held my own with them. In my capacity as producer, I chose to place my 'Lucy Gets Married' monologue as the second last number. By that time the Hearties at the back of the packed room were sitting on each other's shoulders and swinging playfully at each other with empty wine bottles. Down at the front, flanked by two Girton girls in taffeta, the ruffles on the expensive dress shirt of Delmer Dynamo were hanging limply wet, like cabbage bleached by steam. The audience were all so tight that Sir Alec Douglas-Home could have read out the university bye-laws and gone over like Max Miller. At the end of my monologue, I was swept off the stage by a tidal wave of applause. As Romaine went past me in the dark, I tacitly challenged her to top that. For a long while nothing much happened. I peeked around the door. The preliminary cheering had died down to a provisional rhubarb. Some of the Hearties were laughing at Romaine's hat, but all the rest of the audience were refilling one another's wine glasses while she handed her sheet music to the piano player, gave him whispered instructions, stood back, folded her hands, cleared her throat, and nodded for him to begin the accompaniment.

The result was chaos. She sang 'Land of Hope and Glory' with her lips out of synchronisation with the words. When she sang the word 'hope', her mouth was pronouncing the word 'land', and so on. The effect was uncannily funny, as if the world had come loose from its pivot. I saw the normally staid Strad Blantyre pass out from laughter. He was out of his chair and on the floor as if the room was being sprayed with bullets. People were holding on to one another and crying. Delmer Dynamo was removing his clothes by tearing at them, like a sea-lion strangling in its own skin. When Romaine finished the song they made her sing it again. This time she added illustrative gestures, but they were out of synchronisation too. She marched on the spot when she should have looked maternal, smiled winsomely when she should have looked martial, laughed when she should have wept. The audience rocked back and forth as if lashed by the gale of their own laughter. When I led the rest of the cast on for the closing number it was like setting up a Punch and Judy show after the battle of El Alamein. I did my best to look proprietorial, as if the whole idea had been mine. This strategy must have worked at least partly, because from that day forward I was able to run up debts on my college bills, and an *exeat* was always easy to obtain. When I said I had important business in London, I was believed. I had become a tolerated eccentric. This had been, was, and probably still is, one of the undeclared side-benefits of the Cambridge system. Within broad limits you can make as big a fool of yourself as you like, and still be put up with. In that respect, on the day when the ancient universities become efficient they will cease to be productive. Misfits and failures should have room to flourish. The proposition is made no less valid by the haste with which the misfits and failures spring forward to agree with it.

6

Meet Keith Visconti

My important business in London consisted largely of misbehaviour. Charter flights had made Italy cheaper to get to but no nearer. Meanwhile my old life in London could be reached for the price of a student rail fare. Some of my cronies, including the incipient film director, Dave Dalziel, had gone home or gone away, but others had stayed on to enjoy what had become self-consciously an Era. Among these latter was my erstwhile girlfriend, Robin, whom I had helped to become a lapsed Catholic. Since then her personality had flowered, to the extent that the nuns who had brought her up would have sent her to Hell on the strength of her clothes alone. Also she danced well, in a sort of silent frenzy. She was one of those people whose whole bodies have a feeling for popular music, and that was the time when popular music had a feeling for bodies. If you believed the glossy magazines, Swinging London was a place where you could run along the King's Road and meet Julie Christie running the other way. People you knew, or anyway people known by people you knew, were working as extras in Antonioni's *Blow Up*, and sending out reports of how David Hemmings was being pressed flat between ravenous women. The barriers were down, the hunt was up, the game was afoot. Actually it wasn't quite like that. The youth scene consisted, as it always had, of awkward parties with alcohol still the strongest stimulant, apart from desire. This last, however, was rampant, and was flogged on to a new fervour by the music. The music really *was* good. Every new Beatles LP moved things on to a new plane of rhythmic sensuality, as if we were all ascending from floor to floor in a transparent building that swayed more as you climbed higher. Though Robin had good cause to distrust me, in these circumstances she lacked the fanaticism which would have been necessary to fight me off. Her tiny flatlet in Pimlico had a yard consisting of precisely four paving stones. The yard, hilariously called an area, was hemmed in by a wall taller than a man. At three o'clock in the morning I would be up and over that wall like a commando and sobbing at her closed door. What could she do but let me in? Other young women were harder to persuade but the occasional one succumbed, probably because it was too dark to know quite what was going on. In the aftermath I was not always a gentleman. Even more shamefully, I thought I had an innate right to thoughtless behaviour. The *Zeitgeist* had given my Bacchic urge a blanket endorsement. The quantum leap in the efficiency and convenience of contraceptive methods amounted to a mandate. Rubber, however elastic, had been to some extent a restraint. Now the wraps were off. If you looked closely enough at the pill, it glowed with a green light.

On the loose in London, I could fancy myself as a rake. Fancying myself was easier in those days than it became later. Quite a lot of my hair was still on top of my head. My chest, though it showed signs of slipping, had not yet begun to accelerate. As a line-shooter I was indefatigable. I could fall in love in ten minutes and tell her about it for ten hours. I wrote poems on the spot and read them out unasked. Most of what I said, I believed. When I told some pretty dancer that she was a revelation, it was true. True at the time. I had commitments elsewhere but elsewhere was somewhere else. My trick, or condition, of being able to compartmentalise my life allows me to be active in several fields at once. This was already coming in handy as far as writing went: I could write during the day, go on stage at night, and each activity would benefit from the other. But from the moral viewpoint there was another sense in which I needed to be watched. It took me a long time to learn to watch myself, possibly because I didn't much like what I saw when I did.

The return of Dave Dalziel helped to restore my capacity for dedication. Without him, London might merely have been where I went to do a cheap imitation of Christopher Marlowe in his cups. Dalziel had come back out of Africa, and he demanded allegiance. Being a model of seriousness, he got it. He was a man dedicated to his art. That his own art lay mostly in the future merely testified to its purity. In Nigeria, he had put in a punishing year and a half as head of the government film unit. Apart from a couple of local assistants, whom he had to train, he was the whole staff. One of the loveliest of the Australian expatriate girls, a brunette of Irish extraction unbelievably called Cathleen O'Houlihan, had flown out to marry him. Knowing his record, and stung by jealousy, I doubted if the alliance would last, yet I couldn't deny the magnificence of the gesture. It was a leap in the dark. Nigeria was already in a recognisable preparatory stage of the civil war which was later to make the name Biafra notorious. At that time, nobody outside Africa could tell an Ibo from a Hausa. According to Dalziel's letters, however, the lay-out was terrifyingly simple. The Ibos were smart and everybody else hated them for it, so sooner or later there would be a massacre. Meanwhile the Nigerian politicians wanted nothing from the government film unit except to be filmed individually in close-up at all times, even at night. 'You can't turn an empty camera on them, either,' wrote Dalziel. 'They show up at the lab. and demand to see the negative. These guys are *very easy to see* in the negative.'

As conscientious as ever, Dalziel had got on with the charade while sedulously maintaining his lines of communication to London, in the hope of snaring a job that would get him out of Lagos before people started cutting one another up. Utterly without side, he had a great gift for true friendship with the black Africans and didn't want to be there when the inevitable happened. It was already happening when he and the now pregnant Cathleen landed in London. They took a small house in Brixton, where their parlour soon became a gathering point for refugees from Nigeria. You could meet people who had run government departments who would now count themselves lucky if they were allowed to clean trains. I met a tubby, middle-aged, smiling woman there whose whole family had been massacred before her eyes. She was smiling to hold her face together. Cathleen organised the tea and cakes. I listened to the baby in her stomach. It sounded keen to join the party. I had known Cathleen when she had first arrived in Sydney like an inspiration out of an emerald background, an Iseult Gonne transported in space and time. Now she was a wife and soon to be a mother. Dalziel had a new air of — what was it? — sanity. Something was going on that I felt left out of.

Dalziel still had plenty of the old insanity left, however. In Nigeria, on the few days of the month when he was not required to film politicians as they queued up to appear one at a time in front of the camera, he had managed to shoot the footage for a twenty-minute short subject about the only traffic jam in the history of Lagos. It wasn't the most thrilling topic in the world, but the film was put together with such craftsmanship that Dalziel was easily short-listed for the newly created job of running the British Film Institute's Production Board. The successful applicant would be given the task of providing spiritual guidance and practical assistance for aspiring young film-makers. At the interview, Sir Michael Balcon correctly judged Dalziel to be the authentic article, and he was hired. Not even Balcon, a great man with the generosity to relish talent in others, realised just how authentic his new protégé would prove to be. Dalziel was so selfless in his efforts to aid young hopefuls that a mere salary seemed small reward: he should have been canonised. Certainly he had a saint's patience. Some of the aspiring young film-makers were patently crazy. In a few fateful cases Dalziel found this fact difficult to detect. Thousands of applications had poured in from people who wanted to make a film. Many of them loftily left blank the space in the application form reserved for an outline of the film they wanted to make. It transpired that they didn't want to be pinned down by the restrictions of the system. Dalziel was sceptical enough to realise that they wanted the status of film-makers without having to go through the taxing business of actually achieving anything. But if an applicant seemed to have an idea that was even halfway decent, Dalziel would put it up to the board, get a budget, and supply the incipient Fellini with everything he needed, which usually included talent. Like many people with abundant creative energy, Dalziel found it hard to imagine what it was like to be without it. If a young would-be film director stood there without saying anything, Dalziel thought that it was because the hot new prospect was so bursting with ideas as to be inarticulate. If a young would-be film director not only stood there without saying anything but smelled as if he hadn't taken a bath in a long time, Dalziel thought that it was because the hot new prospect was so bursting with ideas he was not only inarticulate, he was beyond being concerned with the petty details of personal hygiene.

I have gone only half way towards describing Dalziel's principal and most troublesome protégé, Keith Visconti. Though Keith's anabasis from the status of comprehensive school expellee to potential *cinéaste* should not be derided even in retrospect, there were several reasons to think that on top of being illiterate and odoriferous he was also clinically insane, with overtones of petty larceny. He had, however, an inborn knack for thinking in sequences. He understood the essential grammar of eyelines and reverse angles without needing to have it set out for him in diagram form. Of no fixed abode, he seemed to live out of the gabardine overcoat which he wore at all times. It shone in a way that any piece of cloth does when it is dirty enough. Clutched tightly against the coat, because too big to fit into either of its bulging pockets, was a ten-minute show reel, made on short ends, which featured a friend of his, dressed unconvincingly as a waiter, serving another friend of his, dressed even more unconvincingly as a businessman, with a cup of coffee. Despite the implausibility of casting, sets and costumes, the action all happened in the right order. This was enough to convince Dalziel that Keith Visconti was a genius, an impression that Keith said nothing to contradict. Keith never said anything. He just stood there in his grotty overcoat, silent and immobile. Dalziel was thus able to read into his new pupil all his own qualities of inventiveness, lucidity and scruple.

The film Keith wanted to make was about a businessman and his wife, or perhaps mistress – the relationship was not specified – sitting in a restaurant and being served coffee. The woman is mysteriously drawn to the waiter, who has perhaps played a role in her earlier life, or perhaps might play a role in her later life, or perhaps both, if not neither. Leaving questions of motivation aside, Keith's screenplay was a small miracle of carefully calculated specificity. Every close-up was thoroughly notated as to expression, the line of the eyes, the intensity of the light. The fact that the whole thing was written out, with very few of the words correctly spelled, in pencilled block capitals on scraps of paper from varying sources, some of the pages being stuck together with gravy stains, did nothing to dissuade Dalziel from the view that here was a talent from Heaven, a technically endowed avatar on the scale of Pushkin, Mozart, Schubert or Seurat. Lacking Dalziel's purity of soul, I was more easily able to spot that Keith was a potential head-case. Actually I was wrong, too. There was nothing potential about Keith's mania. During his first visit to Dalziel's house, he had helped himself to half the contents of the refrigerator. Cathleen had smiled on this Bohemian trait but had been startled to notice, after he left, that several of her brassières were missing. She uttered a clear warning. Dalziel was too caught up to heed it and I was too craven. I was on the set as an unpaid grip when filming began on *Expresso Drongo*. This was Dalziel's working title for the project and showed that he had not lost his sense of humour. But there were some signs that he might have lost his judgment. Keith did at least twenty takes on every shot. Something always dissatisfied him. In the hired studio, it would be the angle of a light. In an exterior shot, it would be the intensity of the sun. He would squint at it as if it were the wrong size. He would complain that his leading actress had moved when she clearly hadn't, because she never did unless told to. All of this would have mattered less if Keith had not arrived late each morning for work. His excuse was lack of funds. Since the film's tight budget ruled out subsidised meals, Keith borrowed from Dalziel against the eventual profits. Taking this handout as his right, Keith complained that there was nothing left over to pay the cost of public transport, so he had to walk, which in turn was very hard on his shoes. His shoes certainly bore out this contention. Once they had been a rather good pair of brogues, but at that time they had probably belonged to someone else. Now they had cracks, thus exposing Keith's socks to the air, with penetrating results. He had feet like dead dogs. The film was four days behind schedule after three day's shooting, a ratio which it was to maintain and eventually exceed. Dalziel was slow to admit the possibility that it was in Keith's interests to spin things out. *Expresso Drongo* was Penelope's tapestry. To put it more plainly, it was Keith's meal ticket. Even after Dalziel caught on, he allowed this state of affairs to continue, hoping that he would be able to work his influence. That, as he saw it, was his job. A less generous man would have hit the silk sooner.

Keith's leading lady was called Nelia. Close interrogation had revealed that Keith's knowledge of the cinema was virtually zero, but apparently he had once seen a French film and been impressed that one of the actresses had been billed under her first name only. Nelia was Keith's discovery. Dalziel objected that the name would only serve to confuse the enormous public which the completed film would undoubtedly attract. Keith dug in his worn-down heels. As out of anything else, there was no talking Keith out of casting Nelia in the twin roles of wife and/or mistress. One of these personages – the one who waited outside the restaurant before coming in, as opposed to the one who waited inside the restaurant and did nothing at all – she played in a blonde wig, which cost a large proportion of the film's budget. The film lacking a wardrobe mistress, Nelia took the wig home with her every night and brushed it herself, presumably for hours, because it shone with a rare lustre. When quizzed closely by Dalziel, Keith avowed, in a few words widely spaced and reluctantly enunciated, that his relationship with Nelia was purely professional. It was hard to see how things could have been otherwise. Keith was so dirty that he had small plants growing on him. Any kind of physical contact with him was clearly out of the question. And Nelia was a zombie. You could simply park her in a chair, go away, come back hours later and she would still be sitting there. She was quite pretty but in a way so lacking in animation that even I had trouble idealising her.

Characteristically I managed it. To those of us who are artists at daydreaming, resistance from the medium is an invitation to invention. Nelia had neat features, a sweet figure, and an uncanny gift of stillness. To my mind it was more than enough. Soon she was my Anna Karina, my Jeanne Moreau, my Monica Vitti. I had ample scope to nourish these fantasies. Each day on the set I tried to make myself indispensable by shifting silver boxes about and helping to place the lights, but when Keith got started on his usual twenty takes there was plenty of time to become acquainted with Nelia if she wasn't in the shot, or even if she was. I could get nothing out of her except a hint that she liked tennis players. 'Tony,' she would murmur, looking at the sports page of some subhuman newspaper it took her all day to read. 'John.' Convincing myself that she had mystery, I perched near her as often as possible, rather hoping that I would be asked to massage her neck, which must have ached from the combined effort of sitting and reading. I thought I was getting somewhere when she asked me to scratch her back: not the whole of her back, just a particular spot in the middle, about three inches below the shoulder blades. I did that several times a day for about a week. Finally I dared to be romantic. 'Is that *the* spot?' I murmured. 'The special place?' In a hitherto unheard-of burst of vivacity she turned her face towards me, instead of just speaking straight ahead as usual. 'No, it's them bras Keith give me,' she said. 'They fit funny.' Years later I learned that she was a notorious tennis groupie who was as much a part of Wimbledon as the strawberries and cream, or the rain. Exhausted players who had fought their way through to the last sixteen would find her waiting for them in their hotel rooms. She would be wearing nothing but a blonde wig. They called her New Balls Nellie.

Not everyone who wants to make a film is crazy, but almost everyone who is crazy wants to make a film. It is just one of the things that crazy people want to do, like starting a law suit or sending long, unsolicited letters to people in the public eye. A letter from a nutter has a recognisable format and orthography, as if all letter-writing nutters have to go through some kind of Top Gun nutter-letter-writing academy. Usually – I think I've said this before, so maybe I'm going nuts too – the letter is written in green ink and its many pages are tied together with a bootlace in the top left-hand corner. Even if typed, however, the letter will continue after the signature in a PS which will run around the edge of the filled page in a dense spiral until the whole of the margin is packed tight. This will occur no matter how many leaves the letter consists of – rarely fewer than twelve – and even if the verso of each leaf is left blank. Usually it isn't. Every space is filled up. Though the combination of energy and futility can be depressing to contemplate, at least the nutter letter can be written on a low budget. The nutter movie costs thousands of pounds at the very least, and if the nutter hasn't got the money himself then he will have to get it from someone else. As the officer designated to provide tyro film makers with operating capital, Dalziel was in the position of a man giving away free meat in Moscow. He was on his guard, but he was handicapped by his correct perception that the partition between talent and obsession is often thin.

The ambiguous case of Keith Visconti would have sapped Dalziel's confidence if it had not been for the continuous, reassuring presence of our old friend and compatriot Alain le Sands. Born Alan Syms in Brighton le Sands, only a mile away from my own home suburb of Kogarah, this conspicuous figure in the history of modern Australian cinema had gone to school and grown up without either my or Dalziel's ever having met him. At the University of Sydney I still didn't meet him, but Dalziel acquired him like a shadow. As I related in the first volume of these memoirs, Dalziel knew the names of the director, cameraman and editor of all the films he had ever seen. Alan Syms knew all those things too. Dalziel made the initial, fateful mistake of assuming that there must be some kind of affinity between himself and this intense young man who followed him everywhere. It turned out that Alan

Syms also knew the names of the assistant director, the make-up artist and the second unit focus-puller. By the time it emerged that Alan Syms not only possessed this information, but was incapable of restraining himself from conveying it unasked, it was too late. That light of excitement in Alan Syms's eyes was the effulgent stare of the true film buff. The eyes were large, with contracted black pupils blazing in the dead centre of the very white whites. They never blinked. His mouth was similarly always wide open. It was equipped with large square teeth, like freshly cut tombstones. Alan Syms talked in a high, piercing shriek. Everything he said was otiose information about movies. He carried a card index.

Alan Syms was one of the main reasons Dalziel left Australia. When Alan Syms showed up in London, changed his name to Alain le Sands and started passing himself off as the leading light of the Australian New Wave, he was one of the main reasons why Dalziel left for Nigeria. At BFI guest lectures given by distinguished visiting American film directors such as John Frankenheimer or Delmer Daves, Alain le Sands would turn up and dominate question time. In a voice like a descending German dive bomber, he asked Frankenheimer for details about his assistant editor on *Seven Days in May*. When Frankenheimer visibly failed to recall exactly who his assistant editor had been, Alain le Sands provided the man's name, address and marital history. It was at this point, I am certain, that Dalziel began to find Lagos attractive. While Dalziel was away, Alain le Sands perfected his act by equipping himself with a screenplay for a short subject. By the time Dalziel got back, Alain le Sands had his film half-made. His own funds – which, judging from his varied supply of leather jackets, must have been not inconsiderable – were all used up. His few friends had been fleeced. He needed completion money. He made Dalziel's life a misery, demanding that the incomplete film be seen and assessed. He would telephone Dalziel in Brixton at three o'clock in the morning, waking up a whole houseful of Nigerian refugees. Finally, for a quiet life, Dalziel agreed to see the incomplete film at a small screening room in Soho. I happened to be in town and was present for the event. Dalziel had stipulated that Alain le Sands himself not be in attendance, so there were no witnesses except Dalziel, myself, and the projectionist, who was the first one to say 'Shit'. The film was entitled *He Alone*. It was subtitled '*un film de* Alain le Sands'. Dalziel was to relate this fact so often afterwards that Alan Parker picked the joke up and made it famous, but I was there at the birth and it was no joke. *He Alone* starred Alain le Sands himself, in a role closely modelled on that played by Charles Aznavour in *Tirez sur le pianiste*. Dalziel, who had wanted to *tirez sur* Alain le Sands for many years, groaned deeply in the dark. Yet Alain le Sands was no slavish plagiarist of Truffaut. Plot, characters and entire scenes had been faithfully copied, but he had an incompetence that was all his own. The deliberate jump-cuts of the *nouvelle vague* were translated by Alain le Sands into simple errors. Playing a young hero of threatening charisma, Alain le Sands would leap instantaneously from one side of the room to the other, his cigarette growing longer on the way. His sleeves would unroll and roll up again from shot to shot. As he advanced threateningly down a hotel corridor, he appeared to be walking between a set of railway lines. They were the dolly tracks of the camera. The cameraman must have been blind not to see them and adjust the framing accordingly. Perhaps he was too busy compensating for an evidently advanced case of Parkinson's disease. The camera shook as if mounted on a billycart. Unfortunately this imposed awkwardness of filmic style gave the central character none of the vulnerability of its model. Alain le Sands was playing the Aznavour character as if he were Robert Mitchum. He was being hunted, but he was not afraid. The point was thus neatly removed, leaving a vacuum. Close-ups were held for a long time. He smiled in every one of them, looking like two cement footpaths which had been freshly laid side by side. Dalziel watched in fascinated horror, audibly calculating the thousands of pounds the thing must have cost. Though it lasted only about fifteen minutes you could practically smell the burning money. Dalziel vowed that whoever else's cash was thrown on fire, it wouldn't belong to the BFI Production Board.

When Dalziel and I emerged shaking into the cold light of Soho, Alain le Sands was waiting for us on the pavement. 'What did you think of it?' he screamed. 'Hopeless,' said Dalziel. 'What are your criticisms?' shrieked Alain le Sands. 'There aren't any,' Dalziel replied wearily. 'It's just hopeless. Nothing works. It's a waste of time. A turkey. Forget it.' Alain le Sands made a strange move sideways. 'Yes, but how about some *constructive* criticisms?' The word 'constructive' was still echoing off the Georgian façades when we noticed the camera crew across the street. Alain le Sands had captured the whole scene. Luckily he could not afford to wear a radio microphone. We couldn't see a sound man. But unless his cameraman was even more incompetent than usual, he had got the picture. Dalziel commendably did not throw his coat over his head as we got into his car. It was a Jaguar 2.4 that was rather like his clothes: bought second-hand off a barrow but it looked terrific. It wouldn't start. The screaming face of Alain le Sands filled my window until the engine fired. 'God knows what he'll do with the footage,' said Dalziel as we pulled away. 'Keith's going to be a relief after that.' We spent the afternoon and early evening watching Keith Visconti shoot the big scene where the woman seated at the café table reveals that she takes sugar as well as milk. Six hours and a carton of sugar cubes dissolved like memories.

My key role in London's upsurgent film *milieu* made me even more determined, when back in Cambridge, to see every movie that came to town. I could not physically watch more movies than I had been watching already, but my newly acquired identity of quasi-film-maker gave new legitimacy to my pretty well constant attendance at the Cambridge cinemas, of which there were at that time half a dozen, most of them showing double bills. Across the river and up the hill, the Rex cinema showed – back to back and without let-up except for a few Pearl & Dean commercials – old and at the time almost entirely forgotten Hollywood programmers and films noirs with titles like *Dateline Homicide* and *Make My Tombstone Thick*. If you counted in the Arts cinema and the film societies, which together took care of the recherché present and historic past, Cambridge offered a chance to see just about every film ever made. I saw them all. In the late mornings I would write and deliver poems. From early afternoon on I was rarely out of a cinema except when I was in Footlights, and most of my time there was spent watching television. Armed with my practical knowledge I analysed every cut and change of angle, communicating my conclusions gratuitously to those sitting near by, even if they were strangers. I was forever drawing the attention of innocent civilians to what I took to be fine points of technique. Most of the time, I have since realised, I was simply wrong. Competent technique is what mediocrity has in common with genius, so there is small point in getting enthusiastic about it. Unless he is an outright hack, a journey-man will be just as careful as Fellini to make his shots match – often more careful. Buñuel, the most inventive of all film directors, resolutely declined to interest himself in any matter he thought merely aesthetic. But a little knowledge, though not always injurious to a practitioner, is invariably fatal to a critic. In recent years I have worked on documentary films at every stage of production and post-production. For any television documentary with my name in the title I have spent at least as much time in the cutting room as on the actual shoot, and often twice as much. I have turned a sentence around to fit pictures and I have asked for a shot to be run backwards to fit words. That kind of finicky labour is an experience for which there is no substitute. Youth, energy and appreciative passion, no matter how blessed they are with insight, aren't enough. There is no comparison between what I know now and what I used to know. Nowadays, after seeing a film or television programme, I wouldn't dream of praising its director until I had seen what he had done with other writers, and especially with other producers. I have seen a producer direct the whole movie. I have seen a cameraman save a director's career. But in my early innocence I fell for the *cinéaste* line full length. A fan of *Al Capone* and *Invitation to a Gunfighter*, I would point out that the director of both these masterpieces, Richard Wilson, had been the assistant editor on *Citizen Kane*, and that this fact should not be ignored when trying to account for their peculiar excel-lence. Though this wasn't a bad point, I was only a step away from sounding like Alain le Sands. Raise my voice three octaves, build my teeth with white plaster, and I could have been him.

7

The Ostrich Alternative

OBSESSIONS ARE WHAT we have *instead* of normality. They aren't a version of it, they are surrogate. My obsession with the moving image was what I was having instead of working on the set books. Out of the three terms of my second and last year as an undergraduate, one and a half had gone by before I could bring myself even to sit down and assess the magnitude of what I had not yet done in the way of preparing to satisfy the examiners. When I finally faced the issue, I quickly realised that I would have a better chance of satisfying them if I offered them my body. To present them with the contents of my mind would be an insult. My first move was to write one of my classic letters to my mother telling her that I was studying hard and not to worry about a thing. More than usually specious, this work of fiction helped get me in the mood for works of fiction composed by other people, such as Dickens and Thackeray. But merely not feeling negative wasn't the same as feeling positive. Enthusiasm was lacking. Why did it have to be Dickens *and* Thackeray? And why were Dickens's novels so very long, not just in thickness but from page to page? He piled it on as if I had all the time in the world to take it off. Jane Austen had had a far better idea of how much time a busy poet and performer had to spare. There was also the advantage that in previous incarnations, while being an aesthete at the University of Sydney or a down-and-out post-Beatnik Bohemian in Earl's Court and Tufnell Park, I had actually read some of her books. Acquiring a working knowledge of her *oeuvre* was thus on the cards. I resolved to concentrate on Jane Austen and thereby reap the benefits of the informed insight that cuts deep, the sharp focus. Whether a sharp focus on Jane Austen would come in handy when discussing the novels of, say, Dostoevsky, was a point that remained moot. A moot point I could always deal with by crossing the river, climbing the hill and hiding from the reality of afternoon in the sweet, artificial night of the Rex.

Most of the films I saw there were like me: rootless, unsung, wandering the universe like a spaceship with a dead crew. When *The Manchurian Candidate* was withdrawn from the screen after the assassination of President Kennedy, it showed up nowhere in the world except at the Rex, where I saw it at least ten times. I could, and at the drop of a hat would, analyse its camerawork exhaustively, but in a more reliable part of my addled brain I must have realised that it was the words which really counted. I learned George Axelrod's perfectly turned screenplay line by line. At that time and for years to come, the muttered question 'Why does your head always look as if it's coming to a point?' was a secret password among those who shared the Manchurian connection. I, however, was the only person I ever met who could correctly recite the key line in *Breakfast at Tiffany's*: 'I've never had champagne before breakfast before. With breakfast, often. But never before before.' The line was Axelrod's, not Capote's. I also knew that the best line in *The Big Sleep* – 'She tried to sit in my lap while I was standing up' – was not Raymond Chandler's. Years before it was rediscovered as a cult classic, the all-time off-beat Hollywood sleeper *The Night of the Hunter* would also show up only at the Rex. The print was full of splices yet the photography retained its lustre and, more importantly, the narrative still flowed. Bowled over by Charles Laughton's talent as a director, I still had enough sense to realise that James Agee's screenplay was the vital contribution.

The second time I saw *Night of the Hunter* at the Rex – once again I was in flight from Dickens – I was one of only three people in the audience. The others were two of the most beautiful people I had ever seen in my life. Both of them were Indians, and before I introduced myself I had mentally transferred to them the title of a piece by Duke Ellington: the Beautiful Indians. The beautiful girl was called Karula Shankar and the young man, if possible even more beautiful, was called Buddy Rajgupta. They looked like a tourist advertisement for Nirvana. It turned out, however, that they were students like me. In some respects they were even my kind of student. They, too, were in flight from the size of Dickens's novels. In other ways they were not students like me at all. Apart from their physical allure, they seemed materially comfortable to a degree unparalleled among the undergraduate population. This I deduced before we had even reached what Karula called Buddy's pad, whither I had been invited back for coffee. Buddy's casual Western clothes he might have worn at a Hyannis Port lawn party and Karula's sari was so subtle in its colours that you had to check your eyes for teardrops. Surely it was a film of water which was supplying the prismatic interplay as she rustled silkily along? No, it wasn't. In the middle of her superb forehead a tiny upright ellipse of scarlet spoke of the mysterious East. Her voice, however, spoke of Sarah Lawrence or Vassar, with the occasional word strongly emphasised, as if she had suddenly moved closer. 'You don't play *bridge*, by any chance?' Already lost, but not so far gone as to have forgotten that a competence at bridge might be hard to fake, I said I didn't. 'Man, have you ever met the *wrong* people. *We* play it *all* the time. We'll have to *teach* him, won't we?' Buddy said nothing for a long while as we walked. I could tell he was thinking. Finally he said: 'Yeah. OK.'

Buddy's pad was behind a heavy door in a neo-Georgian brick façade somewhere near Newnham. I can remember a gravel drive and an overhanging elm which must be gone by now, because the Dutch elm beetle went through Cambridge like silent wildfire later on and missed hardly a single candidate for extermination. I imagine the spacious layout of Buddy's pad has gone too. There can't have been many subsequent undergraduates who would have been able to keep up that level of classy carelessness. By student standards the place was enormous, colossal, outlandish: it was Grand Central Station, the Grand Salon of the Louvre, the Great Hall of the People in Peking. Actually I suppose the main room was only about thirty feet by twenty, but even among all the divans and cushions there definitely would have been room to swing the tiger whose skin was on the floor. The general arrangements were for a Rajah who had been brought up in the Ritz, which was apparently pretty well what had happened. Family photographs indicated that Buddy's forebears had driven at Le Mans, flown in the King's Cup, hunted from howdahs, played host to the Mountbattens. Pretending not to be impressed by all this was made easier by the books, which were loosely shelved by the thousand, and all interesting. Such American avant-garde publishing houses as New Directions and Evergreen were fully represented. These imprints I at least recognised. Others were new to me. Proud of my one-volume collected Nathaniel West, I was rather put out to see his separate novels all lined up in the original American editions, their paper wrappers intact. Undergraduates like to believe that they read adventurously but few of them do. Mostly they follow two curriculae: the official one, and the unofficial one which prescribes books supposed, by general consent among their generation, to be of epoch-making interest. Buddy was a genuine extracurricular reader. He had his own taste and followed it where it led. Nor was he one of those paid-up exquisites who read minor writers because the major ones are insufficiently obscure. He was in search of originality in all its forms. The quest was made only the more impressive by his off-hand manner. Nowadays he would be called laid-back. At that time the word for him was cool. Even in conversation, he never ran to catch the bus. 'Have you read Agee's film criticism?' he asked. 'Yes,' I lied. Buddy crossed slowly to his shelves, took down the relevant book, leafed through it, found some paragraph that he had been looking for, silently read it, closed the book and handed it to me. 'You should,' he said.

And I did. That year I read almost everything on Buddy's

shelves. Constant attendance at the cinema never cut into my reading: only into my official reading. Unofficially I would rather read than sleep. The Cambridge second-hand bookshops always beckoned. By the second week in any term I was usually too broke to buy anything. The University Library, needless to say, was out of the question: it was full of students who were actually studying, a sight which would throw me into a panic. So every few days I took an armful of books back to Buddy's pad, there to exchange them for more. Occasionally I was a fourth in bridge games but I never learned: the Beautiful Indians were too good at it to remember what it was like not to be able to play, so they couldn't teach me. Several times I was paired off with an Italian graduate economist called Mario who could memorise the whole pack at a glance no matter how it was shuffled. I came to dread the moment, usually no more than half-way through a hand, when Mario, Buddy or Karula said something like 'That's it, then,' and they all laid out their cards, having foretold how the hand – or round or rubber or whatever it was called – must play itself out. I had no sense for cards and got no better. Even today, playing gin rummy with my small daughter, I am notoriously easy meat, and have been since she was seven years old. If I make a fool of myself at gin, it can be imagined what a figure I cut at bridge. I just couldn't do it.

Reading I knew how to do: except, of course, when it was prescribed. Buddy was the same way. As far as I remember he never sat for the examinations, and might well already have been sent down without his noticing. Already, on that first afternoon, I envied him his insouciance, although I was too obtuse to realise as yet that it was only part of an aristocratic principle whose other main component was a deep sense of social obligation. Downing the proffered martinis as if they were water, I conveyed to Buddy and Karula my radical convictions, explaining to them the economic problems facing their country and how easily these could be solved. 'Man, that's *crap*,' Karula murmured from her sleepily curled position in a heap of paisley cushions, as if Liberty's had been bombed and geraniums were growing among the ruins. Buddy, smoking a black Russian cigarette so delicately that it seemed never to grow shorter, either listened to my monologue or thought of something else. Perhaps he was thinking of his country, in which, he slyly neglected to tell me, his father was a liberal publisher who had many times laid his life on the line for democracy and would expect his children to do the same. It was a typical Cambridge undergraduate evening: ignorance spoke out confidently while experience waited for it to catch up. Night fell and deepened. Karula rose from her cushions and made for the kitchen. She constructed large, American-style hamburgers. Eating a hamburger without putting down my martini glass made it difficult to talk, but I coped.

It never occurred to me that I should at least have offered to leave the Beautiful Indians together. Anyway, towards midnight I was given the job of escorting Karula home. She lived right in the centre of town, in a suite of rooms in a gingerbread house in a little lane, no wider than a thin man, leading off Market Square. It took a long time to get there because I found her a bit of a handful to escort. In fact I found her at all only with difficulty. The martinis must have had something in them. Alcohol, perhaps. Probably it was the way they made them in India. I tripped over gutters, detoured into bushes, fell down holes in the road. I peed behind a parked Mini and missed it. Karula, perfectly sober, was in hysterics. When we finally got to her place it turned out that she had forgotten her front door key. Luckily her room was on the ground floor. We jemmied her window without much trouble – Karula's peals of oddly accented laughter covered the noise of splitting timber – and I boosted her through. There was so much sari that I didn't really touch her. It was like pushing an unfolded parachute into a dumb waiter. But I felt her. The sweet heat of life. She was lovely and she wasn't mine. I wanted all the lovely women to be mine. If not all, then a few. If that was too much, then just one. Here, now. This instant. I sat down and had a little cry. 'Shit, man,' came that bewitching voice from inside the window, 'go *home*.' But where was home? Far, far away. Using the cool wall as a guide, I edged toward the streetlight at the end of the alley. So cold in England, even when it was warm.

8

Well Interrupted, Pembroke

LET ME NOT convey an impression of time completely wasted. If I had been enrolled to read a science subject and had dodged work in such a fashion, I would have been cheating. But in retrospect it seems possible that I only *felt* fraudulent. Eschewing the set books with unequalled diligence, I read everything else. From the conversations that lasted until dawn, I remembered what I heard in the rare intervals when I wasn't talking. The awkward truth, when it comes to the humanities, is that knowledge, taste and judgment get into us by uncharted routes. Late one night in Footlights, alone with the sputtering black-and-white TV set, I saw and heard Jacqueline du Pré playing the Elgar cello concerto. I saw her before I heard her, and went mad for her smile as I never did for Elgar, but another barrier between me and classical music softly crumbled. Until then I had been convinced, wrongly, that the main stream of great music was in the symphonies and the operas. After that, I started looking for it in the right place, in the concertos and the chamber music. It was her passion that did it. We live more by example than we think. Strong evidence for this view was provided by the disconcerting fact that I was a bit of a role model myself. Undergraduates who were shy about their intellectual or artistic ambitions looked up to me because I was blatant about mine. They believed that I knew a thing or two and I'm bound to say that I agreed with them. When the JCR of my college was invited to send a three-man team to compete in the television programme *University Challenge*, that I should be included seemed natural not just to me but to everyone. The rank of captain being offered, I made no demur. My second-in-command was an American called Chuck Beaurepaire, who was a walking, shouting encyclopaedia. Delmer Dynamo and the other Americans avoided him because of his knack for making his interlocutor redundant. He talked all the time and nothing he said was refutable, because all of it was facts. A formidable practitioner along those lines myself, I had been known to go toe-to-toe with him for a full half-hour before pausing to draw breath, whereupon he swept inexorably into the gap. Beaurepaire talked the way Alexander gave battle. He went straight at you. 'Watch out for Chuck,' whispered Delmer loudly one night in Hall. 'He's got another hole to eat with. The mouth *never* gets tired.' Beaurepaire was sitting only about three places away and should have heard, but he was talking. 'Johnson has the legislative record. Viewpoint of social benefits, Great Society biggest thing since New Deal. Just has a dumb name. Should've called it something else. Fair shake. Free lunch. Whatever. Know what Johnson said about J. Edgar Hoover? You don't? Tell you. Listen, this is great. They asked him why he didn't fire Hoover, right? Johnson said he'd rather have Hoover inside the tent pissing out than outside pissing in. My father was *there* when he said that. Johnson was on the Hill when Jack Kennedy . . . ' Beaurepaire delivered all this in a sustained bellow that made all around him look into their stew as if a tunnel might open through it and lead them to salvation. But from the viewpoint of Pembroke's team for University Challenge, to have Beaurepaire on tap was like being offered the assistance of Otto Skorzeny to pull a bank-raid. The third member of our team was a nice young man whose name I have forgotten. He had been chosen because he knew something about science. Beaurepaire knew all about that too, so the young man never needed to open his mouth, and, being shy, didn't try. Let us call him Christopher, because if his name wasn't that then it was Nicholas. His family had a nice house outside Manchester, where we all stayed the night before we recorded the show next day. In those days, Granada Television ruled the ionosphere with *Coronation Street* and an unrivalled array of classic small formats like *University Challenge, All Our Yesterdays, What the Papers Say* and *Cinema*, which was to be the first programme I ever regularly presented when, some years later, I tentatively essayed what has turned out to be my principal means of earning a living. At that time, however, I had been on television precisely once. It had happened in Sydney. Television itself had been new to Australia. I was one of a team of Sydney University students ranged against a team of journalists in a game of bluff. We had scored precisely no points. I forget the rules, but I never got over sitting there for half an hour without saying a word. This time, I resolved, would be different. In one of Christopher's guest rooms, I lay awake looking at the hammered beams and white plaster of the low ceiling. Outside in the grounds, the moon shone on the lake. I didn't want Christopher's inheritance. I didn't even want, or not very much, Christopher's mother, which was quite mature of me, because she was exactly the stamp of unassuming but self-assured gentlewoman most calculated to arouse greed and resentment. Her husband, I had guessed, must have been that object covered with coats and hats that we passed in the hall. Anyway, he hadn't joined us for dinner, which, excusing herself, she did not change for, merely adding tiny pearl earrings to her ensemble of cable-stitch roll-neck sweater, corduroy trousers and penny loafers. Quality unencumbered by finery, her *soignée* allure was the unfussiest possible interplay of form and content. Serene. What a word. There was nothing ruffled about her image until it reached my eyes. 'You *will* look after Christopher tomorrow, won't you?' I nodded conspiratorially while Beaurepaire told her about the Tennessee Valley Authority.

Next day we were up against an all-girl team from St Hilda's, Oxford. I'm sorry to say that we creamed them. Christopher just sat there and I almost did the same. Beaurepaire was magnificent. Bamber Gascoigne, moderating the programme, could barely begin a question before Beaurepaire answered it. 'It was unhistorical of Keats ...' Gascoigne began. 'Balboa!' shouted Beaurepaire over the zap of his buzzer. He had instantaneously figured out, not only that the question must concern Keats's mistake in putting Cortez on a peak in Darien, but that the question would be about whom he should have put there instead. Bitterly reflecting that 'Silent, upon a peak in Darien' neatly summarised the condition and location to which everyone who knew Beaurepaire would like to see him translated, I was nevertheless pleased that we were cleaning up, and the last bonus question was a personal triumph for myself. The right answer depended on knowing that Leonardo's 'Last Supper' had been painted on a wet wall. Having seen it helped. A man of the world, I struggled not to look too pleased as we swept to victory. The camera probably saw the struggle. Personality is the thing it catches. Everything else it lets go.

You have to realise that in those days the whole country watched every episode of *University Challenge*. They watched it in working men's clubs. The Queen Mother watched it, knuckles white, running to the telephone to place bets. At the time of writing, television in Britain is still, by the skin of its teeth, a communal event – the best reason for being involved in it – but twenty years ago there was no question about it. If you were on television in prime time, the whole population of the country was looking through the same small window right into your face. That night we, the winning team from Pembroke, were given dinner by Bamber and the programme's producer at the Midland Hotel. The losing team was nowhere to be seen. The producer's beautiful researcher had a nice, fresh, land-girl sort of smile which bore up pluckily under a verbal onslaught from Beaurepaire that left Bamber looking thoughtful, as if wondering whether it was all worth it. Some-how I knew that he really thought it was, even if it cost him this, a bad evening out with the cocky youngsters. It wasn't just the money. It was the thing itself. The millions watching. The show. I vowed to myself that they would never get me. Never, never would I succumb to the lure of television. Its mereness I found offensive. Television didn't transform you. You just sat there. Look at Bamber Gascoigne, just sitting there while two pretty girls from the next table leaned over his shoulder – leaned *on* his shoulder – to get his autograph. *Four* pretty girls. It was a moment of truth. Even Beau-repaire stopped talking. Silent, upon a peak in Manchester.

The following week we came back for the next round, against another Oxford college, Balliol. Once again we stayed at Christopher's house the night before the big day. Christopher's father was still nowhere in the picture. Christopher's mother either changed for dinner or else had been wearing that black jersey silk bias-cut scooped-neck top all day, along with the straight plum velvet skirt and the ankle-strap sandals. While Beaurepaire blew a gale I drowned in her eyes. I resolved that when we returned victorious the next evening, I would dare. I had been reading a biography of H. G. Wells which said that when a guest at a country house party he already had a map of the sleeping arrangements in his pocket before he got off the train, with the distances all worked out so that he could get the mother and the daughter before dawn: a brace with one barrel. Along the corridor at dead of night, knock softly on her door, and begin with a discussion of her son's personality problems, currently being exacerbated by unshielded exposure to the overweening self-confidence of Beaurepaire. As she leaned elegantly sideways in the tempest emanating from the latter's tireless lungs, I essayed a small sympathetic smile and was rewarded with a soft lowering of eyelashes like two black moths making a deck landing on stretched silk. I went into battle against Balliol as if her handkerchief was tucked into my tunic, or was fluttering, as it were, from the point of my couched lance.

Boy, did we lose. And it was all my fault. The Balliol blokes knew more than the St Hilda's women and were a lot quicker at hitting the buzzer. Their captain was practically a psychic. He guessed the question before Bamber's mouth was fully open and his reflex speed on the buzzer was like one of those small Australian boys who can bring down a dragonfly by spitting at it. But Beaurepaire was magnificent. He kept us in there, matching the Balliol top gun volley for volley as the afternoon blazed to a climax. The two teams were dead even when it came to the last question, which was about music. I heard two bars and knew it was Verdi. I heard four bars and knew it was *Otello*. I hit the button while the Balliol captain's overdeveloped thumb was still in the air. Beaurepaire hit the button too but the answer was already out of my mouth.

'*Otello!*' I shouted. 'It's *Don Carlo!*' shouted Beaurepaire, louder. Louder but too late. Bamber wrapped it up. 'It was *Don Carlo*, as Chuck Beaurepaire said. Clive James should have waited. Congratulations, though, Pembroke, on being such close losers . . . ' I think I bore up reasonably well. I was told subsequently – I am still told today by anyone I meet over the age of forty – that the tears which I thought were jetting from my eyes merely made them shine, and that if it had not been for my mouth, which went all square like a baby ready to howl, nobody would have known that my world had collapsed.

As we discovered the previous week, losers, no matter how close, did not get invited to the Midland Hotel. All the way back to Christopher's house I explained that the bit of *Don Carlo* they had played was almost identical to the bit in *Otello* just before the whole cast sings at once. Beaurepaire was sulking. Keats would have mistaken him for stout Cortez. Christopher's mother opened the door to us. She looked wonderful. So did her husband. It transpired during supper that he had just got back from Canberra, where he went regularly in order to talk about investments in minerals. 'You're making a mistake, I think,' he told me, 'in selling us the stuff outright. It would be wiser to impose conditions so that nobody could buy anything without processing it out there. That way you'd get a bigger industrial base. At the moment you're just giving it away. The Japanese can't believe their luck.' This was an opportunity for Beaurepaire. His mouth was off and running. I looked at Christopher's mother. I looked at those lashes. They were spread wide while the eyes they protected looked adoringly at her husband. He certainly was quite impressive, if you don't mind them modest as well as handsome, intelligent and rich. 'It must be a bore for you,' I managed to choke out, 'changing planes in Sydney. Must be a hell of a long flight.' He nodded. 'It would be if we didn't have our own. Gives me a chance to keep my hours up.' It turned out that he had flown Meteors in Malaya. I felt terrible. It should have been *Otello*. That bit just before he kills himself, where the strings well up and weep, would have been just right.

9

Wanting and Found Tested

SEXUAL STARVATION WAS the undergraduate's prescribed fate. I considered myself hard done by, having to share it. After all, I was a man of experience: perhaps not precisely a boulevardier, but withal no sprig. I had experimented, and intended to experiment further. In my opinion I was still at a formative stage. I did not yet consider myself responsible enough to settle down. How could I be, when I was scarcely responsible enough to settle a bill? Without wishing to emulate Prince Aly Khan or Porfirio Rubirosa, I yet believed that there was a certain amount of adventuring which a man should regard as his duty; that I had at least made a start; and that if allowed a fair chance I might well make my mark. Consider the evidence. There was my chequered past. There was my long-term liaison in Italy. There was, to make me feel interestingly treacherous, my intermittent imbroglio with Robin in London. But in Cambridge there was, resoundingly, nothing. At the time the number of male undergraduates known to be cohabiting with females could be counted, with difficulty, on the fingers of one hand — with difficulty because the hand would be trembling with envy. A detached observer might have felt that I was already getting my share. As far as I am able to assess the truth by looking back, however, my sense of deprivation was genuine, even though it arose from a compulsively, and possibly psychopathically, inadequate capacity to realise that out of sight should not mean out of mind. People loyal to me I was loyal to only when I was with them. This went double for women. I have learned better since, but very slowly, and the fact that I had to learn it, instead of having the instinct conferred on me by nature, has been a grief to me, although never so much as it has been a grief to others, who always had to grieve first before I noticed that grief might be appropriate.

There was also the consideration that I was very energetic, a condition which time has since gone a long way towards curing completely. Whatever my psychological compulsion towards putting it aimlessly about, sheer physical randiness was a powerful potentiating agent. If the result was priapism, Cambridge might have been specifically designed to put a stop to it. Men of that age, in that epoch, wanted their women attractive or not at all. There being, in the first place, few women *in statu pupillari*, the number of them who might arouse desire by their appearance was few indeed, and these received a volume and concentration of male attention which in some cases ruined them for life. The actresses were the worst. After a season with the ADC and a single appearance with the Marlowe, girls who started off with the self-effacing temperament of voluntary aid workers ended up carrying on like Catherine the Great. Being cast in a play was the merest interlude between bouts of theatrical behaviour extending deep into everyday life. They made entrances. They stormed out. They had the vapours. They did all these things going in and out of the University Library. There were exceptions, but the one I had to go and fall for wasn't among them.

From the wooded slopes of Highgate by way of Golders Green and Tel Aviv, Consuela Schleppkis, though rather younger than I, was at the triumphant end of a university career during which she had taken the starring role, and most of the notices, in every major ADC and college production. A prima donna on stage, she was even more so off it, and after the drama critic of the *Cambridge Evening News* named her as Actress of the Year she went over the top like a regiment. Previously, though she had been unable to cycle up Castle Hill towards Girton without making innocent passers-by suspect that she might be Lady Macbeth, she had been subject to brief bouts of normal behaviour. Now she would take notes in a Sidgwick Avenue lecture theatre with such an air of commitment that the lecturer would break off to ask her if anything was wrong. Actually commitment was what she needed and later on she duly got it, but in the meantime her histrionic intensity was no excuse for my stupidity, whose only mitigating factor was her personal appearance. Consuela would have been a personable girl in any circumstances. In the Cambridge context she was like Marilyn Monroe in Korea. She was slim and dark rather than plump and blonde, but the effect was roughly the same. Blessed with a clear-skinned oval face dreamed by Modigliani in his last fever, she moved well when she was not self-conscious. She rarely wasn't, but moved well enough even so. As the spring of my second year approached, Consuela was rehearsing an open air production of *As You Like It* in the gardens of Clare. Leaning on a hedge, her forehead in her hands, concentrating on her lines, she was so graceful that she made you – or me, at any rate – forget that no one can really lean on a hedge without falling through it. I besieged her with poems. Some of them still seem to me to be pretty good even today. Others were trash. She took them all as her due. They were burning in the fire when she finally invited me to an early tea at her digs near Fenner's. The weather was already warm, but she said we would need a fire if we were going to take our clothes off. Already unnerved by the knowledge that she had asked everyone in Cambridge theatrical society whether it would be wise to sleep with me, I was reduced by the inspiring spectacle of her silky body to incurable impotence. Unaware then, and for some time to come, that what a gentleman should do in such circumstances is to forget himself and think of a few things the lady might like – which is, come to think of it, pretty well what a gentleman should do in any circumstances – I tried everything except ringing up the Fire Brigade. An immediate, frank confession of inadequacy might have enlisted her sympathy to the extent of getting her to drop the play-acting, which would have been a help.

Finally I tried to bluff it out, if that's the appropriate expression. At first Consuela lay back with a show of drowsy, patient sensuality, as if Madame Récamier were receiving Châteaubriand in her boudoir and his dotage. This was not a bad number but unfortunately she must have read somewhere about the possibility of a smouldering simper. She unleashed several of these in succession, decorating them with a flare of the nostrils which would have made the Dalai Lama's robe strobe, but which reminded me of a wild horse I had seen in Taronga Park zoo when very young – when I was very young, that is, the horse being obviously mature, not to say virile. I think it was one of those zebras that have no stripes, but do have a very long and large penis, which, when ready for use, extends so far from the lower abdomen that it will hit the ground unless its owner is standing over a hole. This recollection made me feel even more inadequate than I was feeling already. Desperately I tried to think of stimulating things. Again, here is a technique to which, reputedly, men in that situation often have recourse, but which has little to recommend it. If one is already in the presence of an actual incitement to desire, trying to think of an alternative incitement to desire can only emphasise the discrepancy between one's psychological quandary and the fierce simplicity of one's real-life position. To the part of the mind that watches the mind at work, the disjointure reveals itself as fundamentally absurd. Nothing is sillier to one's superego than to observe one's ego grinding away at the sweaty task of trying to flog one's recalcitrant id into action. I was already far gone in the interior turmoil of this metaphysical confrontation when Consuela put the lid on it by shifting to a new role. She became solicitous, as if I had some rare disease. I got the impression that I had only days to live. Her large and lovely eyes were full of horror and wonder at how God's behest had worked itself out by striking me down, thus depriving her of a great earthly love, but perhaps – who knew? – compensating her with a lasting memory of spiritual grace. If she had left the room, put on a nurse's uniform and reappeared at the foot of the bed holding a hurricane lamp, she could not have done a better impersonation of Jennifer Jones. By now I was ready for the hospital anyway, and would have been glad if she could have left it at that. Unfortunately she saw a further possibility in the scene: a direction in which she might, in actor's parlance, *stretch* herself, since it had long ago become clear that there was no chance of stretching me. She became scornful, as if Lupe Velez, on her famous first tempestuous visit to Errol Flynn, had thrown herself naked on the floor only to find her passion rewarded with a lecture on stamp-collecting. Tossing her head, Consuela made a sudden exit to the bathroom. A bathroom was already a very impressive accoutrement for an undergraduate to have, but the spectacle of Consuela exiting into it was awe-inspiring. She then made an entrance out of it, apparently without having done very much in there except pause for breath and learn her lines. 'It doesn't matter,' she snapped, tossing her head again and gazing fixedly out of the window. 'Let's just say it doesn't *matter*.' What had she seen out of the window? Lohengrin arriving on a swan? It scarcely seemed possible, since the curtains were still drawn. But a certain amount of light was coming through them. Consuela liked looking at light. She liked standing in it. She looked very beautiful there: long-haired, small-bottomed, heroic in her tragedy. My clothes were all over the room. Getting into various bits of them, I couldn't help noticing that I was always looking at her back. 'Look,' she said at last. 'It just doesn't bloody *matter*, OK?'

There was still quite a lot of the afternoon left. Too miserable even to go to the movies, I spent it at the Whim, the Trinity Street coffee bar in whose back room the aesthetes gathered. Except for the Footlights, who were only there in the afternoon when the clubroom closed, everybody in the university's artistic world would use the Whim all day as a headquarters, clearing house, comfort station, watering hole and gossip exchange. The Whim worked on the French café system: you could sit for a long time over a single cup of coffee as long as you didn't mind paying too much for it in the first place. I enjoyed writing there because there was a good chance of being interrupted. This time I worked steadily on a poem – it was one of those threnodies which claim that to say goodbye is inevitable because the ecstasy is too intense to last – without encouraging anyone to join me in conversation. Indeed, I made a point of not lifting my head. A couple of hours went by like that. The place was jammed with its late afternoon regulars when Consuela made an entrance. In full drag as a tempestuous gypsy princess, she was pretty enough to stop a speeding train. A whole room full of aesthetes ceased talking about themselves and looked at her. Meanwhile she was looking at me. She shook her head. She threw it slowly back, raised her clenched fists to her forehead, and rocked as if her body was in the throes of rejecting a brain implant. Then she lowered her arms, looked at me again, shook her head slowly, and made an exit. Everyone looked at me. If she had left it at that, they all might have at least remained in doubt, but over the next few days she told everyone the details individually.

In retrospect I must concede that I was in no position to fault her on that point, because until much later in my life I was terribly indiscreet. Telling myself that to spill beans was a necessary component of a wonderful, warm, openly Antipodean personality, I exchanged gossip with the best of them, which necessarily meant that I also exchanged it with the worst of them. If people asked me intimate questions I would tell them the answers. I told people all about myself. Less forgivably, I told people all about other people too. I can't even say that the concept of privacy eventually crept up on me. It was forced on me, by other people's pain – or, to be less complacent and more accurate, by my pain at earning other people's justified disapproval. In this regard I have become a different person: infinitely more guarded, unforthcoming to the point of paranoia. To embarrass someone by revealing his secret to someone who might damage him with it seems to me, in my later incarnation, a crime worse than breaking wind at an investiture. Having learned something of what malice can do, and of how candour plays into its hands, I am now a clam. In those days I simply blabbed. But I still thought that Consuela was impermissibly revelatory about our unproductive tryst. She did everything but hire a sky-writer. Everyone in town knew. The women who sold cream cakes in Fitzbillie's knew all about it. More than twenty years later I was still meeting perfect strangers who sympathised with me over my fiasco with Consuela Schleppkis. Let me take this opportunity to set the record straight. The truth is that my failed affair with Consuela rankled for a while, but nowadays, far from being still sensitive on the subject, I try to show that I enjoy a good joke against myself, before I go quietly away somewhere to be sick.

There was ample excuse for being unmanned. The Tripos examinations were imminent, and I was scarcely prepared to answer the essay paper, let alone the specialised papers on Swift, on tragedy and on God knew what else. On Jane Austen I had done just enough background reading to convince myself that I knew less about the foreground than I had thought. The mandatory foreign language paper was at least possible now that I had learned some Italian, which enabled me to avoid the French option. Emboldened by having started to get somewhere with Italian, I made renewed efforts to teach myself French, but I was at an early stage, possibly having overtaxed myself by choosing *A la recherche du temps perdu* as a primary reader. After six months I was about half-way through *Du coté du chez Swann* and still looking up every second word in an old Larousse. If I had known then that I would turn bald before I got through the whole thing I would probably have given up. A lack of sense of proportion is one of the big advantages of being young: when we grow out of it, we leave possibilities behind along with the absurdity. Proust remains my idol of idols to this day – and I could not, or at any rate would not, have written that last sentence without his influence. His willingness to generalise about life enthralled me even when I myself knew little about life worth knowing. His specific, concrete observations I admired but thought I understood how he did them. It was the *aperçus*, the aphoristic insights driving deeper than observation, which continually surprised me. His every sententious formulation I underlined in ballpoint, until the tattered, coffee-stained *Livre de poche* was fat with dog-ears and looked blue when it fell open. It was one of the books I carried everywhere in those spring days when I was theoretically gripped by examination fever. Examination lassitude would have been a more accurate expression. It was as though I had been bitten by a tsetse fly. As time grew shorter, I moved slower. Having kept well away from the Footlights May Week revue – I had neither auditioned for it nor volunteered any ancilliary services beyond handing over a few scripts – theoretically I was unencumbered with extracurricular commitments. Thus free to plan my time constructively, I did little except make plans. I constructed elaborate flow charts of what I needed to do, when what I really needed to do was do something. Quietly getting crocked in his college room, my supervisor, nicknamed the Baby Don because his name was Ron Maybey, greeted me with only partly feigned admiration on the one occasion I could bring myself to turn up. 'Remarkable track record,' he said. 'Far as I can tell, you haven't actually *completed* a weekly essay in two years. Fancy a sherry?' It was gallows humour. I should have been in a blue funk.

But the sun was out, the girls were out with it, the punts were on the river and I was lying casually on its far bank, opposite the back lawn of King's, on the edge of the meadow. The pampered cows and expense-account sheep of King's were behind me, grazing plumply among the buttercups. Before me was the prettiest stretch of waterway in the world, bounded on the far side by the austerely satisfying façade of Gibbs's Fellows Building, with whose central arch I would always position myself in line so that I could see through it to the dry fountain in the middle of the front lawn. Wearing nothing but a pair of shorts, I could lie there working on my flow charts. When I broke into a sweat from all that effort I could roll into the river and swim lazily about, just quickly enough to dodge the punts. Of the young men who propelled the punts – of their honking voices, their self-satisfied features and their clothes purchased for a touring production of *Charley's Aunt* – I felt no more tolerant than I had the previous year, but all anger subsided at the sight of their precious cargo. Elegant fingertips of first and second year undergraduettes would trail past at eye level as I lay limp, submerged to the nostrils. The third year undergraduettes, needless to say, were all in their rooms studying for the examinations which, it periodically occurred to me, I would, at this rate, plough like a plane crashing. So I hauled myself out of the water, temporarily put aside the latest master plan for concentrated study, and tried to sketch out a few thoughts relating to the set books.

One of the special papers was on Swift, and there I thought I had the glimmering of an idea. Swift's prose appealed to me so strongly that my enthusiasm had survived a crushingly boring lecture from the current American academic expert on the subject. On a brief visit paid for by some memorial lecture fund, this worthy had packed one of the Sidgwick Avenue lecture theatres with an audience of dons, graduate students and final year undergraduates all eager to hear him on the subject of Swift's sense of humour. By the time the visitor — I recall him as being the Hale Professor of Raillery at Yale, but I must have got that wrong — had finished isolating, exemplifying and analysing what he took to be Swift's techniques of comic invention, anyone present with even a vestige of a sense of humour was, or should have been, praying for death. The professor was a bore on a Guggenheim, a long-range drone, an international ballistic fossil. I spent the whole hour drawing little pictures of hanged men. I was kept from falling unconscious, however, by constantly renewed surprise at the gales of laughter which greeted the professor's every creaking sally. When he quoted something by Swift that he said was meant to be funny, they laughed. Sometimes it *was* funny, although not after he got through reading it out, because he always added a bit of explanatory acting — including, especially, a shrewd, quizzical twinkle which he evidently assumed to be the facial expression Swift might have adopted when regaling fellow members of the Scriblerus Club with a passage of improvised invective. When the professor said something on his own account that was clearly meant to be funny also — you could tell it was a joke because he did everything except lay his index finger alongside his nose — they laughed even louder. It occurred to me that an academic audience — not necessarily individually, but in the aggregate — is like the audience for serious music when faced with the challenge of reacting to *A Musical Joke*. They kill themselves laughing because the only other possible response would be to ask for their money back. They roll in the aisles because they lack the nerve to take to their heels. This was a very depressing conclusion to reach and for a while I blamed Swift himself. Swift himself would have been quick to blame mankind. His misogyny I found off-putting until I read the journals to Stella and Vanessa. The professor was convinced that there could not have been anything between Swift and the girls except a rich exchange of good jokes. This was enough to persuade me that the truth might be different, and I soon turned up enough textual evidence to be certain that the sly old boy had been screwing both of them. Apparently there was still much learned discussion about whether Swift's use of the phrase 'a cup of coffee' was, or was not, a veiled reference to sexual intercourse. Whole academic careers were devoted to this supposed conundrum. To me it looked like the most easily penetrated code since Pig Latin. 'Can't get over that last cup of coffee we had on the floor,' Swift would write, or words to that effect. 'Get ready for three cups of coffee in a row tomorrow night.' Vanessa and Stella were equally scrutable in their replies. 'Must have at least six cups of coffee with you as soon as possible. Love and kisses.' To my mind, the Hale Professor of Raillery at Yale and all his academic kind were wilfully missing the obvious.

It could be said that my mind was not in a very objective state, but whatever the accuracy of its judgments, affection for Swift was fully restored, and I actually got around to reading extensively not just in his major works but in the poems, pamphlets and correspondence. I even read some of the relevant scholarship and criticism. This was the first time in my life that I had ever studied an author against his background at the time I was supposed to, and I was disturbed to find that although I achieved growing intimacy with the author I couldn't make any sense at all of the background. Of the many experts on Swift beside the Hale Professor of Raillery – who had long ago departed by PanAm Boeing 707 to spread his message of cheery bathos to a helpless world – the big cheese was Professor Irvin Ehrenpreis, whose lumbering two-volume work on Swift was mindbending in the completeness of its scholarship. Professor Ehrenpreis knew about every philosophical concept and rhetorical convention current in that part of the eighteenth century. He knew about animism, dualism, Deism, dynamism, Platonism, pleonasm, Whiggery and buggery. Though Professor Ehrenpreis didn't write badly, it was evident to me, in my cocksureness, that he had soaked his brain in the period to the point of its falling apart like dead meat left too long in tap water. According to Ehrenpreis, Book IV of *Gulliver's Travels*, the book about the Houyhnhnms, reflected Swift's attitude to the current Platonic, or was it neo-Platonic, concepts of man, God, society and whatever. According to me, Gulliver felt about the Houyhnhnms the way Swift felt about Sir William Temple and all the other English aristocrats whose high civilisation he admired but on whom it shamed him to dance attendance. The Yahoos were Swift's people, the Irish. He couldn't live with them, but he found little solace, and much more humiliation, in his position of court wit to the English gentry. I had it all worked out. I even drew a little chart.

Actually, after all these years, I still have an inkling that I might have been on the right track. Certainly the scholars and critics were on the wrong track when they suggested that Swift's great writings had been dictated by some sort of synthesis of current thought. That works of art can be inspired only by individual passion is something I am even more sure of now than I was then. Gulliver's love for the Houyhnhnms is made painful to him by their contempt for the Yahoos. His divided feelings are real feelings — Swift's feelings. If I had the time, the qualifications and the academic ambitions I think I could defend that case now. On the eve of the Tripos examinations I was sure I could. I was a man with an idea, and I was angry. Burning in my brain was the memory of the range of gesture and facial expression employed by the Hale Professor of Raillery when he was being amusing about Swift's imitating a horse's whinny and transcribing the sound as the word Houyhnhnm. No doubt that was how it happened, but I knew in my blood and bones that Swift had dedicated his adult life to never being in the same coffee house with a man like the Hale Professor. I was Swift's champion. In my examination paper his great, tormented spirit would rage, laugh, despair and exult.

Unfortunately it happened exactly like that. Casting my eye down the front page of the examination paper, I noted the request to interpret Book IV of *Gulliver's Travels*. Instantly my pen was flying. In a fine frenzy, pausing only to call for another quire of writing paper, I spent the whole three hours answering that one question. We had, however, been instructed to answer four questions. I had left the examination schools, and was standing outside in a pool of summer light trapped by blonde stone buildings, before I quite realised that I had condemned myself to scoring a maximum of twenty-five per cent on that paper even if, which was unlikely, they liked what I said. Instead of cramming for the next day's paper, I spent half the night composing a letter to the examiners begging them to believe that I had failed to read the instructions. The idea that the ability to read instructions was one of the things we were being examined on didn't occur to me at the time.

Ballsing up the Swift paper set the tone for my whole effort in the examinations. The novel paper went only just better. With some ingenuity I answered the questions on the Russian novel by making references to nobody except Jane Austen, but there is a limit to how much you can say about D. H. Lawrence when you have read only *Pride and Prejudice*. As for the English moralists, I was still ignorant as to who they might be, let alone about what they had said. Today it surprises me when I recall how incapable I was of getting interested in anything that smacked of distilled wisdom. If it wasn't Proust, I didn't want to hear it. I valued spontaneity above all else, as if concentration could not be spontaneous too. On my shelves now, collections of aphorisms sit like containers of radioactive material. Just to mention the French, there are Montaigne, Pascal, La Rochefoucauld, Vauvenargues, La Bruyère. Of the Germans and Austrians, there are Goethe, Lichtenberg, Schnitzler, Kraus, Altenberg, Polgar. The pregnant sentence affects me like a lovely woman in the same condition. When Sainte-Beuve said that Montaigne sounded like one long epigram, it was high praise. Thomas Mann's great son Golo is my favourite modern historian because he sounds so like Tacitus, packing a loosely troubled world into a tense neatness. Envious in my youth of what seemed easy, in later years I find nothing more thrilling than the formulation so loaded with meaning that it burns the mind. Only last year, catching Raymond Aron's enthusiasm for Montesquieu, I devoured the *Lois* as if it were *The Lady in the Lake*. My memory is not especially good and as a linguist I am doomed to remain a mere dabbler, but by now I am so drenched in that type of writing that I can quote it off the cuff more easily than I can spit. If only I had had such a facility to draw upon when I sat those examinations! My ignorance of the British moralists might not have been so glaring if I could have imported a few names from the continent. Hobbes, Hume, Locke: how to sum them up, when they had needed such large volumes to sum themselves? I sucked my pen. On the other side of the room, Consuela Schleppkis wrote like a woman possessed. She called for more paper as if she wanted to start her own magazine. I doodled. The clock ticked like a bomb.

On the Italian paper, on the other hand, I lavished a fatal fluency. If Montesquieu had been in my mind to aid me, I might have said something sensible about Machiavelli. I could read *The Prince* in the original, but I had nothing original to say about it, because I had found Garrett Mattingly's theory – that the book was a satirical parody – too attractive not to adopt. An acquaintance with the other masterpiece, *The Discourses on Livy*, would have told me that Machiavelli, far from doing a roguish cabaret number, was founding a tradition of political realism for the modern age. Only in my prose translation of Dante did I really know what I was doing. Françoise had taken me line by line through every dramatic passage in *The Divine Comedy*, so when one of those passages came up it was a cinch. To that extent my satisfaction with the paper was justified, but I should have realised that I would be lucky to get half marks for the whole thing. Allowing myself a measure of elation, however, was the only alternative to despair. I pretended, in the Whim and on the river bank, that I had everything under control. On the day before the last paper, the essay, I lounged at apparent ease under a cloudless sky whose chalky light blue matched the sun dials of Caius. The cows and sheep masticated bucolically behind me. King's College chapel waited for its choir, which duly crossed the stone bridge to my right, the top hats of the smallest boys barely clearing the parapet as they all marched *en croc* for a date with Bach. Was Cambridge getting to me? I had a strange feeling of not wanting to leave – doubly strange because I had approached the examination like someone setting out to be expelled. The prospects of being asked to stay on to do research were dim. I rolled impressively into the water, sank like a hippo under a passing punt full of girls, and damned near killed myself ramming my head against a bicycle stuck in the muddy bottom. It must have been one of the pedals that gashed my scalp. There wasn't much pain but there was quite a lot of blood. It was cowardly not to get it stitched.

Marenko, who knew about first aid, stuck a field dressing on my wound, so it was with my head in a sling that I faced the essay paper next day. I should not have been so surprised to find that I could do it. Who couldn't? The choice of set topics was so wide that even an examinee who had been compelled to silence by all the other papers would have been able to find something to say this time. The only way of stuffing it up completely would have been to get in a dither about which topic to choose. Luckily one of my pet subjects was right there on the paper. I had read Hannah Arendt's book *Eichmann in Jerusalem* when it had been serialised in the *New Yorker*; I had followed both sides of the subsequent controversy; and I had reached my own conclusions on the validity of the catchphrase 'the banality of evil'. One of the set topics was exactly that: *The banality of evil*. My pen fizzed for the full three hours. The invigilators brought me some more paper like coal-heavers feeding a ship's furnace. My pen overheated. On the only occasion when I paused to look around, Brian C. Adams was staring at me as if I was his nemesis. My own fond opinion of what I had written was that I could have published it as a piece in a weekly. More importantly, I got the thing finished before the bell rang. Unfortunately this fact only served to remind me that on scarcely any of the other papers had I actually managed to answer the prescribed number of questions within the allotted time. Elation induced depression. If only I had been prepared for the whole examination, instead of for just one paper!

Outright failure had probably been warded off, but a low 2:2 was the most I could expect and a third was on the cards. As I left the hall, my gown felt like a shroud. Suddenly I didn't want to give all this up.

All this included May Week in its full splendour. Examinations out of the way, the lawn parties flowered. The June sun shone on them as if intent to prove that once in a way it could co-operate. As a minor luminary in the areas of theatre, literature and related arts, I had a fair sheaf of invitation cards – their timings mutually arranged by the hosts so as not to clash – but anyone with half a brain could figure out where the next party was and just walk in uninvited. The basic layout was the trestle table set up on a college lawn. In the men's colleges, mostly the table was bedecked with nothing more grand than a bowl of fruit punch, the bowl borrowed from the college kitchen and the punch concocted according to loudly touted formulae promising instant oblivion to all who drank. Though for some imbibers this proved to be the case, if you kept your head you could move from one party to another and never reach the point at any of them when the ladle scraped the bottom of the bowl and came up with nothing in it except apple skins and orange pips.

If the girls were throwing the party, there was often something to eat and usually something better than punch to drink. I went to a white wine effort in Newnham which not even the presence of Consuela could ruin. She had such a triumph in *As You Like It* that she even forgot to cut me. I watched the production in Clare Gardens and had to admit that as well as looking maddeningly pretty she was actually pretty good. As a rule undergraduates don't act as well as actors and she was no exception: but quite often they speak better, through being less inclined to make the lines their own instead of the author's. Shakespeare, especially, rewards good speakers who are indifferent actors, whereas bravura actors who speak badly can only do him an injury. Consuela spoke surprisingly well for someone so histrionic. She took a long time to come on. There was an ornamental pool in the middle of the Clare Gardens acting area. Consuela held her head so proudly high that I thought she might walk into the water, but the lines fell like pearls.

> Ros. But why did he swear he would come this morning, and comes not?

I could feel the eyes of a hundred of her friends on the back of my neck. No doubt I was being self-conscious. Why not? Everybody else was. It was the right place and the right time. Around the pool, among the flower-beds and between the hedges, the young, would-be, not-for-long actors deployed their hired costumes as they had been taught by some preposterously solemn young director who wanted to be Peter Hall or Trevor Nunn. In their element, the theatrical dons at the back of the natural auditorium threw decrepit fond looks at Orlando. They thought him charming. In that weather I thought them charming. They had their place in this enchanted forest. Absurdly I was sorry that I must soon lose mine.

Buddy threw a party in his back garden. Among the guests were what he described as one or two people from London. The champagne was endless. Under its influence I was able to predict that the young man with the huge mouth would never make it as a popular singer. Susannah York was there. She was so beautiful that I burst into tears. Luckily I was lying down by then, so nobody noticed. Karula dipped a napkin in the iced water of a champagne bucket and spread it over my face. I could see the sun through it. That should have been the most lavish May Week party. It was topped for opulence by Delmer Dynamo, who took over the whole back lawn of Pembroke and slew the fatted calf. Befitting his position as President and sole member of the Aubrey Attwater Society, Delmer had outfitted himself for the occasion in cream ducks, cricket boots, candy-striped blazer, straw boater and a monocle. The ensemble would have been suitable for receiving the Prince of Wales on board the deck of a steam yacht, somewhere around the turn of the century. Delmer could keep his monocle in place only by tilting his head so far back that he was shouting upwards, as if at a passing Zeppelin. Marenko, Strad and some other Americans wore rented white tuxedos with carnation boutonnières. As a barbershop quartet they stood in the rock garden and sang 'The Whiffenpoof Song'. The Master and all the college dons were there. The Dean, somehow managing to keep his champagne glass empty without removing the pipe from his mouth, gazed upon Delmer with transparent fondness. Obviously the college would be sad to see him go. Equally obviously the college did not feel quite the same in my case. Finding myself trapped with the Dean, I was further unsettled to detect in his eyes a look which suggested that he considered himself trapped with me. He sought refuge in the past. 'Brilliant boy, Oppenheimer. Jew, of course, but a real gentleman. Rutherford didn't want to let him into the Cavendish, you know. Said he was too weak on the experimental side. But Thomson believed in him. Young Oppenheimer was really, *really* interested in my minerals. You should have heard him talk about birefringence. Brilliant, brilliant boy. You don't get many like that now. There's Dynamo, of course, but on the whole they're a poor lot now.' The Dean was making it plain that my very existence was an insult to his dream. His whole speech, the longest I had ever heard him give, was an exhalation: one long sigh.

I sighed myself when Delmer shyly confessed that his college had offered him an extra year just so that he could read in preparation for his graduate course at Columbia. 'Hot shit, man,' he crowed. 'They coughed up.' His monocle gleamed in the sunlight. He had done quite a lot of work and deserved his good fortune. I would have found it easier to be warm with fellow-feeling if it were not for the chill wind which I could feel blowing even in the fragrant, stationary air. Where else in the world would I ever fit in except here, where I had never felt the least urge to fit in? And truly I had no social ambitions in Cambridge beyond the tattered pink velvet jacket of the Footlights presidency. The Footlights committee had decided that if I could stay on for a year the jacket was mine for the asking, but the only way for me to remain a member of the university would be to enrol as a PhD student. For that I didn't have the finance, and without at least a 2:1 result in the Tripos I wouldn't be accepted for registration even if I had the money. So it was all over. In the grad pad, Brian C.

Adams commiserated with me. 'You hit the books at least a year too late,' he said sympathetically. 'Still, all that Footlights nonsense should come in handy if you apply for the BBC. Let me buy you another glass of sherry. The Amontillado's really rather surprisingly fine.' Brian C. Adams was taking it for granted that he would get a first. So was everyone else taking it for granted that Brian C. Adams would get a first. There was a rumour that the College was considering taking him straight into Fellowship, so that he could sit up there eating venison where he belonged. Belonging must be a good feeling. Usually it was a feeling I got in or near Footlights, but the May Week revue, when I went to see it on the first night, only made me feel left out. Romaine was in it. She did the 'Land of Hope and Glory' routine with predictable results. There were people rolling about in the aisles like eels. Andy Mayer did his holy roller commercial. 'Write away *right* away . . .' I tried to be elated when my own material went well. It didn't always and it mocked my physical absence even when it did. As far as I was concerned – which on this evidence wasn't far – Footlights was unfinished business. In the Whim I sat anonymously, writing the kind of valedictory ode which treats personal disappointment as if it were the heat death of the universe.

Packed and all set to go, I turned up at Senate House to read the examination results with an air of fatalism which would have done credit to Sydney Carton, the only Dickens character I had managed to mention in the novel paper. (I had read the Classics Illustrated comic of *A Tale of Two Cities* when still a pupil of Kogarah Infants' School.) When I saw that I had got a 2:1 I thought it was a misprint. When Brian C. Adams saw that *he* had got a 2:1 he thought the same. Eventually his fellow members of the Gray Society calmed him down by pointing out the truth: that he was simply too good for the Tripos and should have been doing a PhD all along, like Romaine Rand. For the first few days after he came out of shock, however, nothing except Nembutal would keep Brian C. Adams from throwing himself from his casement window into the courtyard. Exactly balancing his despair was my euphoria. I couldn't see how I had done it, until Ron Maybey the Baby Don, breaking all the rules, told me. 'Never *seen* such a spread of marks,' he said, with evident disapproval. '*Very* good score on the essay paper. Nothing at *all* on the Swift paper. Should be impossible. Ought to get something for writing your name. Think that worked for you in the end. They decided that you'd gone mad that day. No excuse at all for the novel paper. One of the examiners wanted to have you sent down for it. You be staying on?' He was the only don, whether infant or adult, who had ever been sincerely interested in what I was writing, so I told him that I hoped to snare a research grant and be President of the Footlights simultaneously. 'Don't see why not,' he said. 'But I shouldn't actually *tell* them that when you apply. Stress the academic side. Sherry?'

Suddenly it was all at least possible. I applied for a research grant on the basis of a burning desire to evaluate Shelley's reading of the major Italian poets. The university wouldn't actually decide whether or not it was going to finance this scheme until September. Meanwhile I told the retiring Footlights committee, who were about to leave on tour with the revue, that my research grant was in the bag. They handed over the pink jacket, which I stored with the rest of my stuff in the Pembroke linen room. My conscience was reasonably clear, as far as I could tell without actually examining it. If I didn't get the grant, I could always give the jacket back. In the interim it seemed appropriate to go where Shelley had gone, at least up to the point where he drowned himself. Françoise was in Florence. To get there would be expensive. Luckily Robin was still in London. After hitting her for a small loan, I booked myself on the student charter flight which I have already described in my book *Flying Visits*. The reader will permit me the indulgence of making cross-references to my own work when I confess that the journey was never one I have been keen to repeat even in written form. I was exaggerating only when I said the plane swerved to avoid the Matterhorn. It didn't swerve except when it was taking off. Most of the students really *were* seventy-year-old Calabrian peasant women wearing black clothes and carrying string bags full of onions, and I really *did* have a nun sitting beside me who clutched my sweating palm as we came crabbing in to land. It was the way cheap flying was in those days. Today, the nightmare is in the crowded airport. When you get airborne you're relatively OK. Then, the flight was in the lap of the gods. One of David Hockney's early paintings had such a strong appeal for me that I kept a reproduction of it pinned to my wall wherever I moved. I liked its bright colours and cunningly innocent outlines, but most of all I liked its title: 'The Flight into Italy'. Knowing that there was a chance I might have something to come back to made the letting-go all the sweeter, of course. If you can manage it, safe danger is always the best kind.

10

Attack of the Killer Bee

ONCE AGAIN, FLORENCE was my principal destination, but this time I had to go to Venice first, a detour I begrudged. Françoise was there on a fortnight's study leave, to read manuscripts in the Marciana Library in the Piazza San Marco. Proust said that after he got to Venice his dreams acquired an address. For me the impact was, as you might imagine, nothing like so subtle. Never fond of the *Vedutisti* painters – Guardi, I thought, used too much lipstick and Canaletto was patently unreal – I was expecting a picture postcard. I knew all the jokes about Venice, of which the best was Robert Benchley's telegram home: STREETS FULL OF WATER PLEASE ADVISE. The exquisite, I had persuaded myself, held no appeal. Give me the chiselled jaw and marble biceps of Florence every time. Thus prepared to be indifferent, I was in an ideal condition to be floored. Before the *vaporetto* was half-way down the Grand Canal I was already concussed. Heat focused by a nacreous sky like the lining of a silver tureen dissolved the surface of the water into a storm of sparks, which were projected as wobbling bracelets of pure light on the otherwise maculate façades of crumbling plaster and rotting marble. The whole place was being eaten alive by liquid luminosity. It was a vision of eternity as soluble as a rusk, God's love made manifest as a wafer in the world's wet mouth. Françoise had rented a little room just behind the Piazza San Marco. I set up house on her floor. While she read in the library I made a library desk for myself on a café table at the city end of the Rialto, just to the left of where the steps of the approach to the bridge formed a natural rostrum from which the characters of *The Merchant of Venice* might step down into the main acting area. The tourist season being at its height, most of the people who came stepping down were Americans. 'Isn't it *weird*?' a woman in a baseball cap asked another woman in a baseball cap. 'When they say *Accademia* I can understand *them* but when I say ACADEMY *they* can't understand *me* at *all*.' The baseball caps were appropriate because both women were the shape of a baseball. Nothing could break the spell. There I sat reading, periodically lifting my head to confirm all over again that Canaletto had been so literal he might as well have used a Hasselblad. Trying out for the Regatta, the *Bucintoro* swept by with whomping oars, a ceremonial dream boat dripping gold. Every gondolier sang like Gigli. From Françoise I borrowed a volume of Leopardi's *Zibaldone*, the elaborate notebooks in which the great, crippled poet kept track of his vast learning. Religiously looking up every unknown word in a dictionary, I eventually broke through the almost tangible barrier that separates being only just able to read from being able to read with reasonable ease. I started to keep a notebook myself. Dignified with the name of Journal, it would run to a dozen volumes in the next nine years. 'Volumes' is a grand word for tatty exercise books. They must be somewhere amongst my junk. One day I must look into them and see what I thought important. Puerilities, I imagine. But the *soi-disant* journal doubled as a commonplace book, and to that extent it was useful. The habit of copying out was a good one to acquire. Though the main idea was to build up fluency in reading a foreign language, the beneficial side-effect was to fix a lot of good stuff in my head, if only at the level of the half-forgotten. The waiters soon learned to approach me only when I signalled. For a while I thought they were smiling tolerantly because as sons of the Most Serene City they were pleased to see a visitor inspired by intellectual effort. Later I learned that they were being even more tolerant than that. Like all the personnel of the service industries in Venice, they lived in the industrial satellite towns, commuted to work, and would have preferred to bring me a fresh glass of iced coffee every thirty seconds. They needed the tips.

When Françoise got out of the library we would have lunch in a cheap restaurant called the Trattoria al Vagon. You could get there by walking from either St Mark's or the Rialto. The path was a maze in either case, crossing little bridges from island to island, and never turning a perfectly square corner within the island itself. We always had to allow half an hour for getting lost. Years later I tried to find the Al Vagon and couldn't. Perhaps it was never there. It was so good and cheap that it might have been a dream. The pasta was always *al dente*, an expression which could be pressed into service as the name of a ferocious gangster. Lui Medesimo ('he himself') was Al Dente's conceited sidekick. Françoise generously laughed at these heavy jokes while I drank her share of the claret to top up mine. Even for her, who preferred to stay sober, there was always the sense that we were living out a carnival scene by Longhi – another painter whom I had previously despised, and of whom I was now starting to see the point.

Yet again, though, it was the Renaissance that carried the heavy charge. Hungry as always for the main event, I was disinclined to be sidetracked by the quirky, the decorative or the merely pretty. Two minutes' walk from the Al Vagon, Verrocchio's equestrian statue of Bartolomeo Colleoni rode sternly through the Piazza San Giovanni e Paolo. There were pigeons on his helmet and a barge full of empty coke bottles in the canal at his feet, but his *grandezza* was only increased. To every Australian schoolboy of my generation, Bartolomeo Colleoni was the Italian cruiser sunk by H.M.A.S. *Sydney*. The *Sydney*'s bows were subsequently built into the stone harbour wall near Kirribilli pier under the north end of the Harbour Bridge. But in Venice I could see the real Bartolomeo, the *condottiere* four centuries into his immortal ride, his image more immediate than the man himself, or any man alive, even me. The contained energy of that bronze horseman kept me occupied for what seemed like hours. Probably it was less than that, but certainly I stared longer than Byron did, who in one of his plays – either *Marino Faliero* or *The Two Foscari*, I forget which – let slip the opinion that the grim rider was made of marble. It is very doubtful if Byron ever went out of doors in Venice. Recovering in his room between visits from insatiable noblewomen, he would totter asymmetrically to the window, check that the Grand Canal was still there, and turn back wearily to the rumpled couch. Poor bastard.

Françoise believed in her mission to civilise me. When the white heat of the early afternoon sky had eased to a tolerable azure, we would tour the outlying churches by *vaporetto*, on the hunt for Bellini. Most of his capital works were in the Accademia or else in churches close to the centre, but there were others further out, and anyway even his minor canvases were major. Until then, I had been under the impression that all Bellini had ever painted was Madonnas in blue anoraks nursing babies the size of high school children in front of a green shantung antimacassar, with distant landscape an optional extra. Now I saw the range of his humanity, his old men and infantile angels all shaped from pure colour, the painterly monumentality organically complete. In my journal I solemnly noted every painting, enrolling Bellini on my growing list of indispensible seminal figures. His namesake the composer was already on the list. So was Liszt. The honour roll was meant to be growing shorter, but no matter how ruthlessly I pared it down, there was always another genius around the corner demanding to be let in. My appreciation of Tintoretto was not much enhanced by being in his home city, which because of its wet walls has never been kind to the fresco, tempting the business-minded painter towards too-big canvases it took a football team of assistants to help him fill. Most of Tintoretto's best paintings were done on a smaller scale and eventually exported: I had already learned to admire him elsewhere. Titian's last manner, however, was well represented in the Venetian churches. 'Like Shakespeare's sonnets and Beethoven's late quartets,' I remember telling my journal, 'Titian's valedictory paintings have a divine carelessness.' Veronese, I decided, was in Paris and London: to all intents and purposes he had left town. Lacking the means to get out into the surrounding Veneto, we saw little of Tiepolo. I decided to like him anyway: Giambattista, that is, not Giandomenico. I was very strict in my judgments. Françoise, who had heard my unshakeable convictions revised before, patiently upheld the reasonable viewpoint – a propensity which, modest to a fault, she considered her limitation. She also, I need hardly add, paid for the museum tickets, the *vaporetto* rides, most of the meals, and the bus trip to Padua.

Padua was dominated by Donatello's equestrian statue of Gattamelata, a work which I instantly declared inferior to Verrocchio's Bartolomeo Colleoni. This judgment I have since found no good cause to revise, although nowadays I would be less likely to share it with a trattoria full of German tourists. Giotto I had, until then, respected only because Dante thought well of him. Though the big Madonna in the Uffizi was obviously the start of something, I had been able to get interested in the trecento only as a prelude to the quattrocento, which, in its turn – I was suffering from a developmental view of the arts – was clearly only the muted overture to the cinquecento. Françoise had argued wearily against this dogma until it became plain to her that mere reason was powerless. Only evidence would convince me. This was the evidence. In the Arena chapel I stood stunned as the drama unfolded all around me. Drama was exactly what it was, of course: what Giotto had rediscovered, after its thousand years without a voice, was the intensity between human beings. Oscar Wilde had once stood in the same chapel. He, too, had been impressed. You could tell how overwhelmed he was. He was the only English-speaking person to have visited the chapel in the last two hundred years who had not signed his name on the wall. All around the circumference of the chapel, the frescoes were thoroughly mutilated up to the height of an upstretched hand. These graffiti depressed me much more than the missing Mantegnas. Falling out of an erratically flown B-25, practically the only bomb to have hit the historic centre of Padua had gone straight through the roof of the Ovetari Chapel and atomised Mantegna's biggest-ever fresco cycle. But that was just a misfortune of war, a bad spin of the wheel. Vandalism was an endemic human failing. Italy had too many paintings to look after and too little public money with which to hire people to look after them. I didn't mind so much when pictures got stolen: usually they were ransomed back the following week, with tax advantages to both sides.

When paintings got razored I became agitated. The German and Dutch galleries had installed alarm systems whereby no masterpiece could be approached without the offender being instantly gagged, bound and arrested. In the Italian galleries even the guides regularly fingered the paint surface. You would see some idiot bodging his finger into a Botticelli. A reformed vandal with a bad conscience, I began to get very touchy about seeing paintings touched, or even breathed on.

Arriving in Florence just in time for the kind of weather that encouraged the inhabitants to leave, we took a room at the Antica Cervia. The Santa Croce *quartiere* behind the Palazzo Vecchio was the old stamping ground of the *popolo minuto*, in the sense that this was where the little people had been stamped into the ground by a commune which, however egalitarian, had never quite succeeded in distributing its power down as far as the penniless. Still radical enough at that stage to be rather thrilled by my discovery of Gramsci's prison letters, I fancied myself as fitting right in when we dined at the Trattoria Anita with the prostitutes and pimps. In Italy it was a point of style to be a bit red. *Sinistra* was such a thrilling way of saying left wing. *Lotta continua!* The struggle continues! Though theoretically clean shaven at the time, I grew a two-day stubble and tried to look dangerous as I leaned forward over the *spaghetti al sugo*, my intense eye-contact with Françoise perhaps having been unduly influenced by the steely look Giotto had given St Francis. I made it clear to her that the clientele of the trattoria were essentially *my* people: vagabonds, snappers-up of unconsidered trifles, the wretched of the earth. In point of fact most of them scarcely even rated as petty crooks. The boys with the gold chains around their necks who scratched their crotches all the time thought they had done a hard day's work when they succeeded in selling each other a carton of two hundred contraband Marlboros. Otherwise they spent a good deal of time wistfully annoying foreign girls in the hope of forming a profitable liaison, but their hearts and minds weren't in it. The true *pappagalli* would put energy and invention into being pests. This bunch preferred not to work up a sweat. On principle, in the first few days, they eyed Françoise suggestively, challenging her to restrain what they obviously hoped might be an irresistible impulse to cast reason and her clothes aside. After having absorbed the accumulated evidence that she was unlikely to jump into their laps, they relaxed again into their customary torpor. The energy of those brave young men was all for show and their women didn't even bother to show it. To classify them as hookers paid them a compliment. It was a courtesy title. They were too lazy to lean against a wall successfully. Most of the time, when they weren't eating, they sat in the back of a bar complaining in concert about the ladders in their fishnet stockings. A potential customer needed radar to find them.

The only real proletarians present were Anita and her family, who worked their guts out from daylight to midnight, on a profit margin so slim that if a tomato went rotten it was a disaster. Anita could think of nothing more exciting in life than the possibility – a very slim one, given the inefficiency of Italy's educational system – that her clever young daughter might go to university and learn to speak well like Françoise. The daughter, universally called *La Tempesta*, was almost old enough to wait on table. Neither Anita nor her equally hardworking husband wanted the apple of their eye to spend her whole life doing what they had done and their two sons were already doing. These were the kind of proletarians whose only dream was to become part of the bourgeoisie. Gramsci started sounding less convincing. I was still reading him, but not in the restaurant.

Now that I no longer had to, I read all day. Françoise was studying manuscripts in the Laurenziana, in a magnificent reading room at the head of a staircase by Michelangelo. Scorning the gloom of the libraries, I made my base at a bar in the Piazza della Signoria, just in front of a house designed by Raphael. Alas, he had designed it without an awning. As the daily heat increased from merely intense to overwhelming, I changed base to a better-shaded bar near the Badia, whose graceful tower was my personal landmark. The heat was still too much so I transferred to the Biblioteca Nazionale, having decided that the gloom of libraries might be all right after all. In fact there was plenty of light inside, along with the tolerably cool air. With the Arno only fifty feet away, I could sit at a desk for hours on end, reading my way through the collected works of Benedetto Croce, who wrote so much that he made Ruskin look as parsimonious as E. M. Forster. This autobiography is not meant to be a precise intellectual history, which I doubt if anyone can write about himself without fudging the facts. Ideas, even if they come from books, are modified by experience in ways too indirect to be assessed at the time or recalled accurately afterwards. I can state confidently, however, that those weeks in the library in Florence were crucial to my mental development, to the extent that such a thing has ever taken place at all. Croce, in particular, played a vital role in making me feel better about being mentally *un*developed. Formally laid out in his capital theoretical volumes on aesthetics and poetry, and richly applied in countless ancillary volumes of criticism and cultural history, his central concept of the naïve artistic impulse had a strong appeal, perhaps because I was, as I still am, unusually naïve myself. For Croce, the individual creative talent was irreducible. A peasant who could crack a good joke might have it, whereas an educated man who gave his life to poetry might not. The high arts and the low arts were united to the extent that they were inspired. Within the unity conferred by inspiration, all categories were illusory. This was good news for a reader whose devotion to the high arts was continually being sabotaged by the attraction of the low ones. But Croce offered no easy consolation. His position was not an indulgence. It was the outcome of a lifelong, untiringly rigorous process of examining his own omnivorous enthusiasm with a cool detachment. The vehicle of his thought was the proof of his grandeur: his prose, so transparent as to be beyond style, flowed like a river without ever being carried away by itself – or so it seemed. His effect on me, as I progressed from reading with a dictionary to context-reading to reading with ease, was like learning to swim. As I read his pages by the hundred and then the thousand, I tried to remind myself that any great stylist sounds like an oracle until a big enough historic fact contradicts him. After all, I had been equally impressed by George Bernard Shaw until I realised just how wrong he had been about Hitler and Stalin. But Croce's anti-totalitarian credentials were impeccable. Also he was writing in a foreign language. Undoubtedly there was a self-congratulatory element in my thrilled response. Part of the thrill lay in being able to read at all. Careful not to make Leopardi's mistake – he read so much that when he tried to straighten up one day he found he couldn't – I would get up from the desk once an hour, go outside, sit on the river wall and look downstream towards the Ponte Vecchio. Drained by the heat trapped in its etched upper valley, the river was little more than a collection of shallow pools. In the late afternoon sun they lit up white. Fishermen standing in them were silhouettes expounding theorems by Pythagoras. It occurred to me, not as forcefully as it might have, that Florence was my real university, from which Cambridge was the vacation. I was out of phase with my own life. Never would I be able to relax, except when effort was called for, whereupon I would go to sleep. Did this mean that on the day I died I would wake up? *Speriamo*. Here's hoping.

Françoise was there to temper my fanaticism. In theory, a born teacher likes nothing better than a keen student, but there are limits. When we toured the country villas of the Medici, a bronze nymph or satyr disporting on the edge of a fountain would inspire me to give a lecture on the virtues of Giambologna until I found out that it was by Pierino da Vinci. Unabashed, I would give another lecture on Pierino's limitations. Françoise was a very good photographer. That year she posed me against all the fountains of the city and environs, securing a set of pictures remarkable for their composition and for the fact that my mouth was closed. My spoken Italian was not yet good enough for me to join in easily when she was with her friends, so she had to suffer the full spate of my eloquence in English when we were alone. We weren't alone all that often. Her student contemporaries were as gregarious and welcoming as ever, with an extra sense of group identity engendered by the worsening conditions in the universities. Everyone you knew was a red that year. Even Gabriella went to the Communist Party open air festival in the gardens at the Cascine. The dazzling Adriana had changed her thesis topic from Cesare Pavese to Rosa Luxemburg. Older and wiser heads – they had begun to call themselves that more stridently, now that the young were calling them reactionaries – insisted that the growing hubbub was just another case of *fantapolitica*: fantasy politics. To a certain extent that was true, but underneath the posturing there were real grievances. The universities were corrupt. Most of the faculty were behaving like absentee landlords. Even the best students could see no career prospects. *La Sinistra* had become a vocation in itself. It had its own language, its own literature, its own cinema. At its best, the Italian left-wing cinema was capable of an analytical *tour de force* like *The Battle of Algiers*, which I saw three times in a row, resolved to emulate its hard-bitten detachment. But Gillo Pontecorvo was a sophisticate who could read history as a tragedy. The young revolutionaries could read it only as a comic book. Most of them believed that the United States had caused the Second World War. All of them believed that the United States had sabotaged the Italian popular revolution after the war was over. The alleged prosperity of modern Italy was a sham. The elected government was Fascism in thin disguise. It was all the fault of the Americans. The question was simple. Why was the government powerless? The answer was simpler. Because capitalism was powerful. Students gathered around the café tables to examine the implications of this obvious fact. Young men dressed in the Italian bourgeois version of the English aristocratic manner discussed how the wealth of their fathers might be redistributed. Taking drinks in the gardens of her villa under an evening sky strangely rimmed with green radiance behind a picket fence of silhouetted cypresses, Gabriella and her coruscating friends were a cut above all this but they had the same frustrations and the same passions. Adriana being politically passionate was a sight to behold. She was an aria without an orchestra. *Ma donnEEna, figOOrati!* she would wail, the ash from her cigarette powdering the evening air. Watching, I moved my lips silently to match hers, the rhythm of her lilting voice. How could it be translated? But little *lady*. Figure it *out*. The second, stressed syllable of *figurati* was hooted, as in the word 'hoot'. What mad music! I called for madder music, and for stronger wine. Both were immediately forthcoming, especially the wine. Thoroughly committed by now to the study of my second language, I was already realising the benefit I would reap even if I got nowhere: my first language would stand revealed for what it was, a mechanism so complex that it lived. The revelation was intoxicating. I had to sit down suddenly, right there on the parched grass. The Italians, products of a culture in which drunkenness was almost unknown, politely pretended that they thought I might be ill.

During a brief pause in the political discussion we would all go to the movies at the Summer Firefly. A short walk along the dry bed of the Arno near the city end of the Bridge to the Graces, the Summer Firefly charged you almost nothing to get in but broke even by screening old movies at very low standards of projection. At ten o'clock on an August night the heat was killing, but it beat being inside. Indeed the Summer Firefly beat anything. It was the best cinema I was ever in. At first glance an al fresco flea-pit, in its capacity to generate a careless rapture it exceeded even the Rockdale Odeon, the Hampstead Everyman, or that little place in the Rue St Severin where they used to screen old Humphrey Bogart movies in *version original*, back to back, for ever. One of my all-time favourite Westerns, *3.10 to Yuma*, was the Summer Firefly's staple item. Under the title *Quel treno per Yuma* it cropped up every second week, running about fifteen minutes less than its proper length because the print was full of splices. Glenn Ford and Felicia Farr would suddenly switch positions on screen like electrons changing levels. The fact that I already knew all the dialogue by heart in English, however, made the story easier to follow in Italian. We all sat there happily shouting advice to Van Heflin while the other stars, the astronomical ones, sharpened overhead in the deepening purple. At the climactic point where Glenn Ford leans out of the hotel window so that Richard Jaeckel can see him and ride off to tell the rest of the gang, the image on the screen, which had already been flickering weirdly, settled down to show the bottom half of one frame and the top half of another. Glenn Ford's chin and collar were on top of his hat. Electing myself spokesman, I went back to advise the projectionist, who was facing away from the screen while entertaining three friends. They all had glasses of wine in their hands and seemed quite happy to be told that a disaster was taking place. '*Disastro nella proiezione!*' I assured them. '*Glenn Ford si è convertito in una pittura cubista!*' Grammatically questionable, but it worked the trick.

The Summer Firefly's seats were rusty metal folding contraptions that could easily capsize in the gravel if you laughed too hard. The walls of the roofless auditorium were composed of plaited brushwood, intermittently penetrated by children, whose faces appeared like cherubic visitations, abruptly withdrawn when swept by the beam of the usherette's weak torch. Half drunk but fully happy, in the Summer Firefly I hung suspended within reach of the perfect life. It was an illusion, of course: it always is. It can only happen when you have no responsibilities, which is itself an illusion.

On the coast at Viareggio and Forte dei Marmi we swam until August became a slightly more bearable September. Considering the waves to be beneath the contempt of an Australian surfing hero, I sat on the unsatisfactory sand reading the poetry of Eugenio Montale. It was a good location in which to become acquainted with *Ossi di Seppia* – cuttlefish bones. Montale's poetry was difficult for the right reasons. It was reticent, unrhetorical, compressed, permanent. Memorising it line by line, I was put in my place by the increasing weight of what I had absorbed. '*To vanish*,' I mistranslated, '*Is thus the adventure of the adventures.*' During this same educational interlude a Sarah Lawrence graduate student called Lisa joined us, as if to remind our bold young radicals of just how powerful a force American cultural imperialism actually was. She looked like Angie Dickinson, spoke Italian almost as well as Françoise, and was writing a thesis on Castiglione. She drove an Alfa Romeo Giulietta Spider hired with the first example any of us had ever seen of an American Express card. When she appeared on the beach in a black bikini, the boys put off the revolution until the next day. Watching Lisa and Françoise standing waist deep in the flat Tyrrhenian was one of my lasting visions of that impeccable summer. Everything went right. Even the life-transforming message was carried in on cue. Back in Florence at the Antica Cervia, there was a knock on the open door. The proprietress stood there in the compact heat of the gloomy corridor. She was illuminated like a figure of destiny by one of those twelve-watt bulbs of which every Italian landlady has an endless supply, so as to be able to replace them when they burn out once every hundred years. She held a letter forwarded by my college. It informed me that I had been registered for a PhD and that a study grant would consequently be forthcoming.

This news, it was agreed, was too good to deal with on my own. The first instalment of the grant was too far off to borrow on the strength of it. I was hugely in debt to Françoise, whose own finances would have been strained enough without me. Dalziel had offered me three weeks' work on *Expresso Drongo*, which he assured me was making good progress. I would have to go back to London. The Italians would not let me go without a party. More precisely, it would be a dinner: a kind of Last Supper. My perpetual beatific smile must have convinced them all that I was touched by grace. The dinner would be at a special restaurant serving nothing but game. The game was one of the secondary results of the Italian hunting season, whose principal product, as usual, had been an impressive pile of wounded hunters and extinct passers-by. When the bell rang to start the Italian hunting season, devotees of *la caccia* drove at full speed into the woods and shot everything that moved. Since the animals were sensibly lying low, most of the victims were people. Advancing at random through the woods, the hunters – whose minds, like their expensive guns, were on a hair trigger – fired when they thought they saw something. Often they had seen each other. They also killed civilians in nearby villages. The occasional wild animal got hit, but only by a fluke. One man blasted a rabbit that was already hanging from another man's belt. So much frantic vehicular traffic on the woodland roads, however, ensured that a considerable amount of wildlife was run over. The leading all-game restaurant in Florence, I was assured, would be plentifully supplied with pheasants, wild geese, stags, bucks, oryx, ibex and its *pièce de résistance*, wild boar. I was promised the most tearful send-off since Dante went into exile.

With Françoise safely despatched to the library, I spent my last afternoon in Florence luxuriating in sorrow on a stone bench just in front of Santa Maria Novella. I had been inside to commune with one of my heroes, Paolo Uccello, whose frescoes in the Green Cloister had recently been uncovered after about a decade *in restauro*. For once in my life, I told myself, I could take credit for experiencing an emotion appropriate to the circumstances. I knew that I would come back to the city, but that I would never be so happy here again as I had been in this short time. Open in my lap was the *Inferno*, at the great passage where Farinata talks about his banishment. His dignity, I persuaded myself, was mine. I felt that I, too, was a knight in a suit of armour.

Would that it had been true, because at that moment a bee stung me. The bee must have been lurking between my bare forearm – the sleeves of my shirt were rolled up – and my waist. When I shifted my arm slightly, the bee was trapped, and reacted the way bees do. I felt as if a length of stiff copper wire had been shoved into my arm and momentarily fed with the total electric power of an underground railway system. The stab of pain was so disproportionate that I didn't complain until it was over, so instead of emitting an abstract scream I cried 'Jesus Christ!' at a volume that stopped the traffic. It turned out that almost nobody in the square was Italian. A whole busload of English Carmelite nuns stared at me as if I were a blasphemer. They had a point. It was a long way to come to hear the Lord's name taken in vain at ear-splitting volume on the front steps of His own house. A representative of the British Council crossed the square to wonder if I might consider moderating my tone. Only the Americans noticed nothing untoward. They probably thought my outcry had been part of some religious ceremony. The pain was already gone, leaving nothing more than an American man in a baseball cap saying to another man in a baseball cap: 'You mean we gotta spend another three hours in *this* place?' I forgave them, having surmised – correctly, as it turned out – that America was merely first in achieving a level of average income so high that even the mentally underprivileged were able to travel, and that shortly all the other industrialised countries would start exporting idiots too. My senses had never been so sharp. I was clairvoyant. When I met Françoise for drinks at the café near the Badia, I was giggling. When we all arrived at the game restaurant I was already hilarious. The whole bunch was there. The joint was jammed but we had a long table to ourselves. Wild boar with wheel-marks across their backs were hanging from the rafters. I thought it was too funny for words. For the first hour I was the life and soul of the party, in my opinion. My conjectures as to which bits of the wild boar were concealed by the thick gravy were widely received as brilliantly original after Françoise had translated them. Then I got sick. Bee venom and wild boar had done something to each other that a gallon of chianti couldn't fix. In the toilet I was sad to discover that there was no throne I could kneel beside so as to be sick into it. Instead, there were those glorified holes in the ground. Those porcelain efforts that look like plaster casts of the footprints of square elephants. Flush with the ground and they flush all over your feet. Very, very hard to be sick into accurately. Very HAH! That wasn't so bad. Not accurate, though. Not ACK! ACK! I was there a long time. Beppe and Sergio, two of my closest friends in my whole life, arrived to find out how I was. I was OK, but where were the others? They were all my closest friends. Get them all in here. Bring the girls in too. Just a second. YAARGH!

The two guys held me while I tried to regurgitate the wild boar, from which not all the hair, it now became apparent, had been removed. If this kept up, I was going to be sick. The third time that I was helped back to the table, there were suggestions that I should be taken to hospital, but I refused to go unless it was guaranteed that there would be a toilet there. I had seen Italian ambulance crews in action. Manned by volunteers in white Franciscan cowls, the ambulance would scream to a halt at the scene of an accident and immediately the situation would be transformed. Victims lying there with broken backs would be thrown into the ambulance. People bleeding to death from wounds that needed only a tourniquet would be given artificial respiration instead. The volunteers were businessmen with a commendable urge to perform some community service, but they would have done better to sweep leaves. Without the protection of anonymity, they would have stood a good chance of being indicted for murder, if ever the eight differently uniformed Italian police forces could have got out of each other's road long enough to prevent the next crime instead of just arriving abruptly on powerful motorcycles to be photographed beside the results of the last one. No, I didn't want any of that. Just leave me sitting here like a grinning corpse and I'll be fine. Talk among yourselves while I look as if I'm getting ready to vomit a live pig into your lap.

Having thoroughly spoiled my own party, I succumbed to a case of raving, perambulating semi-malaria from which I did not emerge until late next night, when the bus from Luton airport arrived at Victoria. Only then, when all the other passengers were waking up, did I at last fall into a fitful sleep.

II

Full Velvet Jacket

IT SHOULD HAVE been an heroic return. After a mentally improving sojourn beyond the Alps, I was coming back to Cambridge in triumph, at the university's invitation and expense. The reality was less exalted. With my trusty cardboard suitcase full of dirty washing I scaled the outer wall of Robin's ground-floor flatlet in Pimlico. It was after midnight. Safely hidden in the tiny area, I tapped at her door-length window very quietly, so as not to wake the neighbours. I tapped for an hour without waking her either. Finally the window swung open and I was greeted by the glistening point of a carving knife. It was Robin's flat-mate, an English drama student called Alison. Though her terror was not feigned, it was, I thought, excessive. Robin, I was informed, was staying the night at her boyfriend's place in Notting Hill. What boyfriend? Peeved, I set up camp on the floor of the kitchenette. There was plenty of room if I kept my legs folded. When that became impossible, I opened the cupboard under the sink and put my feet in there. Not kicking over the cans of Ajax was harder when I slept. I had to stay awake and concentrate. For three weeks it wouldn't be so bad.

Turning up for work on the set of Keith Visconti's film, I found that there had indeed been developments. Dave Dalziel assured me that the key scene where the girl must decide whether or not she wants milk in her coffee was now in the can. Unfortunately the young actor playing the waiter had temporarily ceased to be available. A childhood friend of Keith's, he was being questioned by the police in relation to an incident at New Cross in which the contents of a van full of the new Japanese portable TV sets had gone missing. He was being questioned, that is, during the previous several months of filming. Now that he had finished being questioned, he had vanished. Apparently some of his friends were looking for him. Not childhood friends like Keith. Other friends. Nelia knew all about it, but she wasn't saying much — not, I think, out of secrecy, but because she couldn't raise the energy. She had started reading a magazine and the effort was wearing her down. It was called *Woman's Realm*. She could just about get an issue finished before the next one came out. Besides, Keith was making her work all the time.

With Dalziel's constant advice, Keith had been using Nelia to get all the close-up reaction shots he could while the search went on for either the original waiter or someone who looked like him. By now it had become apparent that the waiter's scenes would have to be shot again with a different actor. Keith had offered to produce another of his lifelong friends but Dalziel had vetoed this. A proper actor had been hired: one of the Australian expatriates who had been left swallowing engine oil in the burning water after *The Charge of the Light Fandango* had pointed its propellers at the sky and gone roaring down to the bottom. Keith objected that the actor did not look English. Dalziel overruled him. 'I don't think this guy looks especially Australian, do you?' Dalziel asked me this in tones that compelled agreement. The actor, on top of the body of the Man from Snowy River, had the face of Lew Hoad, but I concurred in the judgment that his national origin was impossible to guess. The actor was unimpressed by what I had done for him. All he could remember was *The Charge of the Light Fandango*. Understandably there was a certain *froideur* when he found that my daily presence was part of this deal too. So I did my best to stay out of the way. After doing my bit to shift lights and carry silver boxes I would go outside and sit waiting at the kayf across the road. The studio was in a back street behind Olympia, so it was not a very salubrious kayf. I was writing poems about Florence. They were full of Medici pomp and Machiavellian circumstance, of tasselled banners and blazing trumpets, the sweet waistlines of Paolo Uccello handmaidens and the crackling flames of Savonarola's pyre. All this I wrote about while sitting under a chalked menu announcing that spam fritters with two veg could be followed by spotted dick with custard. Outside the dirty window, rain that for some reason would only make it dirtier fell thinly but persistently, like a small annoyance. The yawning discrepancy between the place I was writing about and the place I was writing about it in, however, seemed to help. I told myself that it was always best to be physically elsewhere from one's spiritual concern: thus recollection was left free to focus. How, for example, would I have come to value the stylish, precisely calibrated density of a tiny Italian *espresso basso* if it were not for the contrast provided by this giant mug of English tea? Tea leaves floated limply on its vast surface. Under the surface there were more tea leaves. A mug of tea of that size and consistency took a minimum of ten minutes to drink, even when cold. If I sipped carefully, opening my pursed lips to the width of a vein, I swallowed only about half a pound of tea leaves, leaving a mulch three inches deep in the bottom of the mug. Yes, this was the real England that Richard Hoggart had talked about in *The Uses of Literacy*. When Raymond Williams complained in *Culture and Society* of the healthy working class traditions that were being lost, this was what he meant.

Dalziel didn't really have enough for me to do during the week. On the weekends it was a different story. His sister was in town. Beryl Dalziel was a sculptress. Like her brother's, her career lay in the future. Unlike him, she did not travel well. Dave Dalziel was famously capable of getting organised. He had a filing system for his correspondence. Some of the clothes he bought off market stalls would have looked incongruous on any man less personable, and the Jaguar he had so proudly bought for a song showed increasing signs of having been overhauled at some stage of its career by someone who might have been a childhood friend of Keith Visconti, but on the whole Dave Dalziel was a scrupulous realist. He did not cause trouble to others. He could get himself from country to country with all his belongings, get the telephone connected, hire a plumber. Beryl Dalziel could do none of these things. She needed help.

Above all, she needed help moving. During the three weeks I was involved with her peregrinations, she changed flats four times, twice on the one weekend. These moves would have been complicated enough if her innumerable suitcases and steamer trunks had been full of air. She claimed to have put her sample sculptures in storage on arrival, but I was convinced they were in her luggage. They were the heaviest bags I have ever carried. In fact there was no question of carrying most of them, even with Dalziel on one end and me on the other. They had to be dragged. Moving her out of the upstairs flat in Maida Vale which we had moved her into on the previous weekend, Dalziel and I began by taking each end of one of the smaller suitcases. I remembered that a week before I had thought it contained nothing except machine tools. This time it must have been packed with uranium. Luckily it was I who was holding the bottom end, or it might have been Dalziel who bore the brunt, with incalculable consequences for the future of the Australian film industry. The thing accelerated down the thinly carpeted stairs. Ignoring Dalziel's exhortations to stop it with my body, I stepped smartly aside while the case boomed past and slammed into the window seat on the landing, staving in its plywood-panelled front. We rearranged the cushions so that the damage hardly showed. The next case we took a step at a time, positioning it vertically and edging it out until it dropped on to the next step down with a thump that shook the house. The landlady was out. Landladies were always out when Beryl took off. She timed it that way. How she managed it when there weren't at least two grown men around was another question, or yet another question. It was already another question how the cases we were taking down had grown even heavier since we took them up. It took an hour and a half to move all twelve cases. We saved the biggest of Beryl's bulk carriers until last. A metal steamer trunk bound about with clasps and hasps, it looked as if it was waiting for a cargo ship. On each side, B. DALZIEL was painted in yellow letters two feet high. I remembered this object vividly from former journeys, but there had been a change. Previously merely backbreaking, it was now immovable. Dalziel and I both got behind it and shoved with all our strength. The trunk reacted like the Albert Memorial. We tried again, this time applying the pressure more gradually, on the theory that a steady build-up would break the air seal holding the bottom of the trunk to the threadbare carpet. We had our eyes closed with the strain, so it wasn't until we had given up that we noticed Beryl had lain down on the bed with her thumb in her mouth.

From long experience, Dalziel recognised this behaviour as a sign of guilt. He demanded that the trunk be unpacked and the contents manhandled separately. His sister sulked. The clock ticked. Not for the first time, I wondered how different my personality – and therefore, presumably, my life – might have been had I grown up with siblings to contend with. Dalziel still had flashes of the old insanity but essentially he was a reasonable man. His sister was essentially unreasonable. Was he like that because of her? Was she like that because of him? It was getting dark. At last she gave in. She unlocked the trunk. It was full of house bricks. 'For my kiln,' she explained. 'Want to do porcelain.' All the other bags proved to have their share of bricks too. Eventually we got everything into the hired Dormobile and set off for Beryl's next address. On the way, at Dalziel's insistence, the bricks were dumped into a builder's skip.

After three weekends of intense body building, my cardboard suitcase was like a feather draped over my crooked index finger when I turned up in Cambridge to claim my inheritance. The place was infested with a new intake of undergraduates, all self-consciously parading in their new gowns, which, had they but known it, were due to be replaced in short order by old gowns whose more experienced owners had seen an opportunity to update their kit. Cambridge was a bit like being in the army: you had to know the lurks. By now I was a lurk man, like Sergeant Bilko. This was nothing to be proud of, so I tried not to be proud of it. As a graduate student I was less of an anomaly than I had been as an undergraduate, but I was still a pretty weatherbeaten customer to have hanging around an institution dedicated to forming the characters of young people and furnishing their minds with knowledge. All I can say now is how I felt at the time: that somehow the fact that I was a few years older than my fellow clerks was cancelled out by my feeling a few years younger than they would have felt had they been a few years older. One day I would catch up with myself and then everything would come out even. Meanwhile, I had been granted the immense privilege of being allowed to live in unapproved lodgings. To put it another way, the college didn't want me making life miserable for any of its registered landladies. With the first instalment of my study grant safely in the bank, I paid back the college what I owed in loans. This left nothing like enough to pay back Footlights what I owed in bar bills, but since I was now President of the Footlights I calculated that I could sway the committee to excuse me my debts until such time as I could pay them back with inflated currency. Retrieving the pink jacket and the rest of my junk from the Pembroke linen room, I staggered along King's Parade, turned right into Benet Street, and moved into the Friar's House, just across from the Eagle.

The Friar's House looked like the best address in Cambridge. It was a half-timbered edifice which had no doubt been built by the eponymous friars. You could tell it went back a long way by all the angles it leaned at. My room was on the first floor. I hadn't been in it thirty seconds before I found out why the rent was so cheap. In those days the ground floor of the Friar's House was occupied by the most popular Pakistani restaurant in Cambridge. I like the smell of curry — rather better than I like the taste of it, in fact — but the fabric of the Friar's House, being so old, was porous. Without going downstairs, I could recite the menu. Another shock was the hitherto unannounced presence of Romaine Rand, who had already taken another room on the same floor as mine. Indeed it was the room *next* to mine. It was the big front room facing on to the street. In something less than a week, Romaine, who in another time and place might have run the sort of salon that Goethe and the boys would have swarmed around like blowflies, had already transformed her room into a dream from the Arabian nights. Drawing on her incongruous but irrepressible skills as a housewife, she had tatted lengths of batik, draped bolts of brocade, swathed silk, swagged satin, ruched, ruffed, hemmed and hawed. There were oriental carpets and occidental screens, ornamental plants and incidental music. The effect was stunning. Aristotle Onassis had married Jackie Kennedy in vain hopes of getting his yacht to look like that. Romaine, however, once she had got her life of luxury up and running, did not luxuriate. She had a typewriter the size of a printing press. Instantly she was at it, ten hours a day. Through the lath-and-plaster wall I could hear her attacking the typewriter as if she had a contract, with penalty clauses, for testing it to destruction. As well as finalising her thesis, apparently, she was working on a book. She definitely would not be available for Footlights, so I could forget it. 'Only a few of them are funny,' she announced, 'and *none* of them can fuck.' I slunk back to my bare room. There was, or were, the flat metal frame of a single bed, a stained mattress, the curried floorboards, a bulb without a shade, and my suitcase. I resolved that I, too, would transmogrify my environment. Picking out a section of the wall where a shelf might go, I tapped it with a testing forefinger. About a square foot of plaster fell off and brained a cockroach.

Making large plans to decorate my eyrie on a scale that would put Romaine to shame, I set off next morning for the Do It Yourself Hire and Supply shop in Hills Road. Somehow I never found it. At the cinema, the DIY Hire and Supply advertisement had always been the one I had most trouble identifying with. It featured an old man with a Ringo Starr haircut who smiled at you while boring holes with a Black and Decker drill. I was well aware of what would happen if I tried to smile at anybody while boring holes. Searching with decreasing urgency for the DIY centre, I happened on a second-hand bookshop and went in there instead. It wasn't a very good second-hand bookshop — mostly its stock consisted of the sort of unsellable item which people nowadays palm off on Oxfam in order to feel charitable — but I had already cleaned all the other second-hand bookshops out. It was a mystery how I managed, on less than no income, to go on building an impressive personal library. From my habit of writing the date when I purchased a book under my name on the front flyleaf, I can now tell that I bought several volumes of Rilke's letters at about that time. Since I would have been able to read no German more difficult than the extracts from *Till Eulenspiegel's Merry Pranks* which had been included in my elementary German textbook at Sydney Technical High School, I must have bought those volumes in the expectation that I would learn the language later on. By that criterion, no purchase was beyond my reach. I brought my trophies home to the Friar's House and lined them up along the edge of the floor where the bookcase would go once I had bored the holes in the lengths of wood that I would be buying in the near future. Until then, late at night when I came home from the Footlights, I lay reading under the dozen blankets I had obtained on a loan from the ladies in the Pembroke linen room. A cold autumn would have made sleep difficult even if there had been a functioning power point for the electric fire I had bought before finding out why it was so cheap. Making sleep impossible, however, was the noise of Romaine's typewriter. Through the trembling partition dividing our two rooms came the frenzied uproar of a belt-fed Mauser MG42 firing long bursts from a concrete pillbox.

She was getting somewhere and I wasn't. Footlights was only one of the distractions that kept me from attending to my principal business, which was meant to be Shelley and his readings of the Italian poets. The luckless man chosen to supervise my PhD thesis was Professor Graham Hough, of whose distinction I was uneasily aware. I went to see him in Darwin. From the time it took me to get there, he might as well have been in Darwin, Australia. Actually Darwin College was only just across the Cam. A hundred yards along Trumpington Street towards Pembroke, turn right down Silver Street, cross the bridge, and I should have been there in five minutes. It took ten times that because I was thinking. When I got to the bridge I looked downriver and thought for a long while. The wooden lattice of Queen's Bridge spanned the river like a quietly exultant reproach. Isaac Newton had designed it, the cocky prick. He hadn't only known what he was doing, he had been mad keen that everybody else should be appropriately cowed, the asshole. During the long vacation I should have got enough of a grip on my subject to make it sound worthwhile for my supervisor to find out about it himself so that he would be able to check up on me as the work advanced. Unfortunately, what seemed a good idea had remained merely a good idea. I had a few citations to suggest that the influence of Dante and Petrarch had been not just thematic, as Shelley himself proudly admitted, but technical, at the level of imagery and rhythmic strategy. Hough wanted to know how this last item differed from the metrical patterns which it was already known that Shelley had taken over wholesale from his Italian models. Sure I was right, but being short of information – always a dangerous state for anyone who is trying to sell someone else on an idea – I struggled to adduce chapter and verse. Hough was patient. As a prisoner of the Japanese in Malaya, he had been through more trying times than this. Younger students than myself might be torn between the brimstone of Leavis and the fireworks of Steiner, but Hough's realistic solidity was what I valued most in a teacher of English. As much for the theoretical dabbling it eschewed as for the pure reason it espoused, I thoroughly approved of his little book *Essay on Criticism*. A poet himself, he wrote the civilised verse of a man who had been far enough into the pit to admire the scenery on the way back out. I didn't want to muck him around. With sherry-fuelled eloquence I conjured visions of the deep studies I would pursue. If not convinced, he was at least lulled. I got the impression that he might be on the verge of nodding off. It was my suggestion, not his, that I should come back when I had something on paper. Instantly he was on his feet with his hand out. I went to shake it, but it was going past me to the door handle.

On the way back to college to pick up my mail, I took the long way around past the pond and over the meadow. At the Mill I stood communicating with the ducks. The river was already closed down for the winter. Raindrops prickled on the dark water just above where it filled with cold light as it curved out to leap through the sluice. It was the kind of thing Leonardo da Vinci liked to draw. Leonardo hadn't been here, of course, but nearly everybody else had. Not only Rupert

Brooke had been down at the Mill, Rutherford had sat here on the wall and watched the atoms pursue their unbroken curve. John Maynard Keynes had looked into that clear declension and seen the economic consequences of the Versailles Treaty. Wittgenstein had seen the silence of what cannot be expressed, Alan Turing the soul of a machine. Apparently there was now some crippled young man at King's who was working on a unified field theory that would explain absolutely everything. Surrounded by these exemplars of mental effort, I couldn't even be sure that I would do the work I had cut out for myself. Worse, I was sure I wouldn't. Somehow I would be drawn aside, into something else. All the ducks knew enough to stay well upstream of where the surface of the water moved faster and lost its comforting darkness. I couldn't stay out of the light. If I had been a duck I would have been down the sluice. I wouldn't even make it as a web-footed water-fowl. Those ducks got on my nerves so much that I wrote a poem belittling their pretensions.

My duck poem took two days of undeflected concentration. If something was irrelevant, I could do it. While I was supposed to be studying the poems of Shelley, I was writing mine. By this time *Granta* was practically my private newsletter. I still contributed, with grand condescension, to *Varsity*, but I was growing sick of its inability to set up my carefully finished copy without including all the same misprints which disfigured the news stories sent in dramatically from the telephone booth around the corner by would-be Fleet Street pie-eating hacks who were all cheap excitement and no sentence structure. The snapping point came when I reviewed Joseph Losey's desperately unfunny comic film *Modesty Blaise*. I compared the undraped Monica Vitti to the Rokeby Venus. It came out as the Rokesby Venue. I might have stood for this if anybody concerned had been ashamed, but student journalists don't learn to take pains until they have to, and perhaps that's the way things should be. It's hard enough crawling out of your shell, without being driven back in by sneers and quibbles. Uncomfortably aware that I had been hanging around too long, I left the junior reporters to get on with it and switched my feature-writing efforts to *Granta* on the semi-fulltime basis necessitated by my having accepted a post as its new arts editor. Taking on this task was sheer folly but I was sick of being at the mercy of undergraduate newspaper editors. Those who edited the magazines had a greater sense of responsibility than the *Varsity* tribe. They also had a bad habit of leaving the printer to get on with it while they toasted muffins in each other's rooms, but at least, as one of them, I would be able to accept my own stuff without demur and make sure that it got laid out with appropriate prominence: nothing too strident, mind, just plenty of white space to set off the body copy, the occasional full-page photograph to remind the readers of who they were dealing with, and a caption prominent enough to make sure that they didn't get my photograph mixed up with anybody else's. Like all previous and subsequent literary editors of *Granta*, I began with confident hopes of securing contributions from world-famous literary figures. If my letters were answered at all, it was in the negative. Jean-Paul Sartre said '*Non.*' The fact that he had said the same to the Nobel Prize committee was small comfort. Dalziel gave me a good piece on the films of John Ford. It needed a lot of subbing, because he had written it in spare time he didn't have, now that the BFI Production Board was pressing him hard to finish *Expresso Drongo* even if Keith Visconti had to be fired.

The one advantage of being *Granta*'s literary editor turned out to be intangible when it really mattered. At the invitation of the Italian department, the great poet Eugenio Montale came to town and sat in the Senior Common Room of Magdalene to be interviewed by the head of the department, Professor Limentani. The room was jammed with members and students of the Italian department plus a couple of hundred others who had all forced their way in to pay homage. Starved of oxygen, Montale sat there under his distinguished cap of silver hair being asked several questions by Professor Limentani. The Prof spoke in a voice that might have just been audible to anyone with an ear-trumpet who had been sitting in his lap. Tired after a long journey, Montale must have thought that to whisper at great length to a huge room full of strangers was an English national custom, like riding to hounds. He whispered too. About two hundred and fifty people all dying of nitrogen narcosis were in there for an hour struggling silently for position so that they could watch two Italian men of advanced years moving their lips. Not for the first time, the extent to which an academic organisation could bungle a big event made me wonder if undergraduates got sufficient credit for the extracurricular things they accomplished. I wrote an article about the occasion for *Granta*, subbed it myself, laid it out and left it for the editor to see through the press. When the issue came out, my article was there pretty much as I had written it, except that almost every detail was in the wrong place. All the paragraphs were out of order, so that Montale – now known as Montela, although sometimes as Mantabe – left Cambridge in the middle of the article before arriving at the end. My critical remarks concerning his famous poem about the lemon trees were attached to a quotation from his equally famous poem about the sunflower. My name was the only item which appeared correctly, thereby ensuring that the blame for the mess would be entirely mine.

At about this time, Florence was hit by a flood that killed a lot of people, played havoc with the artistic patrimony, and transformed the city's way of life. I felt guilty about not being there to help, but not as guilty as I felt about setting out to spread enlightenment and ending up adding to the confusion. There wasn't much I could do about bringing people with lungs full of mud back to life. I felt ashamed of my powerlessness, but the shame was abstract. To have my name on a page of nonsense felt as shameful as having run someone over. Françoise was in Oxford, to start a Bachelor of Philosophy course. After having taken her doctorate with the maximum possible marks – a feat unheard-of for a foreigner, and rare even for a native – she had providentially left Florence before the catastrophe. I was relieved that she was safe. But that, as Gatsby says of Daisy's love for Tom, was only personal. Those columns of pied type were hard to get over. I sent a copy of the magazine to Françoise at Somerville and by return of post she was kind enough to commiserate, although her suggestion that nobody would notice the difference did not have the soothing effect that she intended. No doubt things would have gone better if I had been at the press. I couldn't be everywhere. Certainly I couldn't be at my desk. Shelley would have to wait for a bit.

As usual the thing that demanded most of my attention was Footlights, only now more than ever. In my capacity as President I was in constant attendance. There were more committee meetings than usual because I was intent on delegating every task of day-to-day administration. To delegate successfully, I had to call a meeting, so that everybody could be told what to do. The secretary looked after the finances, the cabaret director looked after the cabaret bookings, the Falconer looked after the clubroom. This left me free to sit in the bar until late at night looking after general policy. My first big policy decision had to do with Prince Charles, who had arrived at Trinity with the whole of Fleet Street just behind him in a succession of hired coaches. It was evident that Footlights concerts and revues, unless an embargo was imposed on his name, would consist of nothing but sketches about Prince Charles. The press was already a gruesome warning of what to expect. Traditionally nuts on the subject of the heir to the throne, they had now gone berserk. Student journalists who had dreamed of joining the World of Paul Slickey were now given good reason to think again. Their heroes, in the flesh, turned out to possess not even the inverted glamour of sleazy corruption. Nothing more complicated was going on than the usual behaviour of a pack of sharks in a feeding frenzy. Determined not to be a prisoner of his fate, their quarry took part in a smoking concert in Trinity. Fleet Street, for which any Cambridge theatrical event is always a Footlights revue – usually misspelled 'review' – ran headlines about his appearance with Footlights. (FOOTLIGHTS CHARLES – PICTURES). Sensibly he didn't come near Footlights. The roof would have fallen in. Thus he solved half the problem himself. The other half was for us to solve. Informing the committee that they would have to agree in advance to pass the motion *nem. con.* – otherwise the mere fact of there having been a discussion would have become a story too – unilaterally I imposed the embargo. This was the right thing to do, but while doing it I felt the sinister thrill of unchallenged power.

Luckily I managed to remind myself in time that as President of Footlights I was not the Shah of Persia, just *primus inter pares*. At very most, as the Dean of Pembroke might have put it, I was *in loco parentis* to those *in statu pupillari*.

Helping to remind me on this point were the club smoking concerts. There was a new bunch of multi-talented performers coming up who had me beaten to the wide, especially when it came to music. Reading for the Classics Tripos at St John's, Pete Atkin was a shy young man with rimless glasses who had an unfair amount of natural authority on stage, as if being in the limelight saved him from self-consciousness. He wrote shapely melodies which, while being completely original, partook of every musical tradition from Buddy Holly back to Palestrina. Footlights had always had a strong musical element. There was always someone who knew all about jazz and someone else who knew all about pop. John Cameron could score for a big band *before* he got to Cambridge, so it was no surprise that he led one after he left. Daryl Runswick was a music scholar in Corpus Christi who could put away the bow and pluck his bass like Ray Brown: later on he was to accompany Frank Sinatra at the Festival Hall. Robin Nelson could write a parody of a Bach cantata that sounded like a Bach cantata. But Atkin knew everything. He was particularly erudite on the subject of Tin Pan Alley. He knew Rodgers and Hart note for note and word for word. The same Mercer and Arlen songs that were my touchstones he could play and sing straight through from memory. Though he wrote excellent lyrics for his own tunes, I was ruthless in planting the notion that he might perhaps consider setting one or two of my own efforts. Cuckoos laying eggs give more subtle hints than I did. Believing then, as I still believe, that a song lyric should be at least as disciplined as a published poem, I produced, in that first flush of collaboration, intricately symmetrical stanza forms which Atkin could inject with music only at the cost of making it evident that he had been required to use a syringe. It was easier to loosen up the syntax when we worked the other way around, with me concocting a lyric to fit a tune he had already written. After a while we met somewhere in the middle, roughing out both melody and story at a preliminary session around the piano. The piano was on the Footlights stage. Late nights in the Footlights grew later. If Atkin had known that we would write hundreds of songs over the next eight years, he might have struck for regular hours. I had a way of catching people up in my enthusiasms. But I don't think he would protest, looking back, that I turned him aside from his studies. Talent will out. It has a mind of its own.

Some people have so many talents that their idea of being normal is to have only one. Russell Davies was also from St John's. He had already taken a double first in the Modern Language Tripos without realising that he had sat the examinations. He thought they were application forms. It didn't occur to him to ask what he was applying for. When people asked him to do things, he said yes. He could do everything except say no. The only reason he was so late getting to Footlights was that he had been asked to play by every jazz band in the area. He played a different instrument in each band. He could play the tuba, the trombone, the trumpet, the saxophone and the piano. When he got to us, it turned out that he could write, draw, sing, dance and act, all better than anyone else. He hadn't quite realised that he could do these things. There hadn't been time.

With Atkin and Davies both around, things were already looking promising for the next May Week revue, of which I intended to be the producer. I had already ruled myself out as a performer. In this company I would be outclassed. As the year developed, St John's proved to be a bottomless cornucopia of gifted new recruits. Atkin and Davies had a friend unromantically named Barry Brown, who wrote and performed surreal monologues. Together they all put on the St John's Smoker. There was an interloper from Emmanuel called Jonathan James-Moore who looked and sounded like a retired colonel invented by Saki. They all seemed to have the kind of stage presence that many professional actors spend a lifetime acquiring, but today they would be unanimous in admitting that they paled into the decor when the spotlight came up on Julie Covington. The decor was in the St John's bike shed, annual home of the St John's Smoker. Atkin and

Brown had discovered Covington at Homerton Teacher's College. Spotlit against inaccurately draped black curtains in the smoky, crowded depths of the bike shed, her prettiness was sufficient on its own to induce a reverent hush. The reverent hush deepened to religious awe when she began to sing. Student singers who could hold a note were rare. Student singers who could hold an audience were radium. Talent-shopping from the back of the mesmerised crowd, I foresaw a whole new era of student revue opening up, in which the lyrical element, formerly an occasional by-product of make-up and drag, would be fundamental.

Inspired to a minimum of half a dozen new song lyrics per week, laboriously I commuted to Oxford by train so that I might read them aloud to Françoise. Her room in the Somer-ville graduate house had the rare luxury of central heating, but I made a practice of reciting all my new lyrics on arrival, before removing my duffel coat. Unaccompanied by music, they were perhaps harder to appreciate than I surmised. The Oxford and Cambridge Ski Club had booked a hotel in Zürs am Alberg for an off-season week in early December. Françoise was going and she suggested that if I wanted to write and recite lyrics without being interrupted by a long train trip via Bletchley, I should come to Austria. Picturing what the officers of the Oxford and Cambridge Ski Club would undoubtedly look like – RAF moustaches and white roll-necked pullovers with Olympic rings on them – I scorn-fully declined. What would a radical socialist be doing mixed up in an upper-crust activity like skiing? On my return to Cambridge, Marenko told me that he was going to Zürs. Blantyre was going too. Even Delmer Dynamo was going. I told them I couldn't ski. 'Blow it out your ass,' said Delmer. '*Anyone* can ski. You just point the things down the *hill*, for Christ's sake.'

12

Hell Below Zero

SOMEHOW THE OXFORD and Cambridge Ski Club got to Austria by train. The club had no officers – it was just a letterhead – so the mass movement was more of an instinctive migration than an organised journey. The Americans caught the train at the last minute. They had planned to go in Delmer's car. It turned out that nobody knew how to fill it with petrol. The filler cap had a combination lock which Delmer had not had occasion to open before because he had never driven the car far enough to run out of fuel. Also there was nowhere to put Marenko's skis. Delmer feared that a roofrack would damage his precious hand-rubbed paintwork. Apparently he had expected Marenko's skis to be much shorter. This was a reasonable assumption. Marenko's skis were made of metal and went on for ever, like two lengths of railway line.

Unseasonably, the snow at Zürs was fresh and deep all the way down into the valley. After hiring boots and skis I headed for the baby slope. I was alone. Françoise had been skiing every year in Australia since the first rope-tow had been put in at Thredbo when she was a child. Instantly she was off and gone. Strad ski'd like a gentleman. He went with her. Delmer spent the whole of the first day buying all his gear instead of hiring it, which promised great things. When he finally emerged from the most expensive ski-shop in Zürs, he was carrying a lot of big boxes and already wearing a sensational pair of boots. In those last days of lace-up boots, experts might wear clip-ons, but scarcely anybody had clip-ons made of plastic. Delmer's were not only brilliant red plastic with silver clips, they had gnurled screws, screwed gnurls, grommets, gauges and three-way adjustable furbelows. 'Get *these*,' crowed Delmer. 'Tomorrow I'll be out of *sight*.'

But by then I had seen Marenko. As I lay there sobbing where I had fallen off the T-bar at the top of the baby slope, I had seen him high above me on one of the lower, slower stretches of a black piste. Unmistakable in his dark glasses and the black one-piece overall of an SS tank commander, he came bouncing down through a mogul field in a dead straight line, slamming from hump to hump, both his poles held by their middles in one hand while he adjusted his collar with the other. What was worse, he saw me. After disappearing behind a clump of trees like a gannet into the sea, he suddenly reappeared on the last, allegedly elementary stretch of red piste on the other side of the T-bar. At first he was going at a scarcely believable velocity, but what was really unbelievable was how smoothly he translated all that impetus into stasis. Changing direction at the last possible second so that he curved up the hill and around the top of the wheel at the head of the T-bar, he just leaned over and stopped, his poles still in one hand. 'This goddam ski-pass keeps flapping loose,' he said. 'Nearly strangled myself up there on the Death's Head. How *you* doin'?'

Though it hurt me to say so, I had to tell him that I wasn't doing very well. For some reason he didn't seem to realise this. He told me to take a run down the slope while he watched. Take a *run*. I took a crawl. Snow-ploughing rigidly with my nose between my knees, I headed downwards at one mile per hour, coming to a halt altogether if someone else had fallen in front of me. Marenko ski'd backwards beside me. 'Don't try to stop the skis,' he said. 'You're choking them. Let them run.' Momentarily I let them run and headed for the village. Between the baby slope and the village was a road. On a collision course from the right came a skidding bus with chains on its wheels and a driver whose arm was across his eyes. Luckily there was a barrier of snow-caked slush at the high edge of the road. While I lay in it face down, sobbing in a muffled manner, Marenko told me I was wasting my time on the baby slope. 'You're a natural,' he announced. 'Tomorrow we'll get you up there on the Death's Head.'

The next day dawned clear and bright, unfortunately. I had been hoping for a blizzard. Everybody was going up to the Death's Head except Delmer. At breakfast he had announced his intention of starting slowly. 'Gotta break in the new boots, men.' And indeed the new boots looked as if they needed breaking in, almost as much as his ensemble needed toning down. A blue and crimson effort with a colour-coordinated beanie, it aroused expectations of speed which Jean-Claude Killy might have found it difficult to fulfil. No stretch pants had ever been so stretched. On the back of the quilted jacket appeared the words DOWNHILL ACTION HI-FI CHALLENGE. On the breast pocket the words RACING TEAM CLUB encircled the face of a snarling tiger. If Delmer had been the right shape for all this it would have helped, but there would still have been a problem. The famous new boots supported him so well that he couldn't bend down far enough to get his skis on. Strad had to help him into them. Delmer looked impatient. Once the skis were on and the bindings were closed, he fell over. All this happened in front of the hotel. 'Blow it out your ass!' shouted Delmer. Some passing Austrian ski-masters, whose walking boots looked as if they had put their legs down the throats of live wolves, looked curious. '*Was hat er gesagt?*' '*Weiss nix.*' We helped Delmer out of his skis and he waved us away, promising to join us later, after the micro-wedge plinth mounting on his boots had been recalibrated to match the barometric pressure.

The idea that Delmer had been wise to cop out early grew on me as we rose in the cable car towards the peak of the mountain known as the Death's Head. My imagination was working overtime as usual. The cable car stopped well short of the peak. The tree line was still in clear view below and the slope looked quite gentle compared to the north face of the Eiger. I hoped it was from the cold that Françoise was trembling. She had advised me to go to ski class but I had shouted her down, keen as usual to take no advice, however sensible, until bitter experience had rendered it imperative. 'This is more like it,' said Marenko. This is more like *what*?

I subvocalised. My lips were too cold to move. I just breathed very quietly through my nose and tried to look at only the first few yards of the slope. The angle it was at looked ridiculous enough by itself, without considering the cliff it turned into a bit later on. The only stroke of luck was that even the vertical bits were covered with fresh snow. 'You can't hurt yourself,' said Marenko. 'If you fall over you'll stop eventually.' But I was already gone, sliding on my face, held back by nothing except the minimal resistance of the snow through whose surface my nose was trowelling a thin furrow. 'Stop!' shouted Marenko as he sliced past at full speed beside me. The clear contradiction between what he was saying now and what he had said just before had obviously not had time to strike him. 'Get your skis below you and you'll stop!' My skis were above me and I wasn't stopping. Marenko cut in underneath me and brought us both to a halt with me crumpled upside down against his ankles. 'That's a good start,' he said, fishing with one of his poles for my left ski, which had come off. 'Shows you're not afraid of the slope.' Françoise and Strad appeared beside us, looking worried. 'You two go on,' said Marenko. 'I'll give him a few pointers.' They wanted to stay but I insisted. I didn't want anyone else to be there while I was being given the pointers.

Each hour that ensued seemed like a bad day. I cried all the time. The tears never fell. They just tinkled in my eyes like Christmas decorations hanging in a window. Before I knew how to traverse across packed snow, Marenko was making me traverse across deep powder. I crashed into snow drifts with both my skis off. The automatic ski brake had not yet been invented. The skis were attached by thongs to your boots, except when the thongs came undone. Mine always did. The bindings, when Marenko rescued the skis from further down the same drift, or from the top of the next drift down, were caked with snow, which at that altitude turned to ice faster than a gloved fingertip could scrape it out. The bindings weren't today's forgiving, apparently simple affairs that you can just step into after a token gesture of knocking the snow off the bottom of your boots with the tip of a stick. They were spring and cable bindings which would not close unless all the snow had been brushed out of them and any hint of ice on the bottom of your boots had been scrupulously removed. Wallowing in a drift, I found these requirements impossible to fulfil. Marenko patiently waited, doubtless thinking about Yeats, while I waded out of the drift towards a firm footing. 'Good training,' he said. 'Just like my first year at Aspen.' He couldn't seem to grasp that the reason I was just lying there was that I couldn't move. 'Don't worry if you feel tired,' he said, blowing on his dark glasses. 'It's just fatigue.'

Though we were on a red piste, which was theoretically much easier than a black piste, there were narrow stretches that I wouldn't have contemplated trying to snow-plough down even in a snow-plough. I took my skis off and walked. On the wider stretches, however, Marenko insisted that I try to do parallel turns. The main difficulty, I found, was to go slowly enough in the first instance so that the turn could be initiated under some sort of control. I was already falling before I turned, so all that the turn did was to alter the direction of the fall. The instruction to lean out into the valley I found impossible to obey, because I had already fallen towards the mountain. The skis having become crossed while my body continued to move, *then* I leaned out into the valley, but by that time I was fully airborne. It was a parallel turn only in the sense that my flailing form was parallel to the snow. On the beaten piste the resulting impact was audible and painful. It was much nicer falling into the drifts. I began to look around hopefully for the next drift. Eventually fatigue reached the point where Marenko began to notice. The piste was about to narrow into a mogul-ridden swoop to the right, with its right edge curving up into the mountain and its high left lip masking a sudden drop to the foot of a clump of pine trees. You could tell how steep the drop was by the fact that only the top halves of the trees were visible. I looked at all this but it must have been clear that I wasn't taking it in. We sat down for a while and Marenko gave me a piece of chocolate. 'You're going great,' he said. 'Only another hour and you'll be down.' At this point Françoise and Strad appeared. They were on their third or fourth run down the mountain. 'He's going great,' said Marenko. All I had to do was sit there until they got bored and went away. Instead I somehow got the idea that it was now or never. In such cases the rule should always be: never. When in doubt, don't. Françoise and Strad fishtailed neatly down the chute and waited at the bottom, looking up. Marenko *schüss*ed in a sweet straight line, his arms held out to the sides like a falling crucifix as he bounced from hump to hump of the frightening moguls. He spun on his skis about two-thirds of the way down so that he was going backwards, drifted to a stop beside the others, and waved a pole to indicate that I should follow.

I should have taken my skis off and walked, but I was too tired. And they had made it look so easy. I started to traverse across towards the outer edge of the piste. After an inspired snow-plough turn I was traversing the other way. But the second turn, which took me some way up the high wall to the right, was of such large radius that it didn't slow me down at all, so when I headed back to the left I was going at full clip. 'Too fast!' shouted Marenko. 'I *know*!' was my agonised reply. Heading up and out over the high left edge of the piste, I tried to stop myself by sitting back. Thus lightened, the skis moved even faster, so I was actually lying down in mid-air as I sailed out into space. 'Death,' I thought. 'This is it. Here it is.' Pine tree branches snapped off in quick succession. They sounded like a pom-pom firing. Their thickness, as it happened, might have been precisely calculated to break my fall instead of my back. My skis came off in the tree, so when I bombed into a drift I was not only moving just slowly enough to survive the impact, I was spared the usual humiliating search for lost equipment. By the time the others materialised below me, having beaten a path through the trees, I had reassembled my stuff and was able to make a brave show of having meant the whole thing. Marenko, in his way, helped. 'You've done the hard part now,' he said. 'Nice work.'

Marenko's teaching methods were, of course, the worst possible for a beginner. Having ski'd most of his life, he had no idea of what it was like not to be able to, and thought that you were incapable from mere recalcitrance, which could be overcome by exhortation. Natural athletes are rarely the best teachers. The person who can teach you something is the one who remembers how he learned it. There was another inhibiting factor. Skiing is a technical sport which has little to do with strength. At that stage I was still quite strong and all too ready to try turning the skis by brute force. It can work only on gently sloping, packed snow. For the last part of the run, some of that was available, and even after my day of torment I was foolish enough to believe that I was getting somewhere. The other three took it slowly so that I could keep up. I fancied that I looked part of the group as we came sweeping down past the baby slope. I rather hoped that Delmer would be there to marvel, but at first there was no sign of him. Then Strad spotted Delmer's beanie. It was sticking up out of the snowdrift at the bottom of the slope. The weatherbeaten, superannuated ski-masters who tended the baby slope were gathered round the beanie. One of them was poking the snow with a long thin stick. Muffled sounds could be heard from under the snow. I recognised Delmer's catchphrase, modulated into fluffy softness as if shouted through a pillow. '*Was hat er gesagt?*' one of the ski-masters asked us. '*Macht nichts,*' said Strad. '*Er sagt nur dass er OK ist.*' I was amazed. I never knew Strad spoke German.

Strad didn't like to show off. He was reluctant to reveal that he was capable of anything until circumstances forced him into it. My own character being incurably different, I envied him his ability to keep his light under a bushel. For me, being able to do something meant that I had to prove it, and being unable to do something was a taunt from Fate. Being unable to ski would have been more bearable in, say, Barbados. In a ski resort it was intolerable. I resolved to dare all. Next day Delmer appeared in full ski kit but without his boots. He had bought himself a pair of yak's hair *après-ski* bootees, and with these crossed in front of him he settled down in a deck chair to cut the pages of his New York edition of Henry James, which had just arrived in a crate. Until the technology had been sorted out, he announced, we would never catch him putting on skis again. His place in the ski class – he had booked himself in for a week of advanced lessons – he kindly gave to me. The ski-masters advised me to swap it for elementary lessons. It was a blow to the ego to be skiing with the children but when they did it better than I the message sank in. Drawing on my usual reserves of fanaticism, I set to work on mastering the stem turn. I mastered it so well that in later years, when the stem turn went out of fashion, it took me an age to unmaster it, and even today, in moments of stress, I find the back ends of my skis drifting apart by that tell-tale inch which brands my generation of skiers more surely than the waffle pattern left by thermal underwear around the thickening waistline. At the end of the week I could get down the red piste on the Death's Head without taking my skis off. It wasn't much of an achievement – there was a six-year-old girl in a crash helmet who would go past me three times while I was coming down once – but it made me absurdly content. What I liked best about skiing was how it made loneliness legitimate. Raised in the hot sun, my idea of romance was to feel cold. North was a thrilling word to me. Balzac said that a novel should send the reader into another country. My dreams were like that. They still are.

On the snow I didn't know what I was doing. As compensation, there was a concert at the end of the week. From the hundreds of student skiers, those who thought they could do a turn came shyly forward. There was the amateur magician with the duff patter and the American girl with the guitar who could sing all the songs Joan Baez sang except that they sounded different and she couldn't remember any of them all the way through. 'Oh Gard, I'm sorry. No, wait . . . No. It's gone.' In this context I was able to shine. I hit them with my 'Lucy Gets Married' number and followed it up with my new one about the lost H-bomb. The Americans, in particular, were delirious. By then the concern with the Vietnam imbroglio had built up to the point where even the Ivy League Americans – and these were certainly those – had doubts about their country's role as a world policeman. As an Australian at a British university telling American citizens how they ought to behave, I was in an anomalous position if I stopped to think about it. It was a less anomalous position than being upside down in a snowdrift, so I didn't stop to think about it. I just rode towards the laughter like a heat-seeking missile. This was the first time I had played to an audience outside Cambridge. I might have been encouraged by the results if I had envisaged a career as a performer. At that time I thought of my own appearances on stage as nothing more theatrical than a form of writing with a light shining on it, like a goose-neck lamp on a desk. It was just a form of expression. I wasn't even sure what form it was. It wasn't acting. I didn't even memorise the stuff. I just read it out. Timing was for real performers: it usually struck me as artificial even when they did it, and when I did it it was ludicrous. Establishing a tacit understanding with the audience that I *wasn't* going to perform, however, generated an air of complicity which I dimly saw might be a way ahead. A ski resort in Austria was an odd spot to be struck with such a formative notion, but that's often how these things happen. Developing a personal style is largely a matter of recognising one's limitations, and the best place to recognise them is somewhere off the beaten track. At the end of the concert I felt pleased with myself. Next day there was a last morning of skiing before we packed up to go home. Pride the night before was duly followed by a bad fall.

I was having one of my customary rests at the side of the red piste on the Death's Head when Marenko appeared from above, heading straight down the mogul field through which I had just spent half an hour painfully picking my way. I was amongst a pack of other heavy-breathing rabbits so he didn't see me. He must have been skiing back the quickest way to the hotel after doing his usual half a dozen black runs in succession. Holding both poles in one hand, he had his dark glasses off and was breathing on the inside of them as his heavy metal skis kissed the crests of the moguls like a flat stone bouncing rapidly across a rippled pond. Below me, where the moguls eased into a smoother piste, he decided he wasn't going fast enough and started to skate. He hooked his dark glasses back on, redistributed his poles so that he had one in each hand, sank slightly at the knees, planted his right pole, and disappeared in a diving turn over the side of the piste. Half a minute later I saw him far below and far away.

He had *schüss*ed across the face of an old avalanche covered with fresh powder. The rabbits around me sighed with admiration.

Deciding that I had not been daring enough, I tried to straight-line the rest of the mogul field. Miraculously I got through it, although my knees, which despite my fear I somehow managed to keep loose, must have looked ridiculous bouncing up around my ears. The predictable result didn't happen until I reached the smooth bit. I was going the fastest I had ever gone and perhaps it was a mistake to be yelling with exultation. 'WEE HAH!' I cried. 'WHOOEE!' The ensuing fall was the most embarrassing kind you can have. The skis went outwards to each side, spreading my legs so wide that they were practically in a straight line. Luckily the bindings snapped open almost straight away, otherwise my nose would have been broken. Like an arrowhead I flew on for some distance, still with a pole in each hand. Making a three-point contact — mouth, chest and seriously shrivelled genitalia — I kissed the piste and slid on at full speed, slowing down only very gradually. The main braking effect was provided by the snow accumulating inside my clothes. About fifty pounds of it was forced into my stretch pants. When I finally contrived to stand up again my pants wobbled like bags full of water. I was so completely winded that I thought all my ribs were broken. Symbolically, my recently eloquent lower lip was badly bitten, the blood seeping through the caked snow around my mouth to give the effect, I was later told, of an Italian raspberry *gelato*. My lucky break was that my skis both missed me. Travelling very fast, they went past me on each side on their way down to the hotel, where I joined them an hour later, feeling chastened. The abyss between wanting to and being able to had once again made itself manifest. A man can fall into that gap and vanish. To him it will be small consolation that those who never aspire never appear in the first place.

13

Fantasy Island

THUS MY FIRST year as a PhD student took shape. The academic year was short anyway, but there was no gainsaying the fact that I was working on my thesis for an average of one hour per month or perhaps less. No gainsaying it by anyone except me. As usual I told myself that everything would change tomorrow. Tomorrow never came, because it couldn't. I just had too many commitments. Alarmed by their number, I distracted myself from them by adding others. In Footlights my new styleless style of performing made enough progress to attract the attention of student producers in other branches of the theatre. It struck someone who shall remain nameless that I would make an ideal Jourdain in the Cambridge Opera Society's forthcoming presentation of the original version of *Ariadne auf Naxos*. I wouldn't have to sing: in the original version Jourdain is the leading role of a play which is eventually, although not soon enough, displaced by the opera. It should have been obvious that if I didn't have to sing I would have to act, but somehow I convinced myself that I wouldn't have to act either. At that time I was enslaved to the music of Richard Strauss. I knew *Der Rosenkavelier* note for note, could do a traffic-stopping imitation of Ljuba Welitsch in the final scene from *Salome*, and would contentedly croon both parts of the long two-girl duet from *Arabella* while sitting in the Whim writing a nit-picking review of *Accident*. Considering that I couldn't sing the National Anthem in a way that made it sound significantly different from 'Rock Around the Clock', this incantatory Strauss-worship must have sounded pretty strange from the outside, but inside my head it had the full, drenching beauty of that reprehensible old opportunist at his most sumptuous: the shimmering swirl of strings that drapes the soprano like a Fortuny gown, the passing phrase, the orgasmic crescendo, the sudden silence. Not too much, in my version, of the sudden silence. In particular I loved the last pages of *Ariadne auf Naxos* where Bacchus got the lion's share of the duet with the eponymous goddess. To all intents and purposes he had a grandstand aria, of which I knew every phrase. Yes, if destiny had denied me the wherewithal to sing Bacchus, at least I could play Jourdain. So what I said to the producer was yes, when what I should have said was no. And if he didn't understand it when I said it in English, I should have sung it in German. *Nein!*

It wasn't his fault. Always in the theatre, as in all the arts, it is dangerous to go against one's instincts, but this doesn't mean that it is always safe to go with them. You can take on a project from the depth of your heart and it will still end up stuck all over your face, like egg. I already knew that, but there aren't many operas with a starring role for a non-singer, and I wanted to be an opera star. So I ignored the law of probability, which declared that no student producer, unless he was Max Reinhardt reborn, would be able to hire the opera singers, organise the orchestra, supervise the designs, stage the main action, and also prevent the play-within-the-opera from sabotaging the opera in a manner less decisive than that which had persuaded Strauss and Hofmannstahl to abandon the original version in the first place. This particular student producer's utter innocence — although a brilliant scholar, he had never produced anything except a weekly essay — helped to persuade me for the first half-hour of rehearsal that he might get everything right by sheer purity, like Parsifal. When he turned out not to be completely certain about the difference between stage left and stage right I started to worry. I should have worried more. For years afterwards, to my shame, I vocally blamed him. The fault was mine for not taking drastic action. Either I should have demanded an experienced producer or else bailed out, if necessary without a parachute. The idea of a non-singing Australian Jourdain was a good one. The idea of a non-singing non-acting Australian Jourdain was a possible one, as long as he learned his lines, hit the marks, and kept his good humour when the set collapsed around him. But with everything else going wrong, I worried about that instead of about getting my bit right. Instead of providing a still centre, I was part of the chaos. The play-within-the-opera was a mess. *Ariadne auf Naxos* was scheduled to go on at the Arts Theatre for four nights running, come what might. Luckily the opera-without-the-play was going reasonably well. Professional opera singers are usually able to produce themselves. Alberto Remedios, appearing in the role of Bacchus, was at that time still on his way up as one of the best Wagnerian tenors in Europe, but he had already had plenty of practice at getting on and off a strange stage at short notice. Despite his exotic name, Alberto was a Scouse plug-ugly with a delightfully foul tongue who knew a potential catastrophe when he saw one. It rapidly became clear that he was unimpressed by the visual aspect of the conditions in which he was being asked to work. 'Shit,' he said when he saw the set. 'Who shat?' And indeed Naxos did look very brown. For an island, it was remarkably short of greenery. The designer had sketched some rocks, which had been faithfully reproduced by the Arts Theatre paint shop. On a large scale the rocks looked like the petrified turds of a mastodon. Ariadne was to be sung by Margaret Roberts, a trouper. It was the other kind of trooper that she swore like when she saw the costume which had been provided for her. Diaphanous in all the wrong places, it looked like Eva Peron's negligée, an impression abetted by the platform mules with pink pom-poms and the sequined cloche flying helmet. A down-to-earth sort of girl, Margaret was prepared to act the temptress, but not in a comedy. Nor was she any more tolerant than Alberto of bright young people dabbling in the arts. She handed back the dress. 'You can burn that,' she said, 'and don't forget to bury the ashes. It might grow again.' From her travelling wardrobe she produced a complete Ariadne costume of her own. Previous experience of semi-professional productions had told her to be prepared.

Alas, not only was I part of the semi-professional production, I exemplified it. For me, *Ariadne auf Naxos* was a personal disaster. I could have called it wounding, but only if I had lived. I died, ten times a night for four nights on the trot. Though the general lousiness of my performance improved toward the merely inadequate as the short run went on, if the show had stayed in repertory for ever I still wouldn't have been able to haul my contribution out of the fire. Romaine Rand, writing a notice for the *Cambridge Review*, said that watching my performance was a strange exercise in compassion, like seeing a man who deserved punishment being beaten up more thoroughly than his crime warranted. She was uncharacteristically kind to the production as a whole, contenting herself with the suggestion that it be sealed in lead-lined containers and buried down a disused coal mine. Looking back on the catastrophe – and even today I look back on it through a veil of tears – I like to think that if I was placed in the same circumstances now I would be able to look after myself, if only by the cheap method of making a virtue of everything going wrong around me. Because everything *did* go wrong, every night. In the play-within-the-opera, a banquet has to be served on stage. On the first night, the banquet was brought in by a single liveried flunkey. There were supposed to be two liveried flunkeys. One of them had gone missing. The remaining liveried flunkey, before he went off to get the banquet, had already entertained the audience by the way his buckled shoes were so obviously a pair of buckles loosely attached to a pair of down-at-heel Chelsea boots. While he was off, we all had a lot of lines about how lavish a banquet it was going to be. When the liveried flunkey reappeared, he was carrying a single tureen. He pretended to stagger under its weight. This merely encouraged the putatively silver cover of the tureen to bounce slightly, as if to prove what the dullest eye already suspected, that it was made of papier mâché thinly caked with silver paint. The audience was thus well prepared to absorb the possibility that the silver cover of the tureen might not conceal anything very wonderful. When the cover was lifted to reveal nothing but a heaped plate of pineapple chunks, however, there were people in the audience who could take no more.

Little could they know how much more they would have to take. When I shut an allegedly heavy ornamental door behind me, it drifted open again to reveal a crouching stagehand in blue jeans. The audience saw him long before I did, so why was he still there then I turned around? It was because he was trying to stop the purportedly massive solid marble fireplace from falling over. He didn't and it did. It floated to the floor and lay there like an extra stage cloth while the cast assembled around it to discuss the unexampled luxury of Jourdain's surroundings. I got exactly one intended laugh. When Jourdain proclaimed his delight at having discovered that he had been speaking prose all his life, the line worked, but that was because it had worked for Molière. The *bourgeois gentilhomme*, however, must have more than one line. He must have character. To be a fool, he must first have his dignity, or he is just ridiculous. My only consolation was that the revival of the original version of *Ariadne auf Naxos*, though worse than a failure on every other level, was a triumph in the musical department – which was, after all, the only thing that mattered. On the last night, the last act sounded lovely beyond description. Conducted by David Atherton, then at the beginning of a glittering career, the orchestra played those marvellous climactic pages in a long, creamy legato line that held Jourdain – watching from a spotlit box but at last released from his terrible obligation to be amusing – spellbound even in the aftermath of his humiliation. Alone on stage among the mastodon droppings, Margaret sent out a languorous invitation to Bacchus that made Sieglinde's song of longing in *Die Walküre* sound like a jingle. The beauty of the music was a sacred rite, but the gremlins had not departed. Alberto's reputed opinion of the set had finally sensitised the student producer to the point where that helpless young man was ready to do anything to put things right. If Alberto couldn't stand the way the set looked, the producer had the solution. As Bacchus, draped in cloth of gold and carrying a priapic stave wreathed with laurels, sang his first heroic phrase and strode masterfully on to the stage, the lights went out. Almost invisible, Bacchus and Ariadne could both still see the conductor, so the sublime duet proceeded on schedule. Indeed it had never sounded better, because now it *looked* so much better. Alberto, however, was not pleased. He controlled his feelings until after the curtain fell. When the curtain went back up again for the first call, the applause for Ariadne and Bacchus was like thunder. You could see the god's mouth moving. It was assumed he was congratulating the goddess. The applause for Ariadne's first individual call was even more cataclysmic, but this time Bacchus, although he was invisible somewhere in the wings, was clearly audible to the whole audience. 'WHICH PRICK TURNED OUT THE FUCKING LIGHTS?' He got a laugh that I walked into, and I was hypocritical enough to bow as if it were mine.

After a cock-up on that scale, Cambridge wasn't big enough to hide in. For Easter I was back in Florence, where the extent and intensity of the destruction caused by the floods put my personal misery into perspective. Though the water had gone down again, the thick tide mark left by the thousands of gallons of spilled oil was still there on the walls, at an impossible height. Everything up to that sinister Plimsoll line had been either washed away or else ruined where it stood. In the *quartiere* between the back of the Palazzo Vecchio and Santa Croce, the fatal black stripe was half-way up the second storey of the buildings. Anita and her family had all survived, but the trattoria was gone, gutted as if by a flamethrower. You would have sworn that fire instead of water had done the work: the walls looked scorched. The whole low-lying little principality of the *popolo minuto* had been soaked with poisons. Sections of the historic centre which lay a few feet higher had suffered less, but more than enough. The cost to the art works and the books was devastating. The human cost was worse than that – it got into my dreams. The underground walkway at the railway station had been full of people when the first big wave had come boiling down the river. People trapped in the walkway had drowned against the roof. None of my friends had been killed, but Florence was my city, so I took the loss of strangers personally. The stricken commune had made it clear that only professionally qualified helpers were welcome. Otherwise, I tried to convince myself, I would have been in there with the first army of saviours. Being useless made the sense of loss more bitter. All over the world, people were horrified by the damage to the patrimony, which they correctly pointed out belonged to all mankind. Would-be realists among them said that the dead people could be replaced but that the works of art should never again be left to chance. They were right. Yet up close it was harder to separate the eternal patrimony from the evanescent human beings who lived and died amongst it. Like everyone else who has ever lived in Florence for however short a time, I had been marked by the city and wanted to feel that I had left my mark on it, even if the mark was only in my memory. In the bar near the Badia, though I hadn't carved my name on the table where I had read and written by the hour, I had been careful to print the table in my recollection. The bar was open again but all the furniture was new. The Biblioteca Nazionale was also, miraculously, open for business, but the desk where I had sat was different and the books I had read were all rebound and their pages were wrinkled from the drying rooms. Somehow the effacement of personal memories was even harder to take than the damage to the Cimabue crucifix in Santa Croce. There was a chance that the Cimabue might be saved. In the Trattoria Anita the decor would never be quite so self-confidently scruffy again. Tat needs to be time-honoured. The level of the Arno had sunk again to the status of a puddle, so we could look over the wall at where the Summer Firefly should have been. It was gone. It has never been put back. With prompt and generous help from America, every shop on the Ponte Vecchio was fully restored, but nobody would bet on the likelihood of people sitting there in the dry river bed to watch *Quel treno per Yuma*. Obviously it was assumed that they would always be listening for another noise in the distance: the roar of water rolling down the valley like a moving wall at the end of an episode of an adventure serial, except that this time, at the start of the next episode, there would be no escape.

At that time I was in one of my beardless periods, so

I found it especially noticeable that some of the young male Florentines among our acquaintances had acquired intentional-looking outcrops of facial hair. Beppe and Sergio both looked like preliminary studies for Titian's portrait of Ariosto. These were the first beards seen on native Italians since the time of Verdi. The floods were the reason. Student life in Florence had been distracted, and had restarted at a broken rhythm, with a new seriousness. The *pappagalli* disappeared overnight, never to return. There had been one notorious occasion when a bus bearing a touring party of French schoolgirls had turned around in front of Santa Maria Novella and gone back to Paris: the teachers in charge had taken one look at the assembled young Italian male pests and decided not to let the girls get off. Now it was different. Foreign girls were no longer followed in the street. In such women's magazines as *Grazia*, which had previously been exclusively concerned with the mysteries of the trousseau, there was new talk of equality. By the following year, the whole of young Italy had become more serious, to the extent that everyone had forgotten where the mood started. But I was there, and I remember. It was in Florence after the flood. The tragedy had worked like a one-day war. Its sheer arbitrariness had concentrated the minds of those who had taken life as it came. They were still subject to intellectual fashion, just as they were still subject to every other kind of fashion. Suddenly all the young men had beards to trim and all the young ladies had blue jeans to bleach. Women in trousers! It was too daring to be true. Yet the surface froth had a deep and potentially violent undertow. There was a demand for justice which the university system was not best placed to supply. You didn't have to be a seer to sense trouble.

Flattering myself that I might do some good, I wrote an article about the aftermath of the Florence floods which I published in *Granta* when I got back. In my capacity as arts editor I allocated to myself three pages of the magazine, with another page for some impressive photographs taken by Françoise. The photographs were rather better judged than my prose, if the truth be told, but the impresario could scarcely be expected to give himself less than star billing. This time I saw the whole thing through the press myself. The viewpoint of the article was perhaps needlessly egocentric – even for myself, I would have done better to leave myself out of it – but there was no chance of muffing the evocation. I could still smell the mud and oil. This article is worth mentioning because it was to have long-term effects on what I have since had to get used to calling my career, so in fairness to an earlier self I should record here that I wrote it out of no great calculation beyond the usual urge to burst into print. At the *New Statesman*, Nicholas Tomalin had just taken over as literary editor, in circumstances which dictated that he find some new book reviewers, and find them in a tearing hurry, because most of the old ones were boycotting him. Tomalin was a feature writer of originality and courage, whose pieces from Vietnam had done a lot to convince Britain – and the Americans in Cambridge – that the United States was in a jungle over its head. The modern determination of the British intelligentsia to keep itself specialised being already far advanced, Tomalin's obvious qualifications as a journalist were held to be disqualifications in a literary editor. Those of the ambitious young who were lit on by his roving eye thought otherwise. Abramovitz, President of the Union in his final term, invited Tomalin to debate some such footling topic as 'This House Would Rather Be Amused'. Abramovitz invited me to be on Tomalin's team. It was billed as a Funny Debate. I had still not learned never to go near anything labelled as Funny. People who tell jokes don't make me laugh. My experience as a guest speaker in Funny Debates at both Cambridge and Oxford eventually helped to convince me that the only place to be amusing is in a serious context. But at that stage I had not yet formulated this important principle, so I agreed to appear in the debate. After the usual interminably facetious opening diatribes by the student politicians, Tomalin rose to speak sensibly about the necessity of writing in an entertaining manner if one wished to convey a serious message. The United States, by bombing Haiphong, had started something which the North Vietnamese army would probably finish. Getting this likelihood across to young Americans before they themselves were drawn into the mud and flames would require all those whose job was to tell the truth to tell it in an arresting manner. There was no use pretending that the story would be a million laughs. Finally what counted was to be serious, a different thing from sentimentality. The Strauss waltzes that had been played in the concentration camps were not only a glaring instance of inappropriate gaiety, they were noxious in themselves. *Der Leichtsinn* was dangerous. Like the official language meant to conceal evil, it really embodied it. Flummery was lethal. Thank you and good night.

Abramovitz understood Tomalin's speech and I could tell from the appreciative laughter that there were some American graduate students in the audience who got it too. For the student politicians it might as well have been a lecture on quantum theory. Why the Oxford and Cambridge Unions should attract recruits of such fatuity is a question that I have never been able to answer. Then as now, they bounced to their feet to make foolish interruptions, gave way, refused to give way, were ruled out of order, and begged the indulgence of the house. Peregrine Sourbutts-Protheroe was there, as usual wearing plimsolls with his evening dress. You could tell he was wearing plimsolls because he was sitting backwards with his legs over the back of a bench. There was a character calling himself Abelard Lakenheath-Bagpuize who shouted at random while eating a raw egg out of his bare hands. It was a madhouse. The libretto was by Tristan Tzara, the choreography by Hieronymus Bosch. When my turn came to speak I let anger rob me of whatever mirth I might have been able to summon. No doubt I deserved to be interrupted by Sourbutts-Protheroe but I refused to give way to him. Nevertheless he unleashed a stream of rip-snorting jokes about the Antipodes, kangaroos, aborigines, and the necessity of walking around upside down in the outback. The audience thought he was hilarious. Even Abramovitz, who was no fool, had been so caught up in the Union's idea of badinage that he felt compelled to laugh. You could tell he felt *compelled* to laugh because he shook his shoulders in a way currently made famous by Edward Heath. Real laughter never looks like that. I was desolate. Tomalin, sensibly, had gone to sleep.

Hours afterwards, when the thing was finally over – there were more student speeches to end with that made the opening ones sound like Plato's *Symposium* – Tomalin took me aside before he climbed into his car to go back to London. 'I liked that thing you wrote about the floods,' he said, looking past me. 'You could do some pieces for me if you've got the time.' With an effortful affectation of off-handedness, I told him that I was busy until May Week but after that I would have some time in hand. Later on I learned he always looked past people. He had a stiff neck. Luckily for me it was only real, and not metaphorical.

My piece about the floods had counted in my own mind as serious writing. It was encouraging to hear that a professional literary journalist concurred in the opinion. Suddenly all my other work in student journalism counted, in my own mind, as serious writing too. I was a serious writer. Whoopee! This was something to set against the nagging fact that I was not doing much serious writing on my thesis. The further fact that I was not doing much serious reading for it either was harder to gainsay. Somehow, along with everything else, I had managed to read a lot, but as usual none of it was immediately relevant to the task in hand. Not having yet accepted that my whole life would be like that, I convicted myself of dereliction. Guilt drove me between the pages of a book – always, since my earliest childhood, my favourite place to hide. In English I read anything at all unless it stemmed from the early part of the nineteenth century, in which case it might have been germane to my subject and thus felt like work. For the only time in my adult life, I became incapable of reading Keats. On the other hand, I could not put Yeats down. The majestic later poems committed themselves to my memory. Where previously I had admired but kept my distance, now I submitted. The long process of growing old enough to appreciate his late achievement was well begun. I tried not to become a Yeats bore. The indomitable Irishry remained an opaque sphere of interest, like the mysticism. But then, as indeed now, I could imagine nothing better than the way Yeats conducted a prose argument through a poetic stanza, compressing syntax as if it were imagery, dislocating rhythm locally so as to intensify it in the aggregate, raising plain statement to the level of the oracular. In my dusty room with the cardboard suitcase open on the curried floor, he was my luxury.

There was now the additional pleasure of being able to read with fair fluency in Italian. I reinforced this nascent ability by raiding the Modern Languages Faculty library, which occupied a floor of the unlovely Sidgwick Avenue site and had a room for each language. I found it hard to keep out of the other rooms as well. The sight of books in languages I couldn't read was a potent stimulus to set about repairing the deficiency. The means of repairing it were near to hand, in an air-conditioned basement under the site. The Language Laboratory looked like the NASA Mission Control Centre in Houston, although — since the space missions had not then yet attained their full glory and coverage — I have always thought of the mission control rooms, whether in Houston or Kaliningrad, as looking like the Sidgwick Avenue language laboratory. The bulky tape decks and discus-sized reels of ¼-inch tape would have looked, to any child of the cassette age who came back from the future, as if they were props from a silent movie about a training camp for mad scientists, but they worked. Picking my way through Proust was a slow way of improving my ability to read French. Studying French in the language laboratory was a faster way. The intention of the course was to teach the student to speak. Leaving that aside until later — decades later, as it turned out — I cashed in on the unintended effect of a language laboratory course, which was to teach the student to read. It was a painless way of absorbing grammar. Over the next year or two I used the laboratory to recapture and improve my primitive German. I also made a good start with Russian. If there had been a Latin course available I would have devoured it. As it was, I picked up a useful if scrappy knowledge of the Latin classics by using parallel texts as portable dictionaries, until finally I could get quite a long way by covering up the page in English and construing the page in Latin from context. But I missed hearing the voices. If Cicero had been on tape I would have memorised the speeches against Catiline and got my quantities right. For me, the language laboratory was the brightly-lit basement shopping mall of the Tower of Babel. I couldn't stay out of it. It was a roundabout and belated way of getting an education. Perhaps it wasn't an education at all. People who knew what I was up to thought I was nuts. They might have been right. There was something pathological about my evasiveness. I hid from my thesis in the pages of books, hid from my native language in a sub-world of smatterings, and hid from myself in the theatre – the place where those who know themselves just well enough to want to get away go to be together.

14

Frisbees Fly at Dusk

NOT THAT THE cast members of the May Week revue were anything like as neurotic as their director – a post to which I had been unanimously elected by the Footlights committee. Since any member of the committee who voted against me would have felt himself obliged to resign on the spot, the unanimous vote was no surprise. I took it as a compliment. I also, I can safely say, took it as an obligation. Night and day, with the exception of the examination period, the whole of Easter term was devoted to rehearsals. Ruling by decree, I had stipulated that the cast would be large. Like many another despot in history, I had talked myself into believing that democracy could be imposed by ukase. I should have known better. I *did* know better, but was carried away by a personal conviction that the club had had its mind on London for too long. Small-cast revues with one eye on the West End had arrived there looking would-be professional and not much fun to be in even when they were funny. A large-cast revue would be a sign that we weren't out for ourselves as individuals. There would be no stars, just a happy ensemble. Though I loathed all of Brecht except the Weill operas, I had been mightily impressed by the Berliner Ensemble when it came to the Old Vic. As Macheath in *The Threepenny Opera*, Wolf Kaiser had writhed against the bars of his gaol in a suitably alienated manner, yet it was the inventiveness of the group movement that had stayed with me. It was like the circus. I liked circuses, too. Though sketches, as always, would be the basis of the show, what attracted me most was the prospect of getting that large cast into concerted action, of creating group effects, of – not yet a word made dreadful by pious use – *improvising*. In the cast there were tall men, small men, thin men, fat men. There were four girls, one of whom was Julie Covington. Normally she would have been the star of the show. In this show without stars I at first looked on her conspicuous ability as a limitation. She was pretty, she could act, she could sing and she could dance. All of that rather got in the road of my general plan to have big production numbers in which nobody would stand out. All day in the clubroom and far into the night, while the smell of fish rose from below like an oily miasma, I carried on like Kim Il Sung, motivating my huge company to perform as one. Possessing an overbearing personality anyway, and fired by the powerful ideals of social engineering, in my ideological determination I was hard for those youngsters to resist. Luckily for us all, they resisted, or there would have been a débâcle.

The show was called *Supernatural Gas* and sold out the Arts Theatre for the whole two-week season. Every Footlights May Week revue always did. At least this one didn't do less. There was oblique evidence that the show was not, in advance at any rate, judged an outright flop. Positive evidence that it was entertaining came from the audience's laughter, which was quite frequent. It might have been more frequent if I had placed due emphasis on the sketch writing. Some of the monologues had not been worked on sufficiently since they had done the usual round of the club and college smokers. Ideally a monologue should be the unique experience of the person who writes it, who, also ideally, should be the same person as the person who delivers it. In reality, scarcely anybody under the age of ninety is self-critical enough to do his own cutting and rewriting. Throughout the Footlight's Dramatic Society's modern history (we had better forget about its ancient history, which was spent, almost exclusively, screaming around in high heels and beads) the best monologues had been worked on by so many hands that they amounted to group creations, like the pyramids or the atomic bomb. I would have done better to apply my group motivation approach to the sketches as well. Instead, I confined it to the production numbers and the mute movement routines. Actually these took so long to rehearse that there was no real prospect of keeping the cast together for further periods of group script editing, desirable though that might have been. Getting the cast together at all proved far more difficult than I had expected.

Russell Davies was in nearly every sketch and musical number. Though the aim was to distribute the plum parts equally, in cold fact he was the best man available for almost everything. No other performer was disgruntled if I replaced him with Davies. Even more gratifyingly, Davies was not disgruntled, or did not seem so. Rehearsing continuously all day and far into the evening, however, he began finding it harder to get up in the morning. We had to send a taxi for him, and it got to the point that if the taxi driver failed to wake him up he would sleep on. It was typical of Davies that he could not bring himself to point out the connection between overwork and narcolepsy. I had underestimated his modesty, and he my insensitivity. The mêlée of an urgent group activity is not as good a time as it is cracked up to be for people to find out about each other. I needed his abilities, so I treated him as if his energies were infinite. They almost were. As for his powers of invention, they seemed to have no limit at all. In a big production number called 'The Fantastograd Russian Dance Ensemble', he played the victim in the Dance of the KGB Interrogators. I was very proud of the whole number and had a satisfactorily dictatorial time making everyone bounce around shouting 'Da!' with their arms folded, but there could be no doubt that the way Davies looked suitably grateful while being straightened out by the heavies – the way he made an actual *dance* of it – was a work of art which brought a lump to the throat. All that inventiveness being lavished on a single moment which would live, at best, in a few thousand memories! Having him to hand was so gratifying that I forgave him his strange habit of falling asleep in his chair and needing to be shaken awake every time the next number to be rehearsed required his presence – which was, in effect, every time.

Robert Buckman, later to be famous as the Pink Medicine

Man on television, was the youngest member of the cast and presented the opposite kind of trouble. He was so energetic that you had to hold a cushion over his face to slow him down. I could cope with him, however, by shouting at him loudly. This did not work with a strange young man calling himself Rusty Gates, who had done some very droll, off-trail sketches in club smokers but who now, having been cast for May Week, revealed an enhanced capacity for obliquity that made him hard to comprehend. He grew his hair in a page-boy cut. He addressed me as 'man'. When he arrived, always progressively later, he crossed one brothel creeper randomly over the other so that there was no telling which wall he would walk into. Either he would stop just short of the wall and address it as 'man' or he would make actual contact with it, but never at sufficient velocity to cause pain. Finally, when he was arriving so late that his eventual appearance was the same as not having turned up at all, he would walk in so slowly that each foot was in the air long enough to make you wonder if paralysis had struck. Even though he is now a highly respected theatre director, he won't mind my saying all this, because his abstracted manner of that time was part of the political position which he has since pursued undeviatingly and with great success. He was the first home-grown English hippy I had met. He regarded me, correctly, as hopelessly square. Certainly I was too square to realise the significance of the hand-rolled cigarettes he smoked in such quantities. In Strad's company I had had the odd puff myself without realising that there was a new religion on the way which would have devotees and would scorn dabblers. Rusty Gates was a hard man to rehearse. He had a manifest contempt for the material. In retrospect I was to decide that he was three-quarters of the way to being right. At the time I regarded him as a disciplinary problem. I condemned him to the worst role, that of the perambulating HP sauce bottle in a clever number called 'Cinquante Sept', written by two exceptionally tasteful young men called Ian Taylor and David Turner, who later on were to do show business a serious disservice by staying out of it. The song had everything. In later days, when I knew more about pacing a show, I would have made it the finale and poured on the effects. As it was, the song had almost the entire cast in it. Even Jonathan James-Moore, who couldn't sing at all, delivered a spoken announcement in the middle of the number. He just read out the label of an HP sauce bottle in a sepulchral voice. He would have brought the house down if it hadn't already been down. The house was already down because of Rusty Gates. His arms imprisoned inside the giant HP sauce bottle, from which only his feet and his closely framed face protruded, he was supposed to toddle out to centre stage and stay still. But a man who, under the influence of the dreaded weed, had an ideological objection to walking straight even in daylight, was unlikely to toe any given line while clad in a papier mâché HP sauce bottle. He wandered around the stage arbitrarily, leaning over at angles from which recovery should have been impossible. The rest of the cast moved smoothly aside to avoid him. It all looked quite meant if you were not the choreographer. I was, and got foolishly annoyed.

Looking back, I am annoyed in a different way, for having become obsessed with technical effects at the very moment when a new maturity of content, made possible by the waning influence of the Lord Chamberlain, was not only possible but called for. The truth was that the theatre, which I had approached, correctly, as a temple, had turned out to be, in the first instance, a box of tricks. Immediately I had become fascinated with the tricks, to the detriment of my sense of proportion. The things that could be done! Normally inhibited young people could be organised into kick-lines wearing funny hats. They could be slung on wires and flown around. They could be made to disappear through trapdoors. Things could be done with lights. Julie Covington looked so elegant singing in a spotlight that I spent hours arranging a slow fade to silhouette and forgot about the songs she was supposed to be singing. Luckily they held the audience, but she deserved better. The whole cast deserved better. I could do it now, but you can't go back into time except through memory, and even that form of transport is dangerous when the question turns on what might have been. At the time it seemed that I had nothing to reproach myself with. Quite the reverse. The show was greeted, if not hailed, as a success. Well, a half-success. It seemed to me that the Six Day War, which broke out at the same time, was a secondary occurrence. I was very pleased with myself and might have modelled my swagger on that of Moshe Dayan. Every night of the run I saw the show and gave notes, but spent little time in the day cutting or re-rehearsing. (In later years I would have rebuilt the show every afternoon until there was not a flat spot left in it.) The mysterious May Week that lasted a fortnight and took place in June was a mystery no longer. It was a time for youth to celebrate itself. I was a tiny bit past being a legitimate celebrant. That just made the feeling sweeter. While the exhausted cast slept the sleep of the just through the long morning, I would walk the gravelled paths of the backs, clutching the jewel of Pembroke's library, Aubrey Attwater's copy of the Leopardi edition of Petrarch. At ease on a bench, with Trinity's Wren Library in clear view and the river dotted with drifting clumps of girls, I would part the gilt-edged pages and imagine myself *Rotto dagli anni e dal cammino stanco*. Broken by the years and by the tired road. God help me, I fancied that what I had faced and conquered had been adversity, instead of just another self-set challenge, easily encompassed.

Marenko and the Americans should have been a healthy antidote. Accompanied by Girton girls who had been carefully chosen and gallantly presented with a bunch of carnations each, they loyally attended the revue but didn't pretend to be impressed by anything except the logistics of mounting such a huge venture when everyone involved was supposed to be studying. They, the Americans, were still studying every day, even though, for some of them, the last examinations were over. A sound mind needed a sound body, however, so in the afternoons they were to be found down in the meadow behind the Mill, benefitting immodestly from the sunlight. Marenko looked so magnificent with his shirt off that a Newnham girl, nowadays world famous as a romantic novelist, rode her bicycle straight into the Cam. For Marenko, exposing his torso to the sunlight was a quasi-sacred act which he called 'baking bod'. At lunch in Hall he would propose this Aztec-like ritual to the assembled company. 'Why don't we all saunter down to the Mill and bake bod?' Delmer Dynamo having copped out on the excuse that his new set of the Nonesuch Dickens needed its pages cut, we would trail down to the meadow and lie around. At one of those meetings — which would have been a bit *Kraft durch Freude* if not for the high quality of the laughter — the first Frisbee I had ever seen was produced. A large black plastic dish with its name, WHAM-O FRISBEE, applied in gold, inevitably it had been imported by Strad. It turned out, however, that all the Americans could make the thing perform. Strad could make it go about fifty yards and then hover like a black and gold halo over Marenko's head. Marenko favoured an underarm flick of the wrist which sent the enchanted disc zipping along about three inches above the ground for an improbable distance until, instead of crashing, it rose remarkably into the air, tipped to one side, and slotted into Strad's upstretched hand as if drawn there by a string. To my shame I went crazy with frustration at being unable to make the bloody thing fly straight. Moving my wrist forward as instructed, I merely delayed the disc's inexorable swing to the right. The accursed object moved to the right like Sir Oswald Mosley. It headed for the Cam like Hitler for the Rhine. Observant young ladies laughed from beneath the willows. When Marenko, like a languishing Discobolus, airily unleashed a fizzer, there were long sighs from the dappled shade. 'Blow it out your ass!' cried Delmer in the distance, appearing in slow stages from the direction of the Mill as he grappled intermittently with a prematurely opened deck-chair. Boatered, blazered and monocled, he sat in full Wodehousian splendour, sending up puffs of smoke from his cigar while his pipe-clayed white shoes acquired grass stains that looked as if they had been brushed on by Monet. When I fluked a straight throw he applauded like a member of the MCC. 'Oh, well propelled, old fruit! Well *chucked*!' The ten-day idyll seemed to last a year. There was the Footlights tour to prepare for. The details must have taken at least a week. Probably it was less than a week, then, that I basked in that perfect light. My whole soul baked bod. At the lawn parties I basked in glory while adroitly dodging Consuela. For someone of my temperament, going over the top is a necessary step towards coming to terms. Those were the days when I gave way to the dementia of celebrity. Critics who think I am out of control now should have seen me then.

And then it was over. Though the tour was no disaster, it was no triumph either. The small-cast show with one eye on London, the kind of show I hadn't wanted, was the kind of show the provincial audiences *had* wanted. It meant nothing to them that the large-cast revue gave the less talented an equal opportunity to share the stage with the more talented. The audience wanted an unequal opportunity to laugh and admire. Sketches which had held the stage in Cambridge ran to comparative silence in Nottingham. They didn't exactly die the death, but they contributed nothing except running time. Standing in the back of the auditorium and wondering how to patch things up sufficiently well to keep the show on the road and some of the cast from suicide, I became a worried man again. At the end of the long vacation I was due to take an abridged version of the show to the Edinburgh Fringe. At that juncture I would have a chance to re-cast along less egalitarian lines. It would be an act of mercy. Performers out of their depth drown. Though they do it in air instead of water, you can see them struggle. Beginning at last to take in, at the level of experience, the lesson which I should have been able to learn at the level of theory, I packed my carry-all and headed for Venice. Françoise was studying there again and as usual she would make all the arrangements, but this time I was not entirely a free loader. In Venice there was to be a major exhibition of Canaletto, Guardi and the rest of the view painters – the *Vedutisti*. To Nicholas Tomalin I had proposed that I should cover this event in a piece for the *New Statesman*. He had agreed. It was a commission. The piece would be paid for. All I had to do was write it.

I wrote it with suspicious ease. Françoise and Venice were at their most beautiful. The wine at Trattoria al Vagon was cheap and plentiful. When I arrived at the exhibition I felt happy and confident. The paintings of Canaletto looked happy and confident. The paintings of his nephew, Bellotto, looked less happy and less confident. Canaletto was light blue but Bellotto was dark green. Guardi was dark blue with too much pink. He was neither happy nor confident, Guardi. You could tell just by looking. I am afraid that my analysis of this entire, quite important movement in Italian painting was all on an elementary, not to say infantile, level. With a set length of only fifteen hundred words in which to express my opinions, a paucity of information was an advantage. As far as I can remember – it wasn't far even at the time – I wrote the piece in a matter of hours. Looked at again today, it has a speciously authoritative bravura which I can only envy. Nowadays a piece the same length, on any subject, would take me at least a week. My brain has grown sclerotic, my wind short, and with experience I have become more fearful instead of less, but the main reason for being slower to get things done now is that I know more about them. Possessing more information than will fit easily into the space, I must sweat at the task of choosing what to leave out, and of making what I put in imply the rest. Though often accused of putting everything I have in the shop window, it is no longer among my vices. In the days when I did, I wrote like lightning. At the bar at the foot of the Rialto, Françoise read the finished piece through, suggested a few corrections, and looked, I thought, slightly ashamed, as if she had taken up with a confidence man – which, at that time, was exactly what I was. Not only was I out of my depth, I was staging an aquacade instead of calling for help. She particularly deplored, I suspect, my knack of suggesting that what I was saying was only the tenth of the iceberg that showed above the water. She was well aware that what showed was all there was: the tip of an iceberg floating on a raft. Dead on cue, seven gondolas lashed side by side emerged from under the bridge. Full of Americans, they rode low in the water while the massed gondoliers provided choral accompaniment to a plump middle-aged tenor who stood in the prow of the central gondola facing backwards. His mouth opening wide enough to swallow a melon, he uncoiled the high wailing melodic line of a love song. He was a professional and so was I. You have to start somewhere, and you can't do so without taking the risk that you might one day end up somewhere else than the place you hoped to reach. A scholar takes a job. A writer takes a chance. Carefully I explained this to Françoise over several carafes of wine paid for by her. Arriving at the post office, where with her help I planned to send the piece off to London by registered mail, I was feeling pretty dauntless. During the long process of acquiring the right stamps, stickers, sealing wax and bits of string I gradually sobered up, until by the time the parcel was ready for acceptance I had qualms. What if it got rejected? Why, indeed, should it be accepted? Three days ago I had scarcely known the *Vedutisti* from the Watusi, Canaletto from a can-opener, Guardi from a mudguard. All I had ever done was look at the pictures. That, basically, Françoise assured me, was all that anyone had ever done. She was a model of strength as I sat there sobbing. The Italian post offices were temples of bureaucracy in those days, sufficient all by themselves to cause a breakdown in civil order. Constantly mutating meaningless regulations ensured that your parcel, when you finally got to the head of the queue, would never be accepted the first, second or third time. Even when you had the right gauge of brown paper, thickness of string and redness of sealing wax, unless you timed your run for the end of the day they would have introduced some new rule about writing the address four times or tying the thing up with a pink ribbon. Coping, Françoise grew cooler as I grew angrier. Finally, when I was down on the floor on my knees, pounding my fist into the tiles, she was smiling seraphically at some official in a cap. He was the one who said there was no problem; of course we shall accept your parcel; he couldn't understand how the difficulty had arisen; was the *signorina*'s friend perhaps the victim of some unfortunate mental disease?

In debt to my college and with a long, long vacation ahead before the next grant cheque came through, I was dependent on Françoise for the necessities of life. This drain on her resources left nothing over for travel, so we were obliged to hitch-hike. In her two-piece raw silk suit and high heeled sandals, Françoise must have been the best dressed hitch-hiker since Lola Montes. On the approach roads to the *autostrada*, Italian male drivers of expensive sports cars were eager to break the law and stop, especially if they thought she was alone. I encouraged this misapprehension by hiding myself behind a bush. If there was no bush available I would conceal myself in the nearest depression, feeling pretty depressed myself. In shallow holes lined with dried mud I would cower cursing. When I heard the shriek of brakes I would dustily emerge and shamble forward. Some of the drivers looked a bit pissed off but very few of them tried to cancel the deal. A guy with an Alfa Romeo Giulia *ti* got us to Bologna in no time. The next bit was the hard part. The recently completed stretch of *autostrada* down from Bologna through the mountains towards Florence had instantly established itself as one of the most frightening experiences in modern Europe. There were three lanes each way. None of them was a slow lane. Articulated trucks with two trailers in tandem swung out from lane to lane without warning just as you were trying to overtake them. The chance of getting cut in half was very high, even if you had a great big car with plenty of hot lights to flash in the mirrors of the trucks. The car that picked us up was a little Fiat Berlinetta whose driver thought he was Eugenio Castellotti, the late lamented Mille Miglia ace revered in Italy for the flair he had shown in driving at 150 miles per hour on the footpath when the road was full of spectators. When a truck pulled out, our boy would try to duck inside, ignoring the possibility that the truck might try to go back to where it had come from, thereby crushing us against the wall of a tunnel or propelling us a thousand feet down into a rocky gorge. All this was happening at about ninety. The hard shoulders of the road were littered with wrecks. Particularly affecting was a Lancia saloon divided into two widely separated pieces. Françoise had insisted on climbing into the back seat with me. Our driver kept turning around to compliment her on the perfection of her Italian and insert his nose into her cleavage. Meanwhile I attempted to draw his attention to the imminent death looming in front. It was a nice exercise in relative time. We got to Florence in a few hours, having aged ten years.

This time Florence was only a staging post. After a night at the Antica Cervia I humped our two bags out to the *autostrada* and we hitched south to Rome. The driver was a gentleman who had a kind word for my Italian as well as Françoise's. That did me the world of good. I forget what make the car was, but in a quiet way of business it was a road-eater. It wasn't an Alfa or I would have remembered. Though the Alfas were fast, they floated sideways on their suspension and had to be steered all the time. This car ran like a train. Probably it was the big Fiat, the one with four headlights. The driver was stopping in Arezzo for a couple of hours. He offered to take us on if we cared to wait. We visited the Piero della Francesca frescoes. I'm glad I saw them then. Later on they were overcleaned and almost ruined. At that time they were as much as I could take in at one sitting – or, rather, standing. I just stood there, with that unmistakable feeling of being returned to the source, of starting again. A clear outline filled in with colour will always be my ideal. Admiring the cinquecento for its intellectual daring, neverthe-less I am a quattrocento man at heart. I like that odour of the workshop; of wood shavings and glue. Behind it, of course, is the odour of the classroom; of paint on the finger. I remembered how I had once decorated the margins of my schoolbooks, and wondered if, had I been born four hundred years earlier, I would have decorated churches. It would have been a perfectly satisfactory occupation, apart from the occasional heresy hunt and visitation of plague.

Rome hove into view and there was a whole new Renais-sance to contend with. This was where even the Florentines came to make it big. The Vatican was their Hollywood. All the paintings were in wide-screen processes. There was nothing smaller than Cinemascope. The candle smoke of centuries having not yet been expunged from the Sistine ceiling, it was up there like a brown cloud, but what you saw stirring in the murk was enough to keep you going, and Christ came hulking out of the Last Judgment like a line-backer unexpectedly carrying the ball. With Françoise's help I was picking my way through Michelangelo's sonnets. I had all the makings of a Michelangelo bore. It was Raphael, however, who did the permanent damage. By being so much more transparent than his paintings in oils, the wide-screen frescoes in the 'Stanze' convinced me that there is a desirable lightness in art which must be planned for so that it is not perfected away: refinement, beyond a certain point, kills itself. That, or something like that, I wrote in my ever-ready journal. Somewhere off the Via del Corso, Françoise had found a room which had once been the bottom half of another room twice as high. Using that as a base, we went out on art orgies. We had a Bernini binge. I fell for him where Daphne flees from Apollo, in the Galleria Borghese. Until then I had been under the impression that I hated the Baroque. By the time we were relaxing over an iced coffee at an open air café in the Piazza Navona, I was Baroque-berserk. The horse's head in the central fountain I thought the wittiest thing I had ever seen: light, fluent, poised, graceful, alert with the accepted tragedy of passing things. Anticipating the rejection of my piece about the Venetians, I was planning a second assault on the *New Statesman* by way of an uncommissioned Italian diary. I had already done a short piece about the *autostrada* down from Bologna. Now I added a thing or two about Bernini. This time I made strategic use of a semblance of honesty, admitting that I hadn't thought much of him before. (The admission that I hadn't known much of him before might have unsettled the reader.) This affectation of candour struck me as quite touching. It reminded me of a poignant moment, much earlier in my career, when I had shyly put my hand up to confess that it was I who had broken wind. At that stage in Italy's continuing history of inflation, coins of small denomination were made of an alloy so light that they almost floated. When we threw our coins into the Trevi fountain they took a long time to flutter to the bottom. I wrote a poem about it. Françoise couldn't complain that I wasn't responding to the country she loved. I responded to everything about it, with an intensity that left Shelley himself sounding as if he had gone to Disneyland instead. What she *might* legitimately have complained about was that the huge two-volume American biography of Shelley which I had humped all the way down there with me remained unopened. I had my answer ready. To know how Shelley had been overwhelmed, *I* had to be overwhelmed. Why don't we ask the waiter to just leave the whole bottle of Cinzano here?

After Rome it was Naples, where we set a new all-comers record for not getting robbed. We had nothing to steal so it was easy. Had we possessed anything more valuable than my two-volume biography of Shelley it would undoubtedly have been whipped. This was the town in which, after the Italian surrender but before the end of the war, a fully laden Liberty ship had been stolen, and the skills learned then had been inherited as an art. In a sensationally hot late morning we were sitting at an open air table in front of a café. The open air tables were divided from the street by a line of bushes in concrete tubs. Françoise, whose task in Naples was to visit the museum that had been made of Croce's house, was mugging up on the catalogue. I was busy trying to unknot the syntax of a Michelangelo sonnet. Neither of us was especially delighted when we were joined unasked by Brian C. Adams and his newly acquired wife. They had driven down all the way from Cambridge in order to break into our idyll. What they didn't realise, as they sat there, was that the Neapolitans were breaking into their car. It was parked in plain sight of us all, about ten yards away on the other side of the bushes. All we could see, though, was the top half of the car, which proved not to be enough. Our visitors having turned out to be unexpectedly charming in this alien context, they left us with a cheery wave which was shortly succeeded by a squeal from her and a low, unbelieving moan from him. It could be deduced that the thieves must have crawled along the side of the car, forced the lock, and hooked out the cameras, wallets and passports. Harder to figure out was how they had removed all four of the car's wheels without making any noise. The car was supported on neat piles of bricks, like an art exhibit. Françoise was at her most diplomatic talking to the *Polizia Stradale*. Gallant in their blue jodhpur suits and white Sam Browne belts, they were clearly prepared to give our friends a motorcycle escort in any direction, as long as Françoise came too. Alas, there could be no question of restitution for lost property. Yes, they realised that to the outside observer it might seem remarkable how such a thing could occur in full view of everyone in the street, including the traffic policeman. That sort of thing happened. They forgot to add that in Naples it happened every ten minutes, and had been happening since the famous day in 1943 when the American ship went missing from the harbour. Having returned to our table while these fruitless negotiations went on, I was writing in my notebook. My *New Statesman* Italian diary had acquired another episode.

Relishing the freedom of the unencumbered, after a ritual visit to Pompeii – the heat was so great that I felt I had once shared in its demise – we hitched all the way back up the boot to Florence, where we paused to count our money and lick our wounds. All of the former had belonged to Françoise and was now gone. All of the latter belonged to me. She still looked like a *haute couture* mannequin. I was showing the effects of several weeks of diving into ditches every time we heard a powerful car in the distance. When we checked into the Antica Cervia I was ready to quit.

The staff of life was waiting for me. Tightly rolled up in plain brown paper, like the baton of a Field Marshal in a people's army, were two copies of the *New Statesman* featuring my article on the Venetian view painters. It was the leading piece in the arts section at the back of the magazine. It covered one and a half pages. My name was in the contributors' list on the front cover. I drew Françoise's attention to these points before settling down to read the piece several hundred times. Even then, in the middle of being carried away, I reminded myself of myself: of how, when my first short book review had come out in the *Sydney Morning Herald*, I had bought ten copies of the paper so that there would be one left over for posterity if I were to suffer nine fatal accidents. Before that, there had been my first poem in *honi soit*; and before that, the first thing I ever published – a contribution to the Sydney Technical High School *Journal* which I had based loosely on a piece in an old war-time issue of *Lilliput*, borrowing only the plot, the names of the characters, the descriptive prose and the dialogue. If, in later years, I had become more capable of making up my own words, I had become no more capable of staying calm when I saw them in print. Debarred by nature from becoming blasé, the best I could manage was an affected air of detachment, and even that fell apart at a moment like this, when an important new step had been taken. I saw, stretching ahead, the dazzling prospect of a professional career as a freelance journalist. After telling Françoise all about it until she fell asleep, I sat up all night completing my Italian diary piece in long-hand. Next morning I mailed it to the *New Statesman*. A whole issue would have to go by without me in it, but there was just a chance that I might catch the one after that.

The article safely on its way to London by plane, I followed it by road. Françoise was due to live in Cambridge during the next academic year, as a don in New Hall. This was a major development which would entail, on my part, some large-scale personal stock-taking. For now, until term started, she would be staying in Florence. I, on the other hand, had to get back to London to earn a much-needed week's wages on *Expresso Drongo* before I went back up to Cambridge to begin rehearsing the Footlights late-night revue for the Edinburgh Fringe. Richard Harris, known as the other Richard Harris to distinguish him from the then up-and-coming film star, was an architecture student and Footlights actor-singer who was heading home from Florence at that very time so as to submit himself to my dictatorial discipline. He had a large heart to go with his small car – a glorified Mini that had a vertical radiator grille effect stuck on the front so it could be called a Wolseley. With him and his stuff in the car there wasn't really any room for me and mine, but I soon talked him out of any qualms. After two solid days of filling in forms at the bank, the *New Statesman* cheque had been turned into Italian money. All of this I gave to Françoise as part payment of my debt, before borrowing it all back again to pay for my share of the petrol. I also generously offered to navigate. What I couldn't do was share the driving, because I had never learned to drive. This fact became especially regrettable by the time we were winding up towards Bologna through the same hideous stretch of *autostrada* on which Françoise and I had already faced death coming down the other way. It was getting dark and Richard was tired. When it became evident that we would soon be cut in half by a road train if we kept on, he pulled into a lay-by and we sacked out in the open. If this sounds only mildly adventurous, it is because I have not sufficiently evoked the scene. There was only just enough flat ground to sleep on. A cliff led down to a tumbling river far below. The edge of the cliff had been inaccurately used as a latrine by many a desperate driver. Avoiding all that, we were obliged to lay down our heads within a few feet of the hard shoulder. The wheels of the passing trucks were near enough for us to hear them fizz angrily over the roar of the diesels. On the crappy edge of the precipice, with our naked heads presented towards the sizzling wheels of the juggernauts, we stared straight up and pretended to sleep under the stars, or under where the stars had been before the clouds had covered them. When rain started falling out of the clouds, we retired to the car and tried to sleep sitting up. The result next morning was that we couldn't stand.

Things got better during the day. We stopped in Geneva and I took a dip in the lake, defying a sign that said it was forbidden. I drew a small crowd of curious people. Richard was curious about their curiosity and asked them why they found me so fascinating. A small girl with pigtails and steel-rimmed glasses said that the last man who had gone swimming in the lake was already dying when he climbed out. His skin had turned bright pink, she said, with blisters that dripped pus. Apparently the lake was so polluted that there were no bacteria left in it. Nothing was alive in there. Apart from the fact that she said all this in French, she looked and sounded exactly like one of those terrible girls in Hitchcock movies who point out unpleasant truths. Until we lunched next day in Besançon, I spent the whole time taking my pulse and checking the colour of my tongue in the rear-view mirror. The restaurant wouldn't serve us a half carafe of wine, so I had to drink a whole carafe, because my companion was driving. I felt better after that, and slept most of the way to the Channel ferry. On the ferry I once again had two shares of drinking to cope with. The next thing I saw was London. Either we had got there in twenty minutes at an average speed of 600 mph, or else I had slept the hard-earned sleep of the navigator. Young Richard showed scarcely a sign of his ordeal. Already a gap was showing up between me and those only a few years younger. There were physical things they could do that I couldn't. For instance, some of them, after having had a certain amount to drink, could walk quite a long way before bumping into a wall. I couldn't. Something would have to be done about that sooner or later. Perhaps I could get the walls moved further away.

15

Hit of the Fringe

IN THE WEEK before rehearsals for the Edinburgh Fringe began, I was scheduled to work, for the usual small but significant financial reward, as Dave Dalziel's assistant in the Sisyphean task of keeping Keith Visconti's film from being cancelled. I needed the cash. The *New Statesman* printed my Italian diary, but the cheque vanished into a party. *Expresso Drongo* was now well into its second year of shooting. On behalf of its director, Dalziel had applied for yet another extension to the original grant so that the film's budget could be expanded to meet its burgeoning projected costs. In Hollywood terms, the overruns had taken off. As head of the production board's operational unit, Dalziel had a persuasive voice in the allocation of funds, but finally it was the board that decided. As chairman of the board, Sir Michael Balcon told Dalziel, in the friendliest possible way, that the film had better enter its post-production phase fairly soon, or else it would have to be shut down – and, by implication, Dave's office along with it. Dalziel, in his capacity as Balcon's protégé, felt a crushing sense of obligation on top of his already burdensome professional commitment to finishing what he had started. He was a worried man. At work he maintained his usual cool air. At home he would stare into space. This was made hard to do by the continuing presence of half a dozen Nigerian ex-government officials in exile, but he managed it. In these worrying times for him and Cathleen, I think I helped by eating any scraps of food that might otherwise have been left lying around. My old friend Robin having unaccountably declined to take me in, I was sleeping in the Dalziels' loft. It wasn't a very big loft but my needs were simple. Cathleen was probably more pleased than she looked when I sat up drinking with her husband late at night. It could have made all the difference to his morale. He was a man under threat. He needed someone to confide in. The main thing he had to confide was his dawning suspicion that Keith Visconti was insane. 'He's a few bricks short of a load,' said Dalziel abstractedly. It was the first time I had heard this expression, which now appears in dictionaries of Australian slang. Either Dalziel made it up, or he got it from Bruce Jennings, and he made it up. From his suite at Claridge's, Jennings would arrive by Rolls-Royce to help soothe Dalziel's anguish with a jeroboam of Krug. They would spark each other off. I was content to be an auditor. 'Of course you could always have Keith *killed*,' Jennings would suggest. 'The problem would be disposing of the body. Physical contact *not* advisable.'

In consequence of all the dire warnings, a new urgency could be felt on the set of *Expresso Drongo*. A tricky scene was being shot in which Nelia, in the role of the woman seated at the table in the coffee shop, rises from the table and crosses to the window in order to check up on whether another woman, perceived in the distance, is the Other Woman. In the finished film Nelia would be playing the role of the Other Woman as well. For now, she was still the woman at the table. So that Nelia might adopt the right eyeline when she reached the window, I filled in for the Other Woman. Keith Visconti made me stand the right distance away and then rehearsed Nelia in the tricky transition from the table to the window. The camera would be tracking with her, which involved all sorts of problems in focusing and lighting. Just solving these would have been finicky enough. Keith made things more complicated by deciding that Nelia's eyeline was not at the right height. I was a touch too tall. After Keith called 'Action!' I would have to crouch slowly so that Nelia would be looking at the right place. The first time I crouched too late, so that Nelia's eyes slipped downward. The second time I crouched too far, so that it seemed as if she were looking, Keith said, at a dog. The twelfth time Nelia and I both got it right but a lamp blew out. It went on like that for days, with Keith always finding another reason for calling 'cut'. Dalziel spent a lot of time with one hand over his eyes. Nelia wasn't bothered. Her capacity for not being bothered, I had by now decided, had less to do with inner serenity than I had once thought. Nor could it be put down to avarice. Although it was true that as long as filming lasted she had employment, what really enabled Nelia to retain her equanimity in conditions of stress was her almost complete lack of a brain. Either that organ had been surgically removed, or it had been cut off from all information. She was a monster. By the third day – the big day when I, doubling for the Other Woman, had to turn and walk away – I could feel Nelia's eyes on my spine as if they belonged to Catherine Deneuve in Polanski's *Repulsion*, currently packing them in at the Academy. Dalziel still strove to convince himself that *Expresso Drongo*, if it ever got finished, would have the same effect. He was whistling in the dark. You could tell he knew it. Deep down, where it counted, he was on the rack.

Dalziel would take Keith aside for urgent talks but found it hard to shout into his face. Keith had still not taken a bath. He was even less nice to be near than he had been a year before. 'You can't stand over that guy without a ladder,' said Dalziel. 'And his breath! It smells like a dead bear's bum.' We were sitting in the Jaguar, which had been taking us back to Brixton until something went wrong again in the transmission. Waiting for the RAC man in the middle of Knightsbridge, we watched the girls go by, or rather I did. Dalziel, the married man, had either lost something of his former keen interest or thought fit to conceal it. Perhaps already feeling the weight of gravity myself, I found a certain melancholy invading my fond regard, like smoke drifting into a beam of light. The female figure was at its slightest since the 1920s. Some of the girls had white lips to match their high lacquered boots. Hairstyles were like tight black helmets. A challenging length of leg still showed between boot-tops and mini hemlines, but otherwise the feminine element had become hard to find. On the most obviously fashionable women, creations carried out in Piet Mondriaan plastic had been imposed, drawing their bodies up into an unyielding grid. The sense of confinement was palpable, or would have been if you were allowed to touch it. These flattenings and polishings, this kit of structures, made beauty less unbearable to look at, but to be thus rescued from the desperation of longing was to be made lingeringly sad.

Girls in uniform. There was a regimentation to this vaunted spontaneity which made 'trend' a more descriptive word than it was meant to be: a viscous, inexorable flow in one direction. The generic word 'pop' made me feel old before my time. It sounded like the unavoidable fate of a bubble. But still there, at the centre of the largely manufactured pop era, was popular music, and that was too abundant to stifle, too witty to ignore. With doom staring him in the face, Dalziel threw a tumultuous Thursday night party at the house in Brixton. The Animals shouted from the loudspeakers. The Nigerians danced. All the Australian expatriates were there. Johnny Pitts, the rebel guitarist of the Downtown Push, for a moment resurrected Leadbelly from the distant past, before forgetting the words and falling sideways. Dibbs Buckley drew a mural in the loft. Bruce Jennings arrived with his next wife. He hadn't married her yet, but he was already calling her by his last wife's first name: a sure sign, with him, of impending nuptials. Dandyishly clad, in show-stopping form, he spoke as if he were still on his first drink. 'I did *indeed* peruse your *obiter dicta* on the subject of the Venetian painters, young Clive,' he pronounced with a vulpine leer, 'and I rather got the impression that you had known them *personally*. One of the two of Canaletto's working drawings are in my possession. There is a drawing of a virile head which at one time led me to suspect that the great man had spent some time in Australia. *Now*, of course, I *realise*. He caught your eyes exactly. *Not an easy task*.' In fact he was on his last legs, but there was no guessing until he fell, and the only way you could tell that he was falling was if you knew he didn't dance. He went down with arms flailing, taking his next wife with him. Since everyone else was dancing in roughly the same manner, nobody realised Jennings had fainted. His next wife, pinned under him, cried for help but was not heard. In the clear space around Keith Visconti, I danced with Nelia. I had gone off her, yet there was no denying her gentle beauty, so spiritual-looking if you did not know her. She smiled at me fixedly, no doubt thinking of John Newcombe.

Next afternoon at the NFT there was a BFI production board screening for the board members and journalists. This was an important day in the career of Dave Dalziel. All the short films on which he had given technical advice, and for which the BFI had provided the facilities, were to be screened one after the other in a programme which he had carefully planned so that a finished fifteen minutes of the Keith Visconti film would be next to last, as a quiet interlude before the final, powerfully rhythmic *San Francisco*, a ten-minute documentary montage to the music of an unknown pop group strangely calling itself Pink Floyd. In the crucial spot just before *Expresso Drongo*, Dalziel had carefully placed a short puzzle picture which would ensure that a simple story of a waiter bringing a woman a cup of coffee would come as a welcome relief. The puzzle picture had been directed by the well-known experimental writer J. D. Sullivan, who committed suicide a few years later, some said because of too much competition from other experimental writers. At the time we are talking about, J. D. Sullivan still had the only game in town. His Arts Council grant for experimental writing had been renewed year after year while he turned out a succession of defiantly unreadable experimental books. Years before John Fowles ever thought of it, J. D. Sullivan had written a novel with alternative endings. He had also written a novel whose chapters came loosely arranged in a box, so that you could re-arrange them in any order you pleased, or, some cynics had suggested, so that you could throw away the ones you didn't like. He had published a novel with a hole through the middle so that you could read the last page while you were reading the first. There was nothing experimental that J. D. Sullivan had not done as a writer. Now he wanted to be an experimental film-maker. I had been in on the meeting at which he had first expounded the idea of his film to Dalziel. It had taken place in a Japanese restaurant in Soho. Sullivan, a big man with a bull neck, had explained why Shakespeare was really no good as a playwright. 'People don't talk like that, do they?' he had asked, stabbing a piece of raw fish with his chopstick. '*Do* they?' he had asked again, looking at me. I had had to admit that they didn't. J. D. Sullivan was well organised. Everything Dave taught him, he learned immediately. The film got made. A heavily compact assemblage of cross-cut imagery, so intricately elliptical that it made your brain ache like a sore foot, it had authority: it looked *meant* in its meaninglessness. You could tell, when the screen filled with rotting flesh, that bourgeois society was being somehow criticised. When a building collapsed, it was a fair inference that a rotten social system had been rumbled. J. D. Sullivan's film was a testament. It was dissatisfied. It made *you* dissatisfied. Above all, it made you dissatisfied that it went on so long. Though short, it lasted for ever. Even *Expresso Drongo* would seem sprightly by comparison. A nice sweet dose of Nelia's impassive face would be just what the doctor ordered.

At the screening, J. D. Sullivan's film was barely half over before it became obvious that the packed audience was inwardly begging for relief. They were squirming under the impact of J. D. Sullivan's pitiless symbolism. 'We'll be starting with the shot where Nelia's sitting there with her legs crossed and her mouth slightly open in anticipation,' whispered Dalziel loudly. 'She looks like she's thinking about the pork sword. Ought to go down well.' A female journalist seated in front of us turned round in what I guessed was outrage. Dalziel didn't notice. He was a tense man. A lot depended on the extract from *Expresso Drongo* being well enough received to warrant further financing. Otherwise the single most expensive project the BFI had ever backed would be remembered only as a dead albatross slung around Dalziel's neck. There was cause for hope, however, as the end titles of J. D. Sullivan's film came up, superimposed over a close-up of a calf being born. Polite applause from the audience was punctuated by the occasional muffled cry of 'Thank God'.

For the lovely face of Nelia, that mystery so haunting until solved, a place had thus been prepared, in the audience's collective mind, as yearningly welcoming as the wall of a monk's cell primed with fresh plaster so that Fra Angelico might draw an angel. What we saw next, however, were the words A MAN ALONE, *un film de* Alain le Sands. Dalziel's seat snapped back. He would have been off and running to the projection box if I hadn't stopped him. Caution was the right reaction. If Dalziel had reached the projection box he would have strangled Alain le Sands and thus attained the wrong kind of fame, as a murderer, although it would have been the right thing to do. Alain le Sands was in there, of course. Craning back awkwardly over our shoulders, we could see his wildly grinning face looking out through one of the observation ports. What we suspected at the time later proved to be untrue: le Sands had not held a gun to the projectionist's head. Le Sands had merely turned up during the screening with his can of film under his arm and convinced the projectionist that there had been a last minute addition to the schedule. The projectionist, like many in his trade, had been too blind to notice that le Sands had the eyes and teeth of a fanatic. *A Man Alone* unspooled its familiar, incompetently captured obsessions. It turned out, though, that le Sands had acquired a hitherto unprecedented sense of proportion. His film was no longer a fragment of a feature. It was now a complete short film, with an ending to go after its beginning. There was a last scene. It was set in Soho. There was a doorway. From it emerged Dave Dalziel and myself. A rear view of Alain le Sands lurched towards us. His dialogue was roughly as it had been on the day, but new words had been dubbed over Dalziel's moving mouth. 'Your film is too challenging, Mr le Sands,' Dalziel seemed to say, 'too dangerous to our establishment values. It must be suppressed.' We got into the car and sat there while Alain le Sands lectured us through the windshield. A shot from another angle, obviously secured at another time and with a different car, enabled the lecture to last longer. 'The true creator thrives on frustration,' orated le Sands. 'You and your cohorts can no more stop this new upsurge of . . . than . . . thus . . . '

Surprisingly few among the audience laughed aloud while *A Man Alone* was on the screen, but everyone was well prepared to pick nits by the time the extract from *Expresso*

Drongo came on. The effect was not as planned. Though Nelia looked suitably serene, gratitude for tranquillity was not the prevailing emotion. There was widespread, vocal disbelief at how long it took to be served a cup of coffee. The exquisite touch of the shooting and editing provoked no applause. *San Francisco* saved the day for the screening as a whole, but *Expresso Drongo*, one felt, had run out of its borrowed time. As the crowd dispersed, Dalziel received many congratulations from board members and critics. There was no word of praise for Keith Visconti. Even Alain le Sands was held to have more talent. 'You're on to something with le Sands,' said one film critic from behind the dark glasses he was famous for never taking off. 'I like the way his camera work always *declares* itself. Like to do a piece on him. Give you a bell.' Dalziel nodded glumly. 'That coffee commercial,' said Sir Michael Balcon, 'is the only really big mistake you've made, David.' Dalziel was downcast. As always there was his lovely car to distract him. This time the Jaguar started at the first turn of the key. We had almost reached home before the engine fell out on to the road. Not even the sudden, total loss of power and the shriek of scraping metal from under the car made it easy to believe, so we got out to check up. This was lucky, because the fire started with a thump. A puff-ball of flame filled the front seats where we would have been sitting. 'The guy who sold it to me had great timing,' said Dalziel thoughtfully. 'I only just finished paying for it.' A woman in a nearby house had already rung the police. She came running out with a bucket of water. Dalziel waved her back, telling her it would only help the burning oil to spread. Watching his strength in adversity, I wondered if I had what it took to succeed in the theatre. For a writer to stay true to his gift, provided he has one, is not as hard as writers are fond of making out. To keep going in any of the collaborating arts requires steadfastness. Misfortunes sooner or later must occur. I caught the train back to Cambridge in a pensive mood.

Luckily, when I got there, the task of putting the Edinburgh Fringe Footlights revue together was so pressing that there was not time to brood. Compressing the two-hour May Week spectacular into a one-hour intimate late-night revue, I had every excuse to trim the cast. I might have done this more gracefully, but to lighten the ship was certainly the right approach. As I remember it, the number of on-stage participants went down from about sixty to about six. New opening and closing numbers were written. The Fantastograd Russian Dance Ensemble number was cut in half, making it twice as funny. Julie Covington was unavailable for Edinburgh that year, but Homerton had produced yet another lovely singer called Maggie Henderson, and she was enrolled to sing the two best of the spotlight songs which Pete Atkin and I were continuing to turn out with a great show of dedication on my part, and real dedication on his. Actually, when I look back on it, I realise that I was then understating, rather than overstating, the amount of work we were all putting into every number. I got very little sleep. There was no need, although I behaved as if there were, to purse my lips and make tired noises. My tired eyes must have conveyed the message. My wisdom teeth were the only part of my body that physically collapsed. They started to ache and there was no time to fix them. Finally, in the Footlights clubroom, with the whole cast singing and dancing its way through the intricacies of the closing number, the moment came when I had to go to hospital or pass out with pain. The orthodontist at Addenbrooke's hospital looked into my mouth and said, 'How long is it since you've seen a dentist?' I told him. He nodded. 'We'll get the wisdom teeth out straight away. They're all impacted. But you've got plenty of other things wrong that you'd better have seen to fairly soon. Fact is, it's a while since I've seen anything like this. I'd like to get some photographs of your mouth for a paper I'm doing. With your permission of course.' I signalled my compliance, unable to speak because by that time he had my mouth propped open with a metal jack. The wisdom teeth were cut out under general anaesthetic and I was back at work next day with enough stitches in my rear gums to make it feel as if I were half-way through swallowing a rattan mat. On a diet of antibiotics, Dexedrine and creamed potatoes, I finished rehearsals and we headed north in a fleet of cars. Once again I was Richard Harris's passenger. While he drove all the way to Edinburgh I sat hanging in my seat belt, delirious. In a day made dark by rain, huge illuminated signs said THE NORTH. I dreamed my primal dream of inadequacy, the one in which I am trapped with no pants on up a tree in a playground of the girls' high school. They pretend not to notice me. Many hundreds of times I have woken up sweating from this dream, without ever being able to decide which kind of fear it is meant to embody, the fear of being humiliated or the fear of being ignored.

In Edinburgh the latter fear receded, temporarily if not permanently. The Footlights late night revue was the hit show of the Fringe. This was not as remarkable an occurrence as I was later able to make it sound. There were hundreds of events on the Fringe. Most of them were starting from zero and not likely to get even as far as square one. The universities were able to mount a concerted effort, and of the universities Cambridge was the one with the glowing theatrical tradition, so the audience came anyway. And of the various plays and shows put on by Cambridge, the Footlights was the one with the internationally resonant name. The theatrical correspondent of *Die Zeit* had us on his must-see list. In Lauriston Hall, the best venue on the Fringe, we were the last show of the night for an audience that had spent the early evening being less than thrilled by the official production of *The Rake's Progress* in the Assembly Hall. Sold out for every night of the run before we even opened, we couldn't lose. It is nice to be able to report in all objectivity, however, that the show was pretty good. If it was running tonight and had my name in the programme, I would still be proud of its precision, energy and sheer glamour, although some of the material would look more out of date than the flared trousers, zipped boots and velvet jackets that adorned the male members of the cast. Most of these items of clothing have since come back into fashion, if only as parody. Much of the apolitical, would-be surrealist verbal humour, however, would now seem irredeemably passé. Striving to separate itself from previously successful styles, it sounded like all of them without attaining any lasting originality. In the technical sense, it was reactionary. The writing was attempting *not* to do things – always a choking brief. It was trying not to sound like the Goons, like *Beyond the Fringe*, like *Cambridge Circus*, like ten other things. Almost the only area left open was television parody.

My own best monologue, delivered by Jonathan James-Moore far more funnily than I could have done, was a lampoon of one of those BBC winter sports commentators who wore white sweaters and beanies and told you nothing useful. (Nowadays they wear parti-coloured Goretex anoraks and tell you nothing useful: they have gone down-market without uprating the info.) This was my first fully effective monologue from end to end. I had kept cutting it and sharpening it up until there wasn't a line in it that didn't work. Having a thousand people a night laughing as one at every gag was a great pleasure, and the editorial rigour I developed in this way was to stand me in good stead in future years. If I hadn't written those monologues, and especially that one, I would never have known how to write a thousand-word column with a cumulative effect. But when you took the thing apart, it was standard stuff. I was merely doing a more refined version of what I had been doing since I was in high school – raising a laugh by guying some recognisable, self-revealing speech mannerisms on the part of the prominent. My winter sports commentator, Alexander Palace, patronised foreign competitors while confidently predicting success for the British ones. Everyone knew that this was what BBC sports commentators did, so there was a yelp of recognition when a fictitious BBC sports commentator stood there doing nothing else. To this day, the laugh of recognition remains the one I seek. It comes from values communally shared. At its best, that kind of humour can push back a barrier, by articulating what is already suspected but nobody has yet dared to say. At its worst, it is complacent. At the time we are talking about, I was more comfortable than courageous.

In retrospect the discrepancy between what was going on in the world, and what I was prepared to say about it, seems glaring – at least to me, the only person really interested. Then, however, I struck myself as adventurous enough in what I wrote, and for stagecraft I was ready to take any kudos going. After the evening performance of *Love's Labours Lost* there was only thirty minutes to erect the Footlights set, so it had to be simple. I made a virtue of this, personally designing a three-piece hardboard screen like a triptych, with a doorway in each of the side panels. The screen was painted white and covered in learned graffiti done by me and Atkin with black and red felt-tip pens. Slogans like IT DON'T MEAN A THING IF IT AIN'T GOT THAT SWING (Duke Ellington) and MEREDITH IS A SORT OF PROSE BROWNING, AND SO IS BROWNING (Oscar Wilde) proclaimed our ideals of catholicity without eclecticism, a universal intensity of effect, etc. Lit brilliantly by the Fresnel spotlights on the gantries, the screen looked like the wall of a loft that had been inhabited by all the students in history. In its disfavour it could be said that it was exactly the appropriate setting for a clever-dick undergraduate revue, but it had a conspicuous virtue. The next act could be prepared behind it and come on in the dark through one door before the previous act had finished going off through the other door, so there was no gap between numbers. This gave an exhilarating effect of speed. The jazz band led by Robert Orledge could be positioned conspicuously in front of the screen and still leave plenty of acting area down-stage. To isolate a monologuist or singer, all we had to do was switch off the spots and floods of the general lighting and switch on one of the two limes positioned high in the gallery at the back of the hall. Picked out in the soft circle of a lime, Maggie Henderson sang a song by Atkin and myself called 'If I Had My Time Again' to such effect that Harold Hobson, the *Sunday Times* critic, made public love to her in his column. I was proud, no doubt too proud, of the precision of all these effects. Nothing was allowed to go wrong. It turned out that Jonathan James-Moore, after he had finished his winter sports monologue, had trouble getting off the stage in the dark. His spectacles didn't work without a modicum of light. On the first night, he groped his way into the drum-kit, turned around, and groped his way off the front edge of the stage, which was about four feet from the floor. He fell into the front row and sat there between two members of the audience for the whole of the next number. They were stunned, but not as stunned as he was. The risk was eliminated from the second night onwards. Someone was detailed to go out and get him and lead him off. Every move, including this, was plotted on the stage manager's chart. I monitored the show every night, ran drills each day to eliminate faults, and one way and another indulged myself in the role of overseer.

Actually all these refinements, once the aim of slick, high-speed, value-for-money, stop-for-nothing efficiency had been decided on, were matters of simple mechanical deduction. I had more right to be proud of the production numbers, in which cutting and long rehearsal had improved already successful pieces into gosh, how-did-they-do-*that*? *coups de théâtre*. Squeezed to half its original length and re-rehearsed so that every move was a gag, the Fantastograd Russian Dance Ensemble made the ideal pre-closer. Russell Davies did one of those Cossack dances performed in the sitting position, with the cocked feet kicking sideways as if at two soccer balls placed a couple of yards apart. He had never had any dance training but once he had seen or heard anything, he could copy it. When he folded his arms, squatted and kicked, the audience rose to its feet in a panic. After about a week of bringing the house down, Davies mildly complained that his feet were hurting a bit. I slapped his back with comradely understanding and discovered only several nights later, when he held up one of his boots in the dressing room and blood ran out of it, that he had been kicking his way towards hospital. His dedication to the show went beyond the heroic. Suicidal was a better word. The whole cast was motivated like fanatics.

It was my misfortune, however, not to be in the show. Having my name on it wasn't enough. Even after running drills and re-rehearsing for a couple of hours a day, I still had too much time on my hands. The Scottish National Gallery had some useful Poussins but I couldn't look at them for ever. At the Traverse I joined in discussions, usually unasked, but the Americans from the La Mama company liked their own voices too, and they had a social revolution to proclaim. I saw matinée performances by other revue groups. Some of them were rather better than I was prepared to allow: the Scaffold, for example, were on at the Traverse and performing material which must have made our stuff look class-ridden to anyone with an objective eye. But most of the revue groups, especially the ones from other universities, were just less disciplined and more thinly cast versions of ours. There was no point going on with the search. Anyone who saw everything on the Fringe would end up in a basket. So with Daryl Runswick and his band I organised a poetry-and-jazz programme for the afternoons, featuring my poetry and his jazz. It is a matter of regret among poets, however, that poetry lovers, or at any rate poetry lovers who turn up to poetry readings, are not a glamorous bunch. Everything E. M. Forster says about his fellow music lovers applies with bells on to poetry lovers. They wear personally-knitted beanies. They bring their own sandwiches. Intoning my translation of Montale's *The Sunflower* while the Daryl Runswick trio backed me up with dulcet riffs, I gazed out over the thinly populated hall – they all sat a long way apart, so as to facilitate concentration – and resolved to try something more ambitious next year. That I would be back next year I didn't doubt. It felt like home. Like all those who have left home, I know exactly how home feels when I find it again, wherever that might happen to be. Haunting the second-hand bookshops, swaggering along the Royal Mile, taking an ill-advised short-cut through the Grass Market late at night in the sad hour before the alcoholics so far gone that they were eating boot polish had crawled away to sleep, I treated Edinburgh as if it were at my feet. Actually I was at its. The strict romance of the city had found a suitably compliant devotee.

16

Black Tie, White Knuckles

BACK IN CAMBRIDGE, I should have settled to my studies. It hardly needs saying that I was unable to. Instead of disappearing into the University Library I disappeared into the language laboratory. If I could have my way, I would still be down there, learning Persian by now, or perhaps Basque. The language laboratory was my bunker. In it, like Hitler in his last days, I could plot the manoeuvres of phantom armies and hide from the implications of the flashes in the distance, the trembling of the earth, the drone from overhead. Another bunker was the Copper Kettle, which at that time began rivalling the Whim as a hangout for the aesthetes. Internally, the difference between the two places was no more striking than that between, say, the Deux Magots and the Flore. Through the big front windows of the Copper Kettle, though, a diarist could look across at King's while he sucked his pen. Establishing rights to a small table by the simple expedient of piling my books on it, I sat for hours bringing my journal up to date and pursuing my brilliantly successful strategy of adding depth to my view of Shelley by reading anyone except him. Wittgenstein induced the same passion as Croce but at a different temperature. Wittgenstein was liquid helium. Saturated arguments crystallised out as aphorisms. I read him as literature: an approach which, I much later realised, is probably the correct one for anyone except the professional logician. Nowadays I can see his sentences, each resonating like a leaf of a xylophone made of ice, as part of an Austro-Hungarian imperial tradition which he fits as surely as

Schnitzler or Klimt, as well as part of the larger German aphoristic treasure-house that includes Lichtenberg, Schopenhauer and Goethe himself. But if that whole expressive effort is now one of my touchstones – one of the things I would like my work to be *like* – then Wittgenstein was the way in, and still rules that long corridor by a tall, uncompromising head. It is so hard to register the thrill of discovery. You have to think yourself back to a time when part of what built you was not there. You have to unbecome yourself. This much I can say for sure, however: Wittgenstein's demonstration that the multiplicity of the self could not only be lived with, but could actually be an instrument of perception, was a revelation to me, and partly because I already knew it. The things that influence our lives don't necessarily just give us the courage of our convictions – they usually help to alter those, or at least refine them – but they do usually make us feel better about our propensities. Croce had made me feel better about being unable, or unwilling, to distinguish between high art and popular art. Wittgenstein made me feel better about being unable, or unwilling, to construct a coherent self. Intelligence had pulled him apart. In Sydney, when I was first a student, Camus had helped console me for the feeling that my life was in pieces. Everybody's life, he said in *The Rebel*, feels like that from the inside. I had acknowledged his assistance by cultivating an existentialist air of amused resignation: a set of the eyebrows which incorporated, no doubt too successfully, the concept of the Absurd. But a wish that the pieces might one day be reintegrated was hard to quell. Now here was Wittgenstein, whose personality was in a million fragments. They shone. I got his aphorisms by heart. They were a star catalogue. Croce had carried me away. Wittgenstein carried me back to myself. There must have been a self there of some kind, or I wouldn't have been able to register these comings and goings. I luxuriated, however, in the awareness of an undiscovered country in the mind. Every man his own *terra incognita*. With the slim volumes of Wittgenstein's output piled up like poetry, I sipped coffee, scattered ash, and soaked up the *Philosophische Bemerkungen* like a parallel text of the *Duino Elegies*. It was a cool love and that could be why it has lasted. Even today, in moments of depression, I still visit Trinity College chapel and commune with his brass plaque. Now he *was* depressed, and look what *he* got done. How? Because he knew that his unhappiness was only personal.

Other bunkers were the various cinemas, at which my attendance increased, as if that were possible. The *Cambridge Review* appointed me film critic. In London, recent *cinéaste* publications such as *Movie* magazine had already imported the *Cahiers du cinéma* approach into English. In Cambridge, it was still unheard-of for anyone to take Hollywood movies as seriously as continental art films. Treating movies and films as if they were part of the same continuity was a kind of heresy. As always, heresy made for more sparkling copy than orthodoxy. There was no particular posturing involved on my part. The propensity to take popular art seriously was in me by nature. Week by week in the *Cambridge Review* I would talk about Fellini or W. C. Fields, Kurosawa or Don Siegel, as if they were in the same business, which I believed they were. I explained, perhaps too confidently, why Fritz Lang's best film was not *Metropolis* but *The Big Heat*. I was tireless. I was tiresome. I was omniscient. I was a pain in the arse. But my *Cambridge Review* film critic's job, though unpaid, was invaluable practice at writing a thousand-word column each week. Employing my Footlights monologue training, I shaped each column as a performance, with a set up, an early pay-off, a development section, a late pay-off and a closing number. I learned that it wasn't necessary to cram one's whole *Weltanschauung* into this week's piece: save some of it for next week. Above all, I learned how to make the writing not sound like writing. If a parenthesis grew to such a length that it would have sounded unnatural read out, I recast it as another sentence. I tried to make every sentence linear, so that the reader never had to look back. This trick, the essence of writing for the theatre or television, is not so necessary when writing for the page, but readability depends on it. Well before my year as a film critic was up, I had evidence that I was getting somewhere. Since everyone, even the dons, went to the cinema, everyone had his own opinion. Since everyone, even the dons, saw the *Cambridge Review*, he wanted to discuss his opinion with me, especially if his differed. The *Cambridge Review* had an illustrious heritage. It had prestige. But that wasn't why I enjoyed writing for it. What I enjoyed was the communal aspect. It was like preaching a weekly sermon and then having to justify it to a rebellious congregation filing out of church. There was an aspect of showmanship that suited my temperament, and an aspect of obligation to the complexity of events which suited the only sense of responsibility I had. Already the evidence was accumulating that whatever I eventually wrote, I wouldn't be writing it in an ivory tower. A circus tent would be more my pitch. So even when I was lounging in the dark I was thinking about the hot lights. The only reason I was hiding, I told myself, was that I was in a false position. My ditherings were nothing to those of my nominal thesis subject Shelley, whose two-volume biography I finally got around to finishing, with some alarm at the erratic nature of the hero I had chosen. Here was another lesson. Since then I have selected my role models with more care.

In the underground maze which I mentally, and to a great extent physically, inhabited, the connecting tunnels that led from the language laboratory to the coffee bars to the circuit of cinemas led on, I need hardly add, to Footlights, where I would finish the day by adding to my already monumental bar bill. With Barry Brown now safely installed as President, I had no duties except to fill my self-elected office as elder statesman and wise counsellor. After a special screening of *The Bank Dick* in the clubroom I gave a detailed lecture on the art of W. C. Fields. 'He never *led*,' I announced, as if I had learned the lesson myself. 'He just let himself be overheard.' Ruthlessly exploiting my friendship with Joyce Grenfell, I arranged for her to be guest of honour at the Footlights annual dinner. The first great lady most of the club members had ever seen in action close up, she wowed them with her perfect manners. I was pretty proprietorial about her afterwards. Far into the night I laid down the law about Ealing comedy. Why had it gone so far and no further? Because the social forces that gave it shape held it reined in. Why were the Americans so much more penetrating? I had my theories. I expounded them. Another round? Put it on my card.

Looking back, I can now see that I must have been a bit of an Ancient Mariner, telling tales of old that held people riveted only because I had them pinned against the wall. Yet some of the time I spent haunting the place was spent well. Atkin and I seemed always to be writing at least four songs at a time. One of the best things about our collaboration was that I received more instruction than I gave. Atkin's justified enthusiasm for the Beach Boys and the Lovin' Spoonful he passed on to me. An instigator, he organised the recording of a limited-edition disc of what we fancied to be our best songs. The edition was limited to whoever could be persuaded to fork out for a heavy shellac pressing in a cardboard cover. A surprising number of people did. Atkin and Julie Covington did the singing. I forget where the recording sessions took place, but remember well that they didn't happen in a proper studio. The venue must have been somebody's college rooms. I recall that a grey blanket was hung up to make a sound booth. The sound quality was frightful. Julie's voice came purely through the static as it would have come purely through a war, but in all other respects the disc caused us misgivings even in our moment of creative euphoria. We distributed it with solemn warnings to ignore its limitations. This was a grave mistake. Nothing except a finished product should ever be put up for judgment. Art is a matter of deeds, not intentions. That art was what we were involved in we had no doubt, and might even have been right. The title of the disc was taken, in all solemnity, from Eliot: *While the Music Lasts*. Later there was a sequel called *The Party's Moving On*. Today, copies of both change hands at too high a price for either me or Atkin to buy them up and melt them down. Our songs always had fans. Just why the fans, over the next six or seven years of hard work, never accumulated into a listening public big enough to keep us alive, had better be the subject of another, and different kind of, book. This is a book about becoming, not being, and it is getting near the end, because by this time my extended apprenticeship was clearly in its terminal phase. If I wasn't quite ready to ply my trade, whatever that was, I certainly couldn't go on preparing for it much longer. There was a credibility problem. In London, among Nick Tomalin's hard-bitten Fleet Street friends, I was known as the world's oldest student. In Cambridge I was known as an aspiring Grub Street scrivener living cheap on college food, or a would-be theatrical assiduously preparing for his advent into the West End. These contradictory views both had something to them. I was caught in the middle.

As a Footlights sketch writer and performer I might have, and perhaps should have, gently faded away at this stage. To inspire an Indian summer of activity in this area, Tony Buffery returned from post-graduate studies in psychology at Toronto. When an undergraduate in Cambridge he had been the member of the original *Cambridge Circus* cast who had pulled out because he wanted an academic career. In his absence, many Footlights cognoscenti, Eric Idle included, had assured me that Buffery was the most inventive cabaret talent ever: not as aggressive as John Cleese, perhaps, or as intellectually wide-ranging as Jonathan Miller, but with an ear like Peter Cook and a mind from outer space. Though some of this sounded like legend-building, it is always interesting when people adverse to that activity make a common exception. When Buffery returned to Corpus Christi as a don, I was ready to find him remarkable, although I didn't expect to see much of him. After a week of the port and walnuts, however, he was up the wall, over it, and into Footlights as if he had never been away. Very tall with thick glasses and curly hair like Harold Lloyd, he was so lacking in arrogance that the young made him nervous. He couldn't have been more approachable, so I approached him. Partaking of the strong Footlights oral tradition by which fragments of sketches are passed down from one intake to the next, Idle had once told me a killing line from a Buffery sketch in which the Queen Mother, played by Buffery in a floral hat, made a speech to open a redbrick university, which was gradually revealed, as the speech proceeded, to have very little going for it. 'Plans have already been drawn up to equip the seventeen-storey science block with a lift. Or a staircase.'

'He used to take the laugh after the bit about the lift,' Idle had explained, 'and then hit them with the staircase. They were helpless.' Remembering this vivid fragment, I now asked Buffery what had come next. 'I can't remember,' he said, with a slight stutter. 'I kept changing it all the time and never wrote it down. I remember she said: "I name this library, Library." They liked that. But I never finished anything. Lacked discipline. Still do, really. Why don't we write something together?'

I had some notes for a sketch about the Olympic games in my pocket. After my tried and tested winter sports number I wasn't too keen on the idea of another monologue. Maybe it would work better as a two-hander. I read out some bits of it to Buffery, suggesting that we could share it out for two voices. 'No, you do the words,' said Buffery, with a light switching on behind his spectacles, 'and I'll be the athletes.' After a grand total of about two hours' rehearsal we tried the number out at the next Footlights smoker. From off-stage I supplied a BBC-type commentary full of the usual wretched optimism about British athletes who had no chance. Buffery kept crossing the stage in various *personae*. He was the German superman Hans-Heinz Reichstagger. He was the Russian female javelin thrower Olga Stickintinskaya. He was Tomkins, the perennial British loser with the pulled hamstring who might have done so much better. Hidden in the wings, I sometimes lost my place in the script, so entranced was I by the way Buffery became these people. Without leaving the ground, or not by much, he could mime Reichstagger doing a sixteen-foot pole vault, clicking his heels in mid-air as if he had suddenly met a superior officer. Russell Davies was still the most protean performer I had ever met, but in his case there was one dour and reticent personality holding it all together. Buffery had multiple selves. By day he was a scientist, probing the human brain to find out which sections of it did what. By night, as a performer, he was a dozen other people. He was also a married man with children. Dr Jekyll and Mr Hyde weren't in the running. Neither of them ever made anyone laugh. Buffery made people laugh until they ached. If he wanted to work with me, I would be crazy to turn the chance down.

I was also, considering my other obligations, crazy to take

it up. My best excuse was that the collaboration provided a modicum of extra income. The Footlights fielded a cabaret team which would perform anywhere in Britain for a suitable fee. When half the fee was given to the club and the rest was divided amongst the participants, it was an unsuitable fee, but it helped me believe that I could earn my own living. It was more fun than supervising undergraduates in Sidney Sussex and easier on the nerves than trying to sweat a thousand words for the *New Statesman* into a gleaming block of lapidary prose – both of which things I was doing as often as I could, although without showing any signs of digging my fingers into the slipping side of the pit of debt in which I helplessly trod slime. I was still in hock to Footlights and now that I was an ex-President the Senior Treasurer tended to clear his throat significantly when we met. A don from Selwyn called Harry Porter, he was a sweet man and a great friend, but neither the university bye-laws nor his own impeccable probity allowed him to encourage the notion that a club could be a bank. My levels of expenditure effortlessly outsoared my levels of income. Even the train journey to Oxford cost money. When Françoise moved to Cambridge in order to become a don at New Hall, domesticity loomed, with all its requirements of financial equilibrium. Also there was the challenge of performing away from the home patch, where the audience would not be so indulgent.

I was right about that. At Goldsmith's College Ball in London, John Cleese, by then an ex-Cambridge professional and already well known, was the first act on. His monologue was brilliant. The huge audience, pissed and impatient to dance, barely heard him out. I watched one purple-faced student at the back of the crowd shout 'Harold Wilson!' over and over while Cleese was performing. Cleese was pretending to be a wartime air force officer in a hurry to recruit new pilots. 'Can anyone fly a B-17? [Pause] All right, can anyone fly a B-16? [Longer pause] A B-3? [Very long pause] Can anyone *drive*?' I was wide-eyed at the perfection of his delivery, and at his courage, because during all the time he was at work, this florid dick-head at the back was shouting out, 'Harold Wilson! HAROLD WILSON!' Then a newly-formed band weirdly known as Cream came on to play a set. I had never heard such a noise. Until then, my idea of an electric band had been the Dave Clark Five. Cream were more like an earthquake. Loudspeakers the size of coffins emitted sound that compressed the air. It was a beat that hurt. Buffery and Atkin and I, our throats dry from the impact of the tumult, retreated to our dressing room to consult. Our dressing room was, literally, a toilet. 'We can't go on,' I shouted thinly. 'We have to,' croaked Buffery. He was right, as usual. When we were announced, the hissing was not universal: it came only from those who had heard the announcement. Luckily the ginger groups in the audience found it easier to attack each other than us. High up on the stage, we were hard to reach except with bottles more accurately thrown than the vast majority of those that flew towards us. Buffery's song about Richard III made a few nice girls laugh. Riding on the shoulders of their partners, they were within earshot. Our Olympics number, however, went for nothing. Working on a bare stage, Buffery had no wings to disappear into and re-appear from, while I found it impossible to raise my voice above the growing *brouhaha*, in which the only words that could be heard clearly were the first and last names of the Prime Minister, piercingly repeated like a horn motif in a Mahler symphony. We managed to make our act look meant, though. An objective observer would have found it impossible to tell if we were failing. Perhaps we were succeeding at some mimed ritual.

The Footlights cabaret team was well rehearsed and usually got away with it. Often we did better than that. Natty in our dinner jackets, we felt pretty pleased with ourselves as we sang a planned encore after slaying them for a solid thirty minutes. Audiences who had once been undergraduates themselves liked us best. There could be an awkward amount of chippy social edge if they thought we needed reminding of our advantages in life. Facing some revelling groups, we wondered why we had been booked. Apart from the Gold-smith's inaudible non-event, which could largely be put down to bad acoustics, we had but one unarguable disaster, explicable only in terms of a mistake on somebody's part. Coming after a string of successes, it was a failure on a scale that builds character, but while the fiasco was in progress we would have given a lot for a hole to open in the floor so that we could have disappeared into it, still waving and singing. The audience was composed of the farmers of Needham Market, a town within easy driving distance of Cambridge. We imagined the kind of prosperous farmers who drove Aston Martins and in January took their elegant wives to ski at Davos. When we came dancing into the dining room, the farmers were all sitting there as if a giftless artist had drawn them. They didn't have the word 'Farmer' written on their hats, but there was something on their shoes that looked like loam. Perhaps loam was what they had been eating. They looked glum and we did nothing to cheer them up. Buffery and I did our Olympics number to less reaction than we would have earned by slowly deflating a large rubber raft. The farmers looked resigned, as if waiting for the death of a sick cow which had never been very valuable when well. It wasn't just that they didn't laugh. They didn't smile. They hardly breathed. A carefully planned half-hour of entertainment was all over in seventeen minutes. When we went dancing off, there was a perceptible difference in the quality of the silence. Throats were being cleared in relief. As we stood white-faced outside in the foyer discussing the details of our escape, a representative of the farmers' committee joined us. 'Do you get *paid* for this sort of thing?' he asked with open scorn. 'We certainly do,' said Buffery. 'The agreed fee. And we might as well take it in cash, if you can arrange it.' I was very impressed with that. It was a good lesson all round. Jokes aren't necessarily pearls just because they fall before swine, but a deal's a deal. A performer always feels guilty when he fails. If his guilt overcomes his business sense he will quickly starve. To flop is already penalty enough. Don't punish yourself. The audience will do it for you.

17

With a Human Face

WINTER WORE ON and the very idea of my PhD thesis slipped
further back into the past. Spring was in the air again but my
heart was heavy with undeclared anguish. Fooled by an early
mild spell, the crocuses came up along the barbered edges of
the backs, were duly filled with snow, survived for a few
hours like candy baskets of sorbet, and so died. Reality had
intruded. A similar crisis was being played out in my soul.
My nagging conscience was partly stilled by Stakhanovite
devotion to whatever work I was doing instead of the work
I was being given a grant for. Everything the *New Statesman*
asked me to do, I did, even if it was beyond me. In Prague,
Dubcek's life was on the line. Now was the time to come to
the aid of Socialism with a Human Face. Socialism with an
inhuman face had already impressed me as the salient moral
fact of the twentieth century, a disaster outstripping even
Nazism, which has at least worn its true colours on its
sleeve. Weighed down by the evidence of history, my erstwhile
radicalism had modulated into a version of social democracy
which, while still hospitable to the idea of universal popular
enfranchisement, was concerned about the milk being de-
livered on time to the doorstep. In short, I was no longer a
revolutionary. No doubt the *Zeitgeist* would have been re-
lieved to hear this news. I did my best to let it know. Nicholas
Tomalin sent me books to review that were hard to make
relevant to the temper of the times. I developed a technique for
turning any subject into an occasion for an anti-totalitarian

essay. I tried to write as if George Orwell were looking over my shoulder. When Eric Bentley's excellent short biography of George Bernard Shaw was reissued, I identified, surely correctly, Shaw's failure of imagination with regard to Stalin as clear evidence that the creative mentality should guard itself against its own inevitable pretensions to omniscience. Less correctly, and ignoring my own homily, I signed off by lamenting that Bentley, presumably through ignorance, had paid so little attention to Shaw's music criticism – a body of work with which, I made it plain, I was intimately familiar. When the piece appeared in the magazine it struck as having the effortless *auctoritas* of holy writ. This mood was punctured when the *New Statesman* forwarded me another book by Eric Bentley, sent, not for review but for my information, by Bentley himself. It was a reprint of *Shaw on Music*, edited, with a long introduction, by Eric Bentley. He could have humiliated me much more thoroughly by writing a letter of protest to the magazine. Thankful that he had taken such a generous course, I resolved never to fudge again. The intellectual community is self-policing. Nobody who tries to pull a fast one will get away with it for long. Also the memory plays such cruel tricks that you will make enough embarrassing mistakes just writing about what you are sure of.

Shamed into flight by the unremitting uproar of Romaine Rand's supercharged typewriter, I had left the Friar's House and gone into exile in digs across the river. My new nest was a front room with a bow window on Alpha Road. The light bulb had a shade. There were shelves for some of my books. I was half way to respectability already. New Hall was only a few hundred yards up the hill. Françoise lived there in a set of rooms whose austere white walls and plain wooden appointments did not preclude an air of luxury verging on decadence. There was so much shelving that even after all her books had been installed there was room for the rest of mine. I also installed my ashtray: a hubcap off a Bedford van, it could hold the stubs of eighty cigarettes, so I only had to empty it once a day. Life was beginning to seem settled, apart from the nagging disjunction between my nominal role and my actual practice. Even the saintly Professor Hough was showing disturbing signs of having at last remembered that I was supposed to be writing a thesis. I promised to show him the finished article soon. It was easier than telling him I hadn't started. The only finished articles I was turning out were for the *Cambridge Review* and the *New Statesman*. Then *The Times Literary Supplement* – in the person of its assistant literary editor, Ian Hamilton – asked me to review some poetry books. Contributions to the *TLS* were still anonymous in those days. This policy didn't suit my lust for glory but it had the merit of not tipping off the dons that my whole attention had turned towards London. It would have been a false conclusion anyway. The university remained, in my mind and feelings, the one place where I could be everything I wanted to be all at once. To a certain extent I feel that even today. Certain kinds of people belong *only* in universities. Later on they make more or less, usually less, successful attempts to convert the rest of their lives into yet another university. Although nowadays I have to get up early in the morning, on the whole I have been lucky enough to arrange my working life along university lines. Mentally I am still *in statu pupillari*, still pursuing extracurricular activities, still torn between all the attractions of the stalls at the Societies' Fair.

The difference is that nowadays I am not so worried about living out an anomaly: let the public judge. In the spring of 1968 I was less confident, and, being that, more strident. If Cambridge thought of itself as the centre of the world, I was determined to take it at its own estimation. With the universities in turmoil throughout the free world, the Cambridge undergraduates regarded their own activities as being of planetary importance. Apart from Delmer Dynamo, who was engaged in an extensive tour of Britain at the wheel of the Bentley which he had at last coaxed out of the car-park, most of my Americans were gone. It didn't need the débâcle of Tet to tell them that the war in Vietnam was a national catastrophe. They had a real moral decision to make. Some of them went into the Peace Corps to do good in Africa, some into the American universities to avoid the draft, some into battle against Mayor Daley's police, some into a long, cold exile. As fast as they left Cambridge, however, more Americans arrived: a new, more vocal bunch who preached direct action. Rome university closed in March. Danny Cohn-Bendit became famous at Nanterre. The new Cambridge Americans wanted to be noticed too. King's College, with a typically canny diplomatic stroke, provided facilities for a Free University. Essentially the facilities were a large room with unlimited supplies of instant coffee, but they were sufficient to supply what the student revolution really wanted – the opportunity for a perpetual meeting. Elsewhere, the world shook. LBJ called it quits on a new term. Bobby Kennedy ran for President and died in the attempt. Martin Luther King was murdered. In the Free University at King's, the rhetoric reached a pitch of ecstasy. A list of Demands was drawn up. A Demand for the complete restructuring of Western civilisation was high on the list. Imported simulacra of Abbie Hoffman and Jerry Rubin called for an assault on the university's property, whereupon, it was promised, the repressive nature of the institution would reveal itself. Called upon to speak by a chairman who was later universally upbraided for truckling to bourgeois elements, I argued against the notion of making demands that could not be met, and thereby provoking a confrontation. There were legitimate demands that *could* be met. The whole apparatus of *in loco parentis*, for example, could be dismantled, with no loss of jobs among the townspeople employed in the colleges and a clear gain in freedom for the undergraduates. This part of my address was listened to in a silence which I construed to be respectful, but when I got to the point of casting doubts on the efficacy, or even the feasibility, of direct action there were snorts of derision from the radical young academics standing at the back, which were soon accompanied by pitying smiles from the undergraduates sitting at the front. I argued against the proposed defacement of King's College Chapel, on the grounds that it would dramatise nothing except propensities towards vandalism; that it would alienate the proletariat, who, if they didn't care for great architecture, cared for militant undergraduates still less; and that there were students in Prague ready to die for the freedoms which in Cambridge were being condemned as illusory.

I was more proud of this impromptu speech than the occasion warranted, because it changed nothing. Speeches rarely do. What changed things in Cambridge was the demonstration outside the Garden House Hotel, staged for a reason now lost in history. Either the hotel had been too hospitable to some representative of the US government, or it had not been hospitable enough to Rudi Dutschke, or perhaps both. Anyway, the students besieged the place. During the siege, a few of them picked up stones and threw them at the windows. All the rest suddenly realised that they liked the talking and shouting part of the revolution but didn't like the part where things got broken and people got hurt. The student revolution in general, not just in Cambridge but in Britain as a whole, was over as from that moment. Effectively the same thing happened in Paris, where, although many more and much bigger stones were thrown, the rhythm of events was dictated by the clubs of the CRS, which descended with a precisely calculated force so as to induce headaches that felt like death but were not it. May of 1968 was theatre. I was glad to be in the cast, if only in a bit part, but like almost everyone else involved I had no intention of relying for long on the unrestrained instincts of my fellow man. The perpetual meeting of the Free University should have proved conclusively to all those in regular attendance that they didn't even know how to conduct a meeting, let alone run a society. In Cambridge the real May, as always, was in June. Well before exam time, indeed well before the time for final revision, the Free University had dissolved, leaving nothing but a rump of misfits who had declared their intention of existing on a single bowl of rice a day so as to dramatise their solidarity with the great, continuing social experiment of the Chinese People's Republic. China was their dreamland. Critical, with some justification, of institutionalised power in the democracies, they managed to believe, because they wanted to, that the centralised, perpetuated and unlimited power of a totalitarian nation was somehow more open to argument, more compassionate, more democratic. Impatient for the millennium but oddly prepared to remain stationary until it arrived, they sat on crossed legs and regaled each other with the prospect of what Cambridge would be like when Mao's vision finally prevailed. Whether King's supplied them with their daily bowl of rice I can't be sure, because by then I had gone too, back to Footlights with a new faith in the validity of the purely frivolous. The impurely frivolous had been on display for a month, and I hadn't liked its inhuman face. The undergraduates could be forgiven their ideals. Experience and knowledge are required before one can accept that an ideal can be murderous, and perhaps they should not come too early. The young dons who had urged the students on, however, were in a different case. Preaching cold-eyed against Repressive Tolerance, safe in their own jobs while urging their pupils to opt out, they were hypocrites and pleased about it: with the taste of cynicism in their tight-lipped mouths they reminded themselves of Lenin, a name they often invoked. Still working out where I stood, I knew where I didn't stand – with men like them. Not just as a displacement activity, but in a kind of wordless affirmation, I directed, for the last Footlights smoker of the year, a sketch baldly entitled 'Slow Motion Wrestling'. Russell Davies was the referee. Robert Buckman, who was very agile, and Alan Sizer, who was large and very strong, very slowly wrestled each other. Russell Davies very slowly tried to stop them cheating. The whole thing happened very slowly indeed. At one point Sizer very slowly punched Buckman in the stomach while equally slowly lifting him bodily into the air with his other hand. Buckman was airborne for an age, mouthing his agony with agonising slowness, while Davies moved like a glacier to intervene. The audience rioted. I felt cleansed. This was worthwhile. Sartre hailing the Chinese Cultural Revolution as an act of liberation: *that* was a waste of time.

A far bigger success than *Supernatural Gas*, the May Week revue that year was directed by Kerry Crabbe, who generously included 'Slow Motion Wrestling' unmodified as the second-half pre-closer. The audience rioted again. I had other material in the show, including several songs written with Atkin and sung by Maggie and Julie, but 'Slow Motion Wrestling' was my apotheosis in the Footlights. Though all three participants in the sketch contributed to its inventiveness, I was its editor. I took out what didn't work and packed the rest up tight. For hours we shaped the piece until nothing was superfluous and everything flowed. It was a piece of sculpture extended into time, an elastic Laocoön, a brawl by Balanchine. Nothing could justify so much effort and that was its justification. Some of the upcoming Footlights disapproved of us who were now the *ancien régime*. David Hare, a brilliant talent with a capacity for organisation almost unheard-of among undergraduates, had a look on his handsome face that plainly suggested one or two of us, and especially one of us, had been around too long. He had a case. From the viewpoint of a politically committed young dramatist with big plans for a new British theatre of Brechtian social analysis, there *was* something irredeemably insignificant about Footlights. But when I stood at the back of the Arts Theatre and watched hundreds of ordinary members of the public rocking with laughter at the antics of my three inspired clowns, I couldn't persuade myself that such a moment of communal joy was reprehensible, even if it was socially irrelevant. No society worth living in is without the irrelevant.

I wasn't at the back door of the Arts Theatre every night. Only every second night. Twice with Buffery and once as a solo act I went through the gruelling experience of a May Ball cabaret. There was applause to be garnered but you had not to mind that it was mixed with the popping of champagne corks, the braying of imported Hooray Henriettas, and the splintering sound of furniture being reduced to toothpicks by a scrum of Hearties. The Pembroke May Ball was the occasion of my solo appearance. Somewhere at the back, the Hearties were duelling with empty bottles of Bollinger. Broken glass fell like rain. On the river that year, Pembroke won the Bumps, or the Lumps, or whatever it was called. The runners-up consoled themselves by burning their boat and throwing the college cat on the fire. David Hare and his admirers would have plenty to react against. They would never forgive themselves for having been at Cambridge. I, on the other hand, had always known that I was just passing through. I took the place for what it had to give, gave back what I had in me, and kept the soul-searching to a minimum, protected by a natural capacity for putting off the moment of reckoning. Everything was a prelude.

18

The Kid's Last Fight

MAY WEEK WAS not only in June, it was two weeks long. Did I remember to say that? In the second week Françoise and I got married. My sole but sensational contribution to the organising of the event was to schedule the reception so that it took place before the ceremony. In the garden of New Hall's Storey's Way annexe the Footlights gathered, along with all the editors and leading contributors from the university magazines I had burdened with my contributions. Françoise's friends, some of them from Italy, looked on with apprehension as the theatricals and the *literati* tanked up on white wine. It was a bright day and the heat helped. Just in time, the whole party headed off down Castle Hill towards the register office. Françoise and I were in the lead, she looking stunning in a white silk two-piece ensemble, I looking stunned in a grey Carnaby Street suit which had already started to fall apart. Stomping along at the rear came a jazz band featuring Atkin, Sizer, Buckman and Davies. They had played better in their lives, but not when as drunk as that. When the registrar recited my full name there was spluttering in the congregation. Clive Vivian Leopold James wasn't feeling very solemn either. Or perhaps he was, and was covering up. It would have been characteristic. I always was the kind of Bohemian who had to work hard to keep the bourgeois within himself from breaking out. *For how but in custom and in ceremony/ Are innocence and beauty born?* I wasn't innocent and I wasn't beautiful, but she was both. I swayed while she stood still. Then we all went up the hill again to continue the party. The lawn was so crowded that the jazz band had to stand in the flower-bed. Strad Blantyre had flown in, on the way through to Germany for one last grand tour before he left for Africa. He had news of Marenko. After long thought, Marenko had burned his draft card. This should have given me pause, but there was no pause to be had. Delmer Dynamo arrived. His tour of Britain had ended in Scotland, when the Bentley got stuck on a narrow stone bridge high over a little river. 'I was actually in a phone booth calling the AA,' shouted Delmer happily, 'when I saw the motherfucker start to roll. She swerved off the end of the bridge, she nosed through this *ridiculous* little wall, she bounced down into the river and she ended up on her back in about three inches of water. I sold her to the guy who owned the pub for a hundred quid and came down by train. Let 'em have it. You can blow it out your ass.'

As happens with all empires, the moment of fruition marked the beginning of decline. My academic career was to linger for another six months before I packed it in, but effectively it was all over. My time at the university was almost up. Later that year I directed the Footlights for the Edinburgh Fringe and had the biggest success I was ever to experience in the theatre. If the show had come to London it would have run for a year and my life might have taken a different course. Equity wouldn't let the show transfer. At the time I thought it was a personal tragedy on a Sophoclean scale. I fought a long delaying action in a doomed attempt to regain the lost momentum. Probably it would have made no difference in the long run. Theatre didn't really suit me. It didn't occur to me that this was because the audience was too small. I thought it was because the audience was too large. My picture of myself was as a lonely writer. On a trip to London I met Ian Hamilton at a pub called The Pillars of Hercules in Soho. He had asked me, by post, to write for his influential little magazine *The Review*. I was already working on my first article, a long piece about E. E. Cummings. Other poets and critics from whom Hamilton had commissioned or was about to commission articles dropped into the pub on the strict understanding that they were staying for only one drink or perhaps two. Ten rounds later they were all still there. Almost instantly I felt about Soho the way I had once felt about Cambridge. Over the umpteenth combination of a pint of bitter with a straight scotch for a chaser, I explained to Hamilton that I had reached another decisive point in my life. 'You're a very complicated character,' Hamilton observed sardonically. I wasn't, but I resolved to become one as soon as possible. Literary London! I could already see myself in that setting: shy, self-effacing, trembling on the edge, but *there*. The metropolitan critic.

That story, if I tell it at all, belongs in another book, which will have to be a collection of fragments. It might be a more reliable account than the one I have written up to now, but of necessity it will be less complete. My unreliable memoirs, in which I have tried to tell the full story even if only in edited form, must now come to an end. I could give up my own privacy as I chose. Where other people are concerned there is no choice. Nor should there be. Beyond the point when it ceased to be my own, my life gets harder to write about, and not just because I must tread carefully. There is so much more to say. In a multiplicity of nuance, only fiction can catch the essence. To rearrange the facts is no longer enough. A young man on the make is a comparatively simple mechanism.

Let us take a last look at him, in Cambridge, in that lovely late spring of 1968. The poetry magazine *Carcanet* has brought out a special issue with a lot of his poetry in it and not much of anybody else's, which is not *necessarily* the way he likes things, but if that's the way they feel, well, let them be happy. A finely burnished piece called 'Cambridge Diary' has just appeared in the *New Statesman*. In the Arts Theatre, actors are saying his words. His songs are being sung. He has married a don. He is on top of his little world. Against a willow tree across the river from the Wren Library, he sits writing in his journal. He has just told it that he is reasonably satisfied. The insistent suspicion that he has not yet begun, and has nothing to show, is too frightening to record. For someone who has good reason to believe that he doesn't exist apart from what he does, to doubt that he has done anything worthwhile is to gaze into the abyss. On the surface of the water, a midge vanishes into a hungry ripple. *I'm not ready yet.* He wonders why, at his age and having come so far, he still feels that. The culmination of his luck is that he doesn't yet realise he will never feel any other way.

Epilogue

ALL I CAN DO is turn a phrase until it catches the light. There was a time when I got hot under the collar if the critics said I had nothing new to say. Now I realise that they had a point. My field is the self-evident. Everything I say is obvious, although I like to think that some of the obvious things I have said were not quite so obvious until I said them. In my younger and more nervous years, I sustained myself by thinking myself remarkable. It took time to accept the fact that I was ordinary, and more time to be thankful. Born without a sense of proportion, I had it imposed on me by the weight of evidence. My solipsism was already crumbling when I played my World Record Club 12-inch LP of Beethoven's 7th Symphony over and over at top volume until it drove my mother mad. It was in the glazed-in back verandah of our house in Kogarah, the year I turned eighteen. My Pye carry-gram, with the lid that split into two stereo speakers, had been hefted into position on a chair, with a book underneath to bring it level. Willem van Otterloo conducted the Concertgebouw of Amsterdam. I danced to the scherzo. During the adagio I sat on another of the wooden chairs, closed my eyes, and rocked slowly back and forth so that the front legs of the chair lifted an inch off the linoleum. That must have been how Blinky bought the farm. Blinky was my mother's budgerigar. When the day was cool enough to permit the closing of the Cooper-Louvres, Blinky was allowed out of his cage to roam the floor. On that day he must have roamed under one of the front legs of the chair and been crushed just enough to limp away and die under the crockery cupboard. Though I decline to admit culpability, the thought was never to leave my mind that I might be someone who loved art so much he could kill while in its thrall.

My mother survived the shock of Blinky's death, and of all the other outrages I have since perpetrated. Readers of the first two volumes of this autobiography often ask me whether she lives and thrives. The answer is that she does both, although she is a different person from the one I have portrayed – no less kind and brave but much more sophisticated, a natural psychologist whose prose, in her letters, has a rhythm and an easy-seeming perspicuity of detail which I would be pleased to hear it said that I had inherited. The point is that I didn't realise any of that until later. Not realising things until later is the story of my life. This applied, still applies, to the awkward philosophical problem generated by the existence of other people. Even the people I knew best I seldom paused to appreciate. There have been those I loved who had to disappear before I saw their outlines. Usually it was only my story that they dropped out of, so as to continue theirs. Perhaps, in order to forestall enquiries, I should close by giving a quick account of those personages in these three volumes who, having played a formative part in my own dazzling course, influenced it still further by their daunting ability to have destinies of their own. The Australians, in particular, showed a disconcerting tendency to forget that I was meant to be the captain of the ship they filed aboard, laughing and waving, on that summer night, almost thirty years ago, when the band played and the cicadas sang and we all went sailing to adventure.

As I recounted in *Falling Towards England*, Lilith Talbot went home to marry Emu Coogan. She thought better of it when she got there, perhaps because as a husband he would have been out of his role, which was to be a radical, a gambler, a battler and a legend. A woman can marry a man like that and still stay sane, but she can't teach school, which was Lilith's vocation. The year after she went home, Lilith was taken ill with meningitis, and for a further year was on the point of death. Her great beauty melted into the pain. But she was saved, and her marvellous looks returned, and now, at a huge school in the Western Suburbs of Sydney, she has taught a whole generation of young Australians from different ethnic backgrounds how to construct an English sentence – the lesson at the foundation of our democracy, and one which the old country needs to learn again. Much loved by the thousands of pupils who are the children she never had, Lilith lives alone in an apartment at the edge of the harbour. From her window in the evening can be heard the tinkle of the moored yachts, like wind-chimes in a water garden. After twenty years I found her again, and although I do nothing for her except invite myself to tea, I am a better suitor to her now than I ever was when we were lovers. My past, of which she was a crucial part, served to civilise my future, and now, in the present, and despite the handicap of my frozen heart, our friendship, restored through good fortune after being broken by neglect, will last until one of us dies, to be mourned by the other.

Robin was three different women, all Catholics: a Holy Trinity. With an overwhelming two-thirds of this group I failed to establish the intimacy here recorded. One by one they went home to Australia, where they now think of London as a part of their upbringing, in which – so one of them secretly assures me – I featured as a marginal, affectionately tolerated part of the geography, like Soane's Museum or Madame Tussaud's. At the time I preened myself as no end of a rogue. Now I see that my love-life was a cliché outclassed by that of any tom-cat. The tremendous, condemnatory last act of *Don Giovanni* was written for Don Juan, not for a feckless young opportunist whose beard had grown because he was too lazy to shave. From the women I did not marry I took what I could get away with, including – a gluttony which can look like generosity in the right light – pride at having given pleasure. More often I gave pain, and probably more often than I thought. It would be hypocrisy, however, to say that I didn't enjoy being a free agent. It would also be ill-advised to say that I did. Marriage is supposed to put a stop to all that. Françoise is not the woman I married, who certainly has the quality of innocence, but only in the sense of being incorruptible by the knowledge to which her high intelligence gives her access. She knew all about me. She knows all about me now, and knows above all that the real blank in this book is not where she should be, but where I should be. In our prurient time, this true age of revelations, even the most sensitive sometimes find it hard to accept that the lasting involvement of two human beings must remain a mystery. The reader has the right to know, however, that something like the wedding in the last chapter happened something like that, and that something like the same marriage is still in existence twenty years later. The long storm of divorce that has blown away the marriage contracts of our generation continues to leave my hair unruffled – what there is of it, and for what such an exemption is worth. Perhaps my house is being saved up for last. Anything more specific I will have to say in a novel, where one can pile in all the right facts, as long as they lead in the wrong direction.

Some of the Australians went home, some stayed away, and much has since been made of who fulfilled his duty and who betrayed it; but the truth is that it all came down to personality in the end. Brian C. Adams, who had struck me as the prototype of the prematurely middle-aged academic, just as I had struck him as the extreme case of the delayed adolescent, went back to Adelaide to begin a university career which I loudly condemned in advance as a caricature. As things have turned out, he has played an important part in furthering the movement to give the study of Australian literature its due dignity without succumbing to provincialism. Particularly impressive, in every article he writes, is his mature, humane judgment, which I would once have said – did often say – that he could never possess. Some people develop, and sometimes they have to do that by throwing off the limiting estimation of those who know them. The privilege I always claimed for myself, of putting off until later the onus of knowing better, I should have more readily extended to others. It might even have been preferable, in the matter of success and failure, never to have judged people at all. Though the Australians who stayed abroad have made their mark, some of those who returned home have changed the history of their country. A few years back, Romaine Rand and I were in Sydney to appear on a television programme together. Romaine's first book, whose early drafts kept me awake while she typed, had long since made her one of the most famous women in the world. We went to see *Il Trovatore* at the Opera House. Romaine, not liking the production, talked to me animatedly throughout the first act. (Proust, when gladly accepting an invitation to the opera from the Baroness de Pourtalès, said: 'I've never heard you in *Faust*.') During the first interval we looked out through the screen of glass at the harbour and the city lights. 'It's beautiful,' I said. 'It's pretty,' said Romaine. 'Venice is beautiful.' She was right, but there was no denying that the city we had left behind had come a long way. The expatriates who had repatriated themselves had realised their dreams at least as well as we had. Australia had done very well without us. We could count ourselves part of it only to the extent that our books were on the racks in the shop at the airport. After the performance we walked, middle-aged and arm-in-arm, up Macquarie Street past the Mitchell Library. In the branches of the Moreton Bay fig trees arching overhead, the possums, driven mad by the spring, were behaving shamelessly. It was a sweet moment, but we didn't even reminisce. We hardly ever meet except in television studios, and even then, for preference, one of us is there only as a satellite image. The stayaways are all like that, more or less. Lost in space, they have only so much time for one another. Huggins, who left us behind in volume one of these memoirs, wrote a book about the early days of Australia that is now being translated into every language on earth. New York, though, is his home. He needs something that tall at his feet. As for Spencer, he is beyond achievement, far gone in a version of our search from which no messages come back. The last I heard of him, he was in Brazil, teaching linguistics. It is less than certain that he will ever go home, and more certain than it should be that he will never publish a thing. He, however, was the man with the gift. Given a brilliance of phrase the way Mahler was given melody, Spencer, if he leaves behind nothing more than a thin exercise book with his ten best poems in it, will be the writer in whose work our wandering generation of Australians finds its purest voice. Why did the children of paradise go out into the world? Why did they give themselves up for lost? We will hear the answer in a cadence.

The same way they had come, on expensive silver wings, the Americans all went home again, because to an American there is so little to be gained by staying away. Sometimes the route home was circuitous, but it always led there. Strad Blantyre was with the Peace Corps in Africa. In his letters he insisted that he could have done the same work in Harlem to better effect. Milos Forman was right when he said that there are only two places where we feel at home: home, and in America. My American friends were fighting for their country, but the war to be won was within its borders: in a cruel dilemma, they grew through the seeking of its cure. Chuck Beaurepaire, who knew everything, put his egregious self-confidence to good use as a lawyer in defence of civil liberties. Even Delmer Dynamo, exempted from the draft on about seventeen different counts of physical inadequacy, lent himself to the struggle. At Berkeley, in the bad days when Ed Meese sent in the cops, Delmer, according to other accounts beside his own, saved the life of the most luscious girl student on the campus by throwing himself on top of her. In his version of the story, he did this several hours before the riot even started. He is probably understating the case in order to sidetrack nemesis, a trick I know well. Delmer is a funny man who makes his friends funny too. I should see him more often, but I am seldom in New York long enough, and the passing of time becomes hurtful between friends if they don't see each other regularly. Strad Blantyre I see often, but that is partly because he is one of my American publishers. It comforts me that he has lost almost as much hair as I have. In New York he takes me to lunch at the Princeton Club; in London I take him to dinner at the Garrick; and it pleases us both to impersonate pillars of the Establishment. What we really share is an unspoken dread of how the dice roll. Stability, for both of us, is a nostrum against caprice.

Marenko is dead. Having decided that the war in Vietnam was a criminal enterprise, he opposed it with a determination and bravery that could have cost him his life, and would certainly have cost him his career if he had not been so – the military word somehow seems apt – outstanding. When the tear gas cleared, the campuses that he had helped turn into battlefields vied to appoint him. His first book of literary criticism carried a charge of abstraction that I was glad to see being partly unloaded in the second, by which time he had become the youngest associate professor in the United States. He married a fellow teacher called Rosalind. They gave their baby another Shakespearian name, Miranda. When they were doing well enough to have a vacation cabin in Maine, Marenko typically built the cabin. I still have a photograph of him, naked from the waist up, hefting an axe and looking like Li'l Abner filtered through a pipe-dream by Thoreau. Miranda, about five years old, looks up at him in adoring awe as he stands there, baking bod, in confident possession of the summer. In the winter of the following year, when he was out with Miranda on the frozen lake teaching her to skate, the ice gave way under her. Trusting his strength, he jumped in with his skates still on. It took him too long to find her and bring her up. They were both already gone when Rosalind got back from the store. My guess is that the little girl died first, and that when he realised this he gave up the struggle, and let the terrible weight of what he had allowed to happen take him down. I knew him, you see. He felt responsible for everything.

Was he wrong about that? I find it hard to be sure. A sense of guilt, it seems to me, is inseparable from having grown up in our share of the twentieth century, when to die young, and for no reason, has been, if not the typical childhood, then certainly the representative one. When I was first old enough to look back on my infancy, I thought it the epitome of dislocation. My mother's fears while my father was a prisoner of war; her grief when he failed to return; her lonely struggle to bring me up – all this struck me as dramatic, and it was a mystery to me why my mother seemed more inclined to count our blessings than to curse fate. I was a long time, by now stretching to a lifetime, in grasping how reality has a texture to which histrionics are an inadequate response. Those millions of young lives apparently rendered meaningless by arbitrary death were taken from us too: a deprivation for which we can compensate only by making ours meaningful. When I was five years old and sobbing in my mother's arms because the bull ants had stung my foot, children my age were being rounded up all over Europe, to be crammed into boxcars and despatched into oblivion. There were mothers who were obliged to kill their children so as to save them from the protracted agony of medical experiments. Compared with that, the story of my mother and her little boy, and of her husband who did not come home, was something old under the sun, and possible to understand if hard to bear. One day, if I am granted life, I will write a book about what happened in the Pacific when two nations, Australia and Japan, strange to each other in every conceivable way, met and fought, and about what has happened since, in the long, blessed peace which by some extraordinary stroke of good fortune has coincided with my own life. If I have an important book in me, that will be the one, but I will have no warrant to take pride in it, because it will be the book into which I finally disappear, having overcome an inordinate need for attention the only way I could, by reducing it to absurdity. For such a book I will need a decade to prepare before I even begin to write, which is asking a lot. Ten years ago, the joke behind the first volume of these memoirs was meant to be that I was too young to be writing it. Now I can hear the clock. As I bring this slight manuscript to an end, in the fiftieth year of my life, and the first year of the Heisei Era, the swags of blossoms on the cherry trees in the many cemeteries of Tokyo are falling softly apart under their own weight, covering the asphalt walkways with faded pink petals. The year before last, at the cemetery in Aoyama, when there was no hint of a breeze, and I saw the petals change their pattern as if driven by the sad cry of the chestnut vendor, I could already feel the texture of what I will one day write. It will be frail, but as the surface of the sea is frail. The transparency which is all I have ever been capable of will have at last justified itself, by joining up. Inside that opalescent bubble, I will be invisible at last. There is not much time left, though. Already I have lived half as long again as my father did, whose fading daguerreotype, as Rilke once said, I hold in hands that are fading too.

Merely to be clear would have seemed an aim too trivial to be considered by the eternal student commemorated in these memoirs, which have that much truth, if no more: they are faithful to my ignorance. Through hindsight, I could have given myself foresight. It would have been a bigger lie than any I have told here. I thought I was Jason the Argonaut, Odysseus the long voyager, or at least one of the children in the radio serial I listened to every week when I was still too young to read – children who never had to go to school, and who were always free to continue their quest, the Search for the Golden Boomerang. It just never occurred to me that the real distance I would cross would be in my own mind. In that respect, I had flown half a million miles before I moved an inch, and these three volumes are just the rattling the side of my cot made when I climbed over, on the first stage of that long, momentous journey across the carpet, towards the light of the open door.

Clive James
Unreliable Memoirs £3.99
The Kid from Kogarah tells all.

'You had better not read the book on a train, unless you are
unselfconscious about shrieking and snorting in public' OBSERVER

'The public's favourite wit and pundit, reduced in imagination to short-
trouser size, wrestling with snakes and aunties and mutual-masturbators in
the bush-bordering suburbs of postwar Sydney . . . called up in the familiar
two-fisted prose. The old boy may be 40, but he times a punchline
disgustingly well' RUSSELL DAVIES, LISTENER

Clive James
Falling Towards England £3.99

'Make no mistake, Clive James is an artist . . . I have my own memories and adventures of youth and early manhood to record, but Clive has done it so well he has done it for us all.' BARRY HUMPHRIES

When we last met our hero in *Unreliable Memoirs*, he had set sail from Sydney Harbour bound for London, fame and fortune. Idealistic and uncompromising, if short on cash, he planned to engage himself in a low-paying menial job by day and to compose poetical masterpieces by night. Having promised himself he would never succumb to such stop-gap occupations as publishing or advertising, he was happily unsuccessful in landing a job in either – at least initially. Positions with London Transport and as a wine expert were likewise denied him.

Scarcely daunted, he moved purposefully beyond 'the Valley of the Kangaroos' (otherwise known as Earls Court) into a bed and breakfast in Swiss Cottage where he thoughtfully practised the Twist in his room, anticipated the poetical masterpieces and worried a little about his wardrobe. Already movie mad, he goes opera mad and persists in his efforts to drive young women mad. No one else could have captured the absurdities and sublimities of the early Sixties of the rigours of being an alien in the motherland with such aplomb.

'A comic triumph, full of terrific jokes and brilliantly sustained setpieces'
IAN HAMILTON/LONDON REVIEW OF BOOKS

'It is something to do not merely with talent but with energy, chutzpah, appetite. James is the funniest man we have . . . He is a master of that kind of light touch which depends on the possession of a vocabulary appropriate to a heavy one. Wodehouse had it, so did S. J. Perelman. Mr James has total mastery of his medium, like them.'
ANTHONY BURGESS/OBSERVER

Clive James
Brilliant Creatures £4.99

'The brilliant creatures of the title live in a world of lost innocence and vast incomes; publishers, writers, media men and consultants, they belong to a charmed circle where everyone knows everyone else's business ... Clive James doesn't miss a trick' THE TIMES

'Nearer to Wodehouse than to Waugh. He is not setting out merely to raise laughs. He takes vigorous swipes at most of the unacceptable faces of society' LISTENER

'Romping satire of London literary life ... the writing sizzles off the page with a rare merriment' ILLUSTRATED LONDON NEWS

'The wittiest novel of the year' BOOKSELLER

'Clive James writes one-liners the way John McEnroe wears headbands' FRANK DELANEY

Clive James
The Remake £4.99
A novel

Twenty years before, in the age of polymorphous perversity, I had played it straight. Now I wanted to know. To find myself through yielding. To be irradiated by the revelation of the Mole's perfectly proportioned, rainwater-pure corporeal presence. Hindering my commitment to this idea, however, was . . . an unavoidable suspicion that I would have felt the same way if exposed to, say, the inner thigh of Linda Lovelace. Maybe I was just horny.

Joel Court had problems. He'd lost his wife, his mistress, quite possibly his career as an astronomical wizard, and had ended up living with Chance Jenolan, to whom success was a way of life, and whose Barbican fortress was protected by a maze that would shame the Minotaur. To make matters worse, there was the Mole. Her heavenly body outshone all the celestial manifestations Joel had ever seen. Pretty soon, he would not be able to bear having her out of his sights . . .

'*The Remake* is a consideration of the artistic and media-star lifestyle, full of brilliant observation'
LONDON EVENING STANDARD MAGAZINE

'As sharp as a tack and as clever as eleven wagonloads of monkeys'
DAILY TELEGRAPH

'The reader is kept busy catching the glancing reflections, fitting together bits of puzzle and enjoying jokes. There is much that cries out to be quoted. Clive James's latest book is funny, serious, challenging, annoying, iconoclastic, elitist, erudite and erotic' ADELAIDE ADVERTISER

'Clive James is the funniest man we have' ANTHONY BURGESS

'Clive James is a brilliant bunch of guys' NEW YORKER

All Pan books are available at your local bookshop or newsagent, or can be ordered direct from the publisher. Indicate the number of copies required and fill in the form below.

Send to: **CS Department, Pan Books Ltd., P.O. Box 40, Basingstoke, Hants. RG21 2YT.**

or phone: 0256 469551 (Ansaphone), quoting title, author and Credit Card number.

Please enclose a remittance* to the value of the cover price plus: 60p for the first book plus 30p per copy for each additional book ordered to a maximum charge of £2.40 to cover postage and packing.

*Payment may be made in sterling by UK personal cheque, postal order, sterling draft or international money order, made payable to Pan Books Ltd.

Alternatively by Barclaycard/Access:

Card No.

Signature:

Applicable only in the UK and Republic of Ireland.

While every effort is made to keep prices low, it is sometimes necessary to increase prices at short notice. Pan Books reserve the right to show on covers and charge new retail prices which may differ from those advertised in the text or elsewhere.

NAME AND ADDRESS IN BLOCK LETTERS PLEASE:

Name————————————————————————

Address—————————————————————————

3/87